Connecting with History

A GUIDE TO SALVATION HISTORY
OLD TESTAMENT AND ANCIENT CULTURES

Companion Reader

Volume 1

Connecting with History
A Guide to Salvation History Old Testament and Ancient Cultures
Companion Reader
Volume 1

Compiled and Edited by Sonya Romens

Book Design by Mary Jo Loboda

Cover Design by Mary Jo Loboda

RC History
www.rchistory.com

Introduction

For many years, I have been collecting short stories and articles written for children with the idea of publishing anthologies to accompany each volume of the *Connecting with History* program. It has been a project that was constantly put on the backburner because of other, more pressing projects that needed to be accomplished. I am thrilled to finally be able to offer this first book in a series of Companion Readers .

This Companion Reader is a bridge between a textbook and living books. It contains simple articles about cultures, places and events from history in more depth than is found in most textbooks, stories to illustrate themes contained in the *Connecting with History* units, and short historical stories written in a friendly, conversational style about real people and events.

Each chapter of this book corresponds to a unit in *Connecting with History, Volume One*. To make them more easily incorporated into your history studies, most of the stories are organized to correspond with the Volume One Daily Lesson Plans. Some topics include multiple selections to appeal to a variety of age levels. Don't feel that you have to assign every story in the book. You may want to assign particular readings to your child; on the other hand, you might not want to assign the stories at all, but let children read and enjoy the stories during their leisure time.

Most of the selections are written for independent reading at the elementary (Grammar stage) level, although older students will enjoy and benefit from them, as well. Many of the stories lend themselves to being read aloud to Beginner level students. You are the judge of what will appeal to your particular child.

The stories have been selected from classic books, most written before 1923. Many of the stories have been edited to update the language and spelling to make them easier to read for modern children. Some stories have been abridged as well. Most quotes from the Bible have been changed to the New American translation.

Above all, the purpose of this book is to make history come to life: to make it interesting, relevant to a child's daily life, and enjoyable. Approach it, not as a textbook, but as part of the fascination of learning about different places and times in which very real people lived.

Thank you to Mary Jo Loboda for all of her hard work in formatting, proofreading, and editing this volume. Many thanks also to Margot Davidson for her constant support, encouragement and mentoring.

Contents

Contents

Unit One: The Early World

Theme: The Justice and Mercy of God

From The Catechism in Examples
By Rev. D. Chisholm

The Cardinal Virtues: Justice

Justice, my child, is the second Cardinal Virtue.

It consists in giving to everyone that which is due. It concerns not only the duties we owe one to the other, but also those which we ourselves must discharge towards God.

Jesus Christ has said: "Render to Caesar the things that are Caesar's, and to God the things that are God's."

"THIS DO, AND THOU SHALT LIVE."

The Ten Commandments prescribe to us our duties towards God and our neighbor; in carefully observing them we will practice in an eminent degree this cardinal virtue of justice, or, in our Lord's own words, we will "fulfill all justice."

The first three Commandments have for their object our duties towards God. "The Lord thy God shalt thou adore, and Him only shall thou serve." Justice towards God requires of us to honor God with a supreme and sovereign honor which can be given to no other, to worship Him as our Creator, our Redeemer, and our Last End, and to obey Him with all diligence as our true and supreme Lord.

In consequence of this He requires of us that we show outwardly a great reverence for His holy Name, and observe with great diligence the external signs of worship He has appointed, and especially by consecrating to His service the days He has appointed for this purpose, not only that we may manifest our submission to Him as our Lord and Master, but also that we may nourish in our hearts a greater love for Him.

The other seven Commandments explain to us in detail how we are to exercise this virtue of justice with regard to our neighbor, whom we must love as we love ourselves. Justice requires us in the first place to love, honor, and obey our parents and those who rule over us in God's Name; secondly, to entertain towards our neighbor with regard to his person, his reputation, and his possessions, the same sentiments which we would desire him to entertain towards ourselves, and not even in our thoughts to bear towards him any feelings which might be to his prejudice.

From this, my child, you can easily see what this virtue of justice means, and how justly it finds a place among the four fundamental virtues of our holy Religion. You have already read in detail these various duties in the instructions upon the Commandments, and you will often think of what you have read there that you may more readily practice this virtue of justice.

A Story About Justice
From Fifty Famous Stories Retold
By James Baldwin

The Bell of Atri

A Story About Justice

Atri is the name of a little town in Italy. It is a very old town, and is built half-way up the side of a steep hill.

A long time ago, the King of Atri bought a fine large bell, and had it hung up in a tower in the market place. A long rope that reached almost to the ground was fastened to the bell. The smallest child could ring the bell by pulling upon this rope.

"It is the bell of justice," said the king.

When at last everything was ready, the people of Atri had a great holiday. All the men and women and children came down to the market place to look at the bell of justice. It was a very pretty bell, and was polished until it looked almost as bright and yellow as the sun.

"How we should like to hear it ring!" they said.

Then the king came down the street.

"Perhaps he will ring it," said the people; and everybody stood very still, and waited to see what he would do.

But he did not ring the bell. He did not even take the rope in his hands. When he came to the foot of the tower, he stopped, and raised his hand.

"My people," he said, "do you see this beautiful bell? It is your bell; but it must never be rung except in case of need. If any one of you is wronged at any time, he may come and ring the bell; and then the judges shall come together at once, and hear his case, and give him justice. Rich and poor, old and young, all alike may come; but no one must touch the rope unless he knows that he has been wronged."

Many years passed by after this. Many times the bell in the market place rang out to call the judges together. Many wrongs were righted, many ill-doers were punished. At last the hempen rope was almost worn out. The lower part of it was untwisted; some of the strands were broken; it became so short that only a tall man could reach it.

"This will never do," said the judges one day. "What if a child should be wronged? He could not ring the bell to let us know it."

They gave orders that a new rope should be put upon the bell at once, a rope that should hang down to the ground, so that the smallest child could reach it. But there was not a rope to be found in all Atri. They would have to send across the mountains for one, and it would be many days before it could be brought. What if some great wrong should be done before it came? How could the judges know about it, if the injured one could not reach the old rope?

"Let me fix it for you," said a man who stood by.

He ran into his garden, which was not far away, and soon came back with a long grapevine in his hands.

"This will do for a rope," he said; and he climbed up, and fastened it to the bell. The slender vine, with its leaves and tendrils still upon it, trailed to the ground.

"Yes," said the judges, "it is a very good rope. Let it be as it is."

Now, on the hillside above the village, there lived a man who had once been a brave knight. In his youth he had ridden through many lands, and he had fought in many a battle. His best friend through all that time had been his horse, a strong, noble steed that had borne him safely through many dangers.

But when the knight grew older, he no longer wanted to ride into battle; he no longer wanted to do brave deeds; he thought of nothing but gold; he became a miser. At last he sold all that he had, except for his horse, and went to live in a little hut on the hillside. Day after day he sat among his money bags, and planned how he might get more gold; and day after day his horse stood in his bare stall, half-starved, and shivering with cold.

"What is the use of keeping that lazy steed?" said the miser to himself one morning. "Every week it costs me more to keep him than he is worth. I might sell him; but there is not a man that wants him. I cannot even give him away. I will turn him out to manage for himself, and pick grass by the roadside. If he starves to death, so much the better."

So the brave old horse was turned out to find what he could among the rocks on the barren hillside. Lame and sick, he strolled along the dusty roads, glad to find a blade of grass or a thistle. The boys threw stones at him, the dogs barked at him, and in all the world there was no one to pity him.

One hot afternoon, when no one was on the street, the horse chanced to wander into the market place. Not a man nor child was there, because the heat of the sun had driven them all indoors. The gates were wide open; the poor horse could roam where he pleased. He saw the grapevine rope that hung from the bell of justice. The leaves and tendrils upon it were still fresh and green, for it had not been there long. What a fine dinner they would be for a starving horse!

He stretched his thin neck, and took one of the tempting morsels in his mouth. It was hard to break it from the vine. He pulled at it, and the great bell above him began to ring. All the people in Atri heard it. It seemed to say,—

> *"Someone   has done   me wrong!*
> *Someone   has done   me wrong!*
> *Oh! come   and judge   my case!*
> *Oh! come   and judge   my case!*
> *For I've   been wronged!"*

The judges heard it. They put on their robes, and went out through the hot streets to the market place. They wondered who it could be who would ring the bell at such a time. When they passed through the gate, they saw the old horse nibbling at the vine.

"Ha!" cried one, "it is the miser's steed. He has come to call for justice; for his master, as everybody knows, has treated him shamefully."

"He pleads his cause as well as any animal can," said another.

"And he shall have justice!" said the third.

Meanwhile a crowd of men and women and children had come into the marketplace, eager to learn what cause the judges were about to try. When they saw the horse, they all stood still in wonder. Then everyone was ready to tell how they had seen him wandering on the hills, unfed, uncared for, while his master sat at home counting his bags of gold.

"Go bring the miser before us," said the judges.

And when he came, they told him to stand and hear their judgment.

"This horse has served you well for many years," they said. "He has saved you from many perils. He has helped you gain your wealth. Therefore we order that one half of all your gold shall be set aside to buy him shelter and food, a green pasture where he may graze, and a warm stall to comfort him in his old age."

The miser hung his head, and grieved to lose his gold; but the people shouted with joy, and the horse was led away to his new stall and a dinner such as he had not had in many a day.

FROM THE CATECHISM IN EXAMPLES
By Rev. D. Chisholm

THE SPIRITUAL WORKS OF MERCY

LET US SAY TOGETHER ONE HAIL MARY

A certain man was, on account of his great crimes, condemned to death. A priest, full of zeal for the salvation of his soul, went to him to prepare him to die well. But the wretched man would not as much as allow him to speak to him about God and eternity. The priest wept for him, and besought him with words full of earnest entreaty, and even threw himself at his feet, to try to touch his heart. But all was of no avail; the heart of the criminal, harder than flint, would not yield.

As a last resource, the priest had recourse to the Most Holy Mother of God; then, full of the most heartfelt compassion for the wretched man, he said to him: "Before I leave you, will you grant me one little favor?"

The man, more to get rid of him than from the desire of pleasing him, answered that he would.

"Let us, then, say together one Hail Mary!

So they began together that holy prayer. But scarcely had they said the first words of it, when there came over the poor man a feeling of repentance. Tears fell from his eyes, and the next instant he was on his knees at the feet of the priest, and when the prayer was ended he begged of him at once to hear his Confession.

He then confessed all his sins with every mark of sincere sorrow, and when the time of his execution came he calmly died, pressing the image of Mary to his breast.

The Vision of Blessed Caprus

In the island of Crete there once lived a holy priest named Caprus. Full of zeal for the glory of God and the salvation of souls, he labored without ceasing to fulfill the sacred duties of his calling.

But Satan was full of rage when he saw how zealously this good priest labored in the vineyard of the Lord, and he raised up a very bad man, who by his example did much harm among the people. Caprus was grieved to the heart when he saw the evil that was done, and wondered how God could permit a man to live who was the cause of so much evil.

But God was pleased to show him in a vision how dear to him is every soul, even the soul of the most obstinate sinner, and how much he desires us to pray for the salvation of all, both good and bad. The following is the vision he had as he himself told it: "Satan stirred up a certain man who was leading a very bad life to do a great deal of evil amongst my flock. The first great evil that he did was to lead into sin a man who was very pious, and to make him also very wicked.

"I was full of anger when I saw this, and instead of praying to God, that by His grace the one who had gone astray might be converted, and that the other who had been the cause of his fall might also by a special grace become a fervent convert like St. Paul, I was filled with great indignation, and my mind was embittered against them to an unspeakable degree.

"In this state of mind I retired to rest one night. About the middle of the night, when I was accustomed to rise for prayer, I awoke, but felt so disturbed in mind that it was quite impossible for me to say my prayers. I knelt down, however, as usual, but there were so many distractions in my mind that I scarcely knew what I was saying. The thought that those two wicked men were going about trying to ruin souls for which Jesus died, and by their wicked conduct leading astray those who were in God's grace, made me feel quite unhappy, and in my zeal I cried out to God: "O my God, it is not just that these two wicked men should be allowed to live and to do so much evil by their bad example; so, my God, I beseech Thee take them out of this life at once, and show them no mercy, since they have done so much harm to Thee, in the persons of those whom they have led into sin.

"But God in His goodness wanted to show me that these two men, wicked as they were, were precious to Him, and that He had shed His blood for them as well as for me. For when in my earnestness I had said that prayer, I suddenly felt the house in which I was, shaken; then I saw it divided into two parts, and the roof taken off; after this there seemed to come down from Heaven a great fire, and it came into the house, and was placed before my feet.

"After this I looked up, and I saw the heavens opened, and Jesus, the Just Judge of the living and the dead, seated on His throne of judgment, surrounded by an immense multitude of angels. Then I saw at my feet, at the side of the immense fire, the ground open, and far below there was a deep, dark abyss, which seemed to have no bottom, and terrible to look at.

"Then I saw standing on the very brink of the abyss the two men against whom I had prayed; they were trembling from head to foot, and their countenances were pale with terror, for they were on the point of falling into it.

"Then I beheld coming forth out of this abyss a great number of hideous serpents; they went straight up to the two men, who, when they saw the terrible beasts, became more and more afraid. Then, I saw the serpents begin to twist themselves round the two men, and by their united force to drag them down with them into the dark dismal gulf.

"I also saw as it were wicked spirits in human shape dancing around them. Then it seemed to me that the two men began to fall into the pit. I was very glad in my own mind when I saw this, and I said to myself: Now they will get the punishment they deserve, and will no longer bring souls to ruin by their bad example.

"Still, although they were tottering on the brink of the pit, they were able in some way or other to keep themselves from falling into it, at which I was very angry, for I was so anxious to see them fall in and disappear from my sight for ever; so I went over to where they were standing and tried to push them in, but I was not able to do it, for just at the moment when I expected to see them fall in, they struggled so much that they kept their footing, even on the brink of the great pit.

Then I became exceedingly angry when I saw that, notwithstanding all my efforts and the united efforts of the wicked spirits and the serpents, these two men still stood safe on the firm ground. In my wrath I raised up my mind to Heaven to ask the Just Judge Who was upon His throne to help me to destroy them, when, behold, I saw a sight, and heard words, which in an instant changed my anger into compassion, and my prayer for vengeance into one for mercy and pardon.

"I saw Jesus sitting as before upon His throne. His face presented an appearance of compassion and of love. He rose up from His throne, and came down from Heaven towards me. There seemed to be tears in His eyes, tears of affection. He went straight to the two men, and instead of pushing them into the pit He stretched out His hand, the hand of forgiveness towards them, and they were full of joy and of gladness when they saw the immense love of Jesus for them. Then He told His angels to go and drive away the evil spirits, and send back the serpents into the pit again.

"After that he turned towards me, and seemed to be very angry with me, for He said: Come and strike Me, for I have such a love for men, and My Sacred Heart is so full of zeal and desire for their salvation, that I am willing to suffer and die over and over again for poor sinners such as these. Oh yes, to suffer and die again would give Me intense joy if only sinners would be sorry for their sins, and resolve never to do them again. And tell Me, continued Jesus, tell Me what good would it do to you if, as you asked Me in your prayer, I had sent these two men into that terrible bottomless pit? What good would it have done you? How much better would it have been both for Me and for them, and for yourself too, if you had prayed for their conversion, that they might for ever live with Me and My good angels in Heaven!

"So saying, Jesus disappeared, and the vision came to an end. I fell down on my knees and prayed, no longer for justice against sinners, but for mercy, for God now made known to me the infinite value of a soul, even the soul of a sinner who had grievously offended Him."

FROM A BOOK OF DISCOVERY: THE HISTORY
OF THE WORLD'S EXPLORATION,
FROM THE EARLIEST TIMES
TO THE FINDING OF THE SOUTH POLE

A LITTLE OLD WORLD –
AN INTRODUCTION TO ANCIENT CULTURES
by Margaret Bertha Synge

No story is complete unless it begins at the very beginning. But where is the beginning? Where is the dawn of geography—the knowledge of our earth? What was it like before the first explorers made their way into distant lands? Every day that passes, we are gaining fresh knowledge of the dim and silent past.

Every day men are patiently digging in the old heaps that were once the sites of busy cities, and, as a result of their unwearying toil, they are revealing to us the life-stories of those who dwelt therein; they are disclosing secrets writ on weather-worn stones and tablets, bricks and cylinders, never before even guessed at.

Thus, we read the wondrous story of ancient days, and breathlessly wonder what marvelous discovery will thrill us next.

For the earliest account of the old world—a world made up apparently of a little land and a little water—we turn to an old papyrus, the oldest in existence, which tells us in familiar words, unsurpassed for their exquisite poetry and wondrous simplicity, of that great dateless time so full of mystery and awe.

"In the beginning God created the heaven and the earth. And the earth was waste and void; and darkness was upon the face of the deep: and the spirit of God moved upon the face of the waters.... And God said, Let there be a firmament in the midst of the waters, and let it divide the waters from the waters. And God ... divided the waters which were under the firmament from the waters which were above the firmament.... And God said, Let the waters under the heaven be gathered into one place, and let the dry land appear.... And God called the dry land Earth; and the gathering together of the waters called the Seas."

Thus beautifully did the children of men express their earliest idea of the world's distribution of land and water.

FROM ANECDOTES AND EXAMPLES
ILLUSTRATING THE CATHOLIC CATECHISM
By Rev. Francis Spirago

CREATION

God created heaven and earth, and all things.

THE ACORN AND THE PUMPKIN

The wisdom of God is displayed in creation. A man was lying in the shade of a spreading oak tree one hot summer's day. As he looked idly about him, he saw a pumpkin vine trained on a fence, from which large, heavy pumpkins were hanging. "That is a very bad arrangement," he said to himself, "that slender, fragile plant bears such large fruits, while a stalwart tree, such as this oak beneath which I am resting, only bears tiny acorns. If I had made the world, I should have ordered things more wisely." As he finished speaking an acorn fell from the tree, and smote him on the nose so sharply that his nose began to bleed. This unexpected blow taught the conceited man a lesson. "I must acknowledge, he said, "that God has arranged everything very wisely. Had the acorn that fell been the size of a pumpkin, and dropped from the height it did, I should have been stunned, or at least my nose would have been broken. What we learn at school is quite true: God has ordained all things in creation with wisdom and forethought." How foolish are those who think they know better than the all-wise Creator?

— ❦ —

God created heaven and earth from nothing by His word only;
that is, by a single act of His all-powerful will.

THE FIRMAMENT IS UPHELD BY DIVINE POWER

If we consider the universe, we shall assuredly be compelled to admire the omnipotence of God. A German prince was one day conducting a foreign ambassador over his palace and calling his attention to the strength of its walls, the beauty of its architecture and decorations. The court fool who, according to the custom of former days, followed his master everywhere and was allowed perfect liberty of speech, put in his word. "Your Highness," he said, "do not boast too much about your palace. It may well stand firm and strong; it has massive columns to uphold it; it rests upon solid foundations. But just look up to heaven. The Lord who reigns above needs neither pillars nor foundations to support the immeasurable dome He constructed; He upholds it by His omnipotent will alone. One must needs respect so great a Potentate!"

— ❦ —

The angels were also created to assist before the throne of God and to minister unto Him; they have often been sent as messengers from God to man; and are also appointed our guardians.

THE SCHOOL CHILDREN OUT IN A STORM

Children are often favored by the miraculous protection of their guardian angels. In the year 1890 the children of a village school near Reichenberg in Bohemia were taken on an excursion into the woods for a treat. While they were at play, a heavy storm came up and the rain came pelting down. A party of children—thirty-one in number—sought shelter under a gigantic fir tree. All at once one of them—a little girl—felt irresistibly urged to leave the shelter of that tree; she ran away, dragging two or three others with her, while the remainder followed of their own accord. They had scarcely got a few feet from the tree when it was struck by lightning, and torn asunder with a terrific crash. Singularly enough, the tree thus struck formed a kind of cross. The parents of the children piously ascribed their rescue from death to the kind protection of their guardian angels, and out of gratitude, they erected a cross on the spot where the tree had stood.

FROM ANECDOTES AND EXAMPLES
ILLUSTRATING THE CATHOLIC CATECHISM
By Rev. Francis Spirago

ON OUR PARENT'S FIRST FALL

The first man and woman were Adam and Eve.

THE HEN'S EGG

The world did not come into existence without a Creator. A young man who had finished his studies at the high school came home with an overweening idea of his knowledge and wisdom. Amongst other foolish theories that he enunciated, he asserted that the world was not made; it came into existence of itself, and was not the work of a Creator. His mother, a simple but sensible woman, let him run on, and listened in silence; at length she said: "Since you have such definite knowledge on all these matters, tell me, did the egg exist first, or the hen?" "The egg existed first," the youth replied, "all chickens come out of eggs." His mother continued: "That is impossible, for the egg comes from the hen; therefore the priority of existence belongs to the hen." Her son answered: "Perhaps you are right, mother." But she said again, "Yet you must not forget that there is never a hen that did not originally come out of an egg." The youth was silent, and looked abashed. "You will never be wise," his mother said to him, "if you do not believe in the Creator. The whole world will be an inexplicable puzzle to you and an enigma. Believe in God, and you will have the key to that enigma. Then only will you acquire true wisdom." The hen indisputably existed before the egg, for the hen lays the egg, and has to hatch it if the young bird is to come out of it. Therefore, God created the first hen.

— ❧ —

To try their obedience, God commanded Adam and Eve
not to eat of a certain fruit which grew in the garden of Paradise.

THE BUNCH OF GRAPES

It is related of St. Macarius, one of the Fathers of the desert, that, having received as a present a beautiful bunch of grapes, though he longed to taste them, he, to exercise himself in self-denial and obedience to his rule, resolved not do so, but sent them with his compliments to a neighboring hermit. He, inspired with the same holy motives, sent them to a third; the third to a fourth, and so on until finally the grapes, having passed through most of the cells in the desert, came back to St. Macarius practically untouched. The latter, on receiving them and on learning after inquiry through whose hands they had passed, gave thanks to God that in the world should be found so many faithful sons of Adam and Eve to make reparation for their parents' transgression.

— ❧ —

On account of the disobedience of our first parents, we all share in their sin and punishment,
as we should have shared in their happiness if they had remained faithful.

THE HEIRS OF AN ESTATE

We are all inheritors of Adam's sin and its consequences. An emperor once gave a large estate to one of his subjects, a man of rank, on condition that he should always be faithful to him, but the nobleman proved a traitor. Thereupon the emperor took his land and his title from him and banished him from his dominions. The man's treachery brought misfortune on his children; they could not inherit either the property or the title that had been their father's. All that he could bequeath to them was a legacy of disgrace and poverty. Our case is a similar one. Our first parents had and lost their supernatural privileges, and we also are deprived of them. They caused injury to both the soul and body; this is handed down to us. Only one thing is beyond our power to comprehend, that we inherit the sin of Adam; this is and ever will be a mystery of faith.

— ❧ —

The chief blessings intended for Adam and Eve, had they remained faithful to God, were a constant state of happiness in this life and everlasting glory in the next.

THE WOODCUTTER'S CONCEIT

We would have fallen into the sin of our first parents much more readily than they did, had we been in their place. In the employ of a prince there was a certain woodcutter who, while he was at work, was wont to protest against Adam and Eve for eating the forbidden fruit, abusing them roundly for having transgressed so easy a commandment and thereby brought such unbounded misery on their posterity. "I and my wife would not have been such fools," he said. His employer overheard this speech, and said, "Well, well, we shall see. From this day forth you and your wife shall live at my expense and have it almost as well as Adam and Eve in Paradise; but the day of probation will come." The wedded couple was given good rooms and grand clothes, they were not obliged to work, their daily food was brought from their master's table, labor and anxiety were at an end for them. Then came the day of probation. One gala day the prince had them to dine at his table, and sumptuous foods were set before them; at last a dish closely covered was placed on the table and their host said: "You can eat of every dish except this one; that is to be left until I return. You must not so much as touch it." He then left the dining-hall and was absent for a long time. The two guests began to get impatient, their curiosity was awakened; it got stronger and stronger. At length the woman could resist no longer; she gently raised the cover. But the harm was done; a beautiful little bird flew out, and disappeared out of the window. Then the master of the house came back, and drove out both the man and his wife, bidding them be wiser in the future. Here we have an example of human frailty.

— ❧ —

Our nature was corrupted by the sin of our first parents, which darkened our own understanding, weakened our will, and left in us a strong inclination to evil.

The Spots of Ink on a New Dress

Disobedience has evil effects. A lady had a handsome dress of sky-blue silk made as a present to her grown-up daughter at Christmas. On Christmas Eve the tailor brought it home. The young lady tried it on at once, to see if it was properly made. To her satisfaction and that of everyone else, it was found to fit perfectly. The lady paid the bill, and said to her daughter, "Go into the next room and bring a glass of red wine for the tailor. But mind you turn on a light before you pour it out." The girl went at once to do her mother's bidding and soon returned with a glass of wine that she handed to the man. He raised the glass to his lips and took a good mouthful, but quickly spat it all out again. Lo and behold! The grand new dress was sprinkled with hideous spots of ink! The girl had not taken the trouble to do as her mother had told her, and turn on a light in the adjoining room; hence it came about that she took the wrong bottle, and brought a glass of ink instead of wine. She was thoroughly scolded by her mother for her disobedience, and all the next year no new dress was given to her. It was through disobedience that our first parents stained the robe of their primeval innocence.

From The Chosen People
By Charlotte Yonge

The Promise

"For creation was made subject to futility, not of its own
accord but because of one who subjected it in hope that
creation would be set free from slavery to corruption and
share in the glorious freedom of the children of God."
—Romans 8:20-21

When the earth first came from the hand of God, it was "very good," and man, the best of all the beings it contained, was subjected to a trial of obedience. The fallen angel gained the ear of the woman, and led her to disobey, and to persuade her husband to do the same; and that failure gave Satan power over the world, and over all Adam's children, bringing sin and death upon the earth, and upon all, whether man or brute, who dwelt therein.

Yet the merciful God would not give up all the creatures whom He had made, to eternal destruction without a ray of hope, and even while sentencing them to the punishment they had drawn on themselves, He held out the promise that the Seed of the woman should bruise the head of the serpent, the Devil; and they were taught by the sight of sacrifices of animals, that the death of the innocent might yet atone for the sin of the guilty; though these creatures were not of worth enough really to bear the punishment for man.

From Book of the Ancient World for Young Readers
By Dorothy Mills

Pre-Historic Times

"Many the forms of life,
Wondrous and strange to see,
But nought than man appears
More wondrous and more strange."
—Sophocles: Antigone

History is the story of the way in which man has learned, and is still learning, how to live: of how through long centuries he has sought to satisfy the practical needs of his body, the questioning of his mind, and the searching of his spirit. It is the story of the greatest adventure in the world, this story of how man, from very small beginnings, has progressed in body, mind and spirit.

There was once a time when the earth was like a wilderness; there were no cultivated fields, no roads, no towns or villages, no houses. The lowlands were covered with vast and almost impenetrable forests and jungles, with wide rolling prairies, open meadows and barren sandy steppes. Strange animals roamed over the land and lived in the water, such as the hippopotamus and rhinoceros and great mammoth elephants; and wild bison and untamed horses lived on the open spaces on the hillsides.

Such were the surroundings in which man first lived. These early men had no houses, no clothes, though they probably had some kind of hairy covering which they lost later, owing to their custom of wearing the furs and skins of other animals; they had no tools or weapons, no tame animals, no jars or pitchers in which to keep food, no fire by which to warm themselves or to cook; they had even no language. The animals were much better off than man, for they had thick fur in which to keep warm, tusks and horns with which to protect themselves, hoofs under which they could trample their enemies, and wings with which they could fly away from danger. Man had none of these things, but he had two other things which the animals had not: he had a brain and he had hands, and when he had learned how to use these, he began to rise above the animal life which surrounded him. History is the story of how many learned to do and think and have all that we do and think and have today, and we owe almost everything we have to the inventions of people whose names we do not know, who lived many thousands of years ago, for everything that is invented grows out of something that has gone before. If we think back far enough in the history of the world, we come to a time when these everyday things had a beginning, when, for example, the first wagon was made because someone had thought of a wheel, and when the load had no longer to be drawn by man, because someone else had thought of taming a wild horse.

History is said to have begun as soon as man had learned how to keep records of what had happened; so these earlier periods when no records were made, because no one knew how to write, are called Pre-historic times. The first things prehistoric men needed were weapons and tools, and as they had not yet learned to work metal, they made these of stone, and the long period when stone was the only material used, is called the Stone Age. We do not know how long this age continued. In the beginning, they no doubt used stones just as they found them, choosing the shape and size that were most convenient; but they presently learned that by knocking and chipping a stone with other stones they could make its cutting edge sharper and blunt off its jagged places, making it easier to hold. One of the earliest tools thus made was the Hand Axe, and for a long time it, and the small splinters and flakes of stone knocked off when they made it, were used for almost everything. By degrees, however, men improved upon it, until they produced stone hammers, axes, chisels, and scrapers. A very important discovery made early in the Stone Age was the use of fire, for then men could warm themselves and cook their meat, and another great advance was made, though much later, when the bow and arrow was invented, for then men could defend themselves at a distance and kill birds for food as well as animals.

In the middle of the Stone Age there took place a very strange thing, which must have been a terrifying experience for primitive man. The climate began to change, and it gradually grew colder and colder, and ice began creeping down from the frozen North, burying everything beneath its weight as it slowly and relentlessly advanced. Geologists have discovered that this had happened three times before and that each descent of the ice had been followed by a long warm period, but we know almost nothing about those very early times. When the ice came down for the fourth time, in the middle of the Stone Age, men were hunters, roaming about with no settled homes. The ice drove them further South and they began to use caves as shelters from cold and storm and wind. Some of these caves have been discovered, the walls of which are decorated with rough drawings, and tools and other implements used long ago have been unearthed in them.

It must have been a strange life that was led by these Stone Age men. Fires were built at the entrance to the caves, and here they would spend the long, dark winter days huddled together. The hearth was the center of all things to them, and as a fresh fire was very difficult to kindle, they never allowed the old one to go out. To the minds of these primitive men there was something very mysterious about fire, it gave them light and warmth, but if they touched it, they received a sharp stinging hurt. So they gradually looked upon the fire on their hearth as the dwelling-place of a spirit, who was sometimes friendly and sometimes the reverse, and if one of their number died, he was buried near the hearth, where he might be warm and comfortable and under the protection of this guardian spirit. Nature frightened these men, there was so much that they could not understand, and in their dim striving to find out the truth about it all, they peopled the world with ghosts and spirits, of most of whom they were terribly afraid, and so, like children frightened in the dark, they felt safer, especially in the gloomy winter, when they were together. But when the spring and summer came and the days grew longer and warmer, some of their terrors vanished, and the men went out to hunt, whilst the women gathered berries, roots and nuts, wild apples and other fruit, and the store house would be replenished for the coming winter.

The next step in advance taken by primitive men was when they learned to plant, and when they began to live in settled homes. The men still went hunting, but the women planted and found out how to weave, so that they had baskets in which to carry things, and then they discovered that clay would harden in the fire, and so they began to make all kinds of pottery. The first wooden houses were built on piles in the lakes and as some of these piles have been found in Switzerland, they are known as Swiss Lake Dwellings. They seem to have been quite comfortable shelters, with rough wooden furniture, and to have contained wooden pitchers and spoons as well as a variety of pottery dishes, jars and bowls. As these men learned how to plant more and to make a greater variety of things, they wandered less and made themselves real homes, where they kept their belongings, where the children grew up, and to which the men returned from their hunting expeditions. At first everything was done by man, but later they learned how to tame the "wild things out of the wild woods," and first the dog, who became the friend of man. He found food and warmth and kindness in the human dwelling-places, and by degrees this all became familiar and friendly to him, and he grew tame, until at last he roamed no more but made his home with man. Then were tamed sheep, goats, swine, oxen and—last of all—the horse.

We know most about pre-historic man in Europe, and at the time of which we are speaking, he had advanced a great deal from the first beginnings. He had learned how to make weapons and tools, to use fire and to cook and make pottery, to make himself a shelter as a home, to plant seeds and to make some kind of rough clothing. Prehistoric man had discovered all these things for the first time; he was the ancestor of the great discoverers, inventors and artists of later times, of all those who have within them a spark of creative genius. But at last he came to a point when he could learn nothing more. His tools and implements were still of stone. He had no metal, so he could not build much or make ships, neither had he learned how to write. Man needed these things before he could advance in civilization: he needed metal for better tools and building and weapons; he needed ships to bring him into communication with other parts of the world; and above all, he needed writing in order to make records of his law and history. To the east of Europe, men had found out how to use metal, to build ships and to write, and very slowly, but very surely, this civilization moved westwards, each century giving something to it, until it became the civilization we have inherited, and which we in turn must hand on, enriched by the new things we have added to it.

From Our Old World Background
by Charles A. Beard

The Early Ages of Mankind

Many an American farmer boy, while strolling along a river bottom or plowing a field, has picked up stone arrowheads or stone hatchets that were made long ago by American Indians. Such weapons have been found in nearly all parts of the United States. They tell us of human beings who lived in a crude and savage condition, without a knowledge of metals, without strong, well-lighted houses, without the comforts and the tools that make it so much easier for people to live and work today.

Now it is an interesting fact that such stone weapons have been found also in other parts of the world; indeed, in nearly every country. In Europe and Asia, however, they are not usually found near the surface of the ground. There they have been buried deep by drifting sand and by the ruins and rubbish left by many generations of people who had learned to use metals and had quit making stone weapons. By studying these stone weapons and the bones and various things found with them in rubbish heaps, scholars have learned much about the way people lived long ago before the invention of writing made written records possible. The long period before the invention of writing is known as the prehistoric ages, "pre" being the Latin word for "before."

The Prehistoric Ages — from Stone to Metals

The Old Stone Age

For many long centuries, all mankind lived very much as the North American Indians lived before white men came to this continent. In France and elsewhere in Europe, there have been discovered deep caves which had been closed for thousands of years. In these caverns, the bones of human beings have been found and, along with them, the bones of animals, like the woolly rhinoceros and the mammoth, that do not exist today. In these caverns, as well as in sand banks, there have been unearthed many rude implements made of stone. Owing to the fact that the implements found at the very bottom of these caves and sand banks were scarcely more than rude flakes and chunks of stone, historians speak of the earliest part of the prehistoric period as the Old Stone Age. How long it lasted we do not know.

The New Stone Age

In the upper layers of the rubbish in caves and in river drift were found better and better tools in ever greater variety; hence the term, New Stone Age. Progress among primitive people was slow, very slow; but there was some advancement. The crude way of chipping stone was improved. Axes, spearheads, and arrowheads came to be made of stone that could be highly polished and brought to a sharper edge or finer point. In addition to weapons, there were bone needles, fragments of pots, scrapers, flint knives, and other things used in making clothing and preparing food.

The Bronze Age

As primitive people became more and more expert in making stone implements, they began to take note of the differences among stones of various kinds. Whenever they discovered a new kind of stone, they doubtless tried to see what they could do with it. Now it happens that one of the few metals that is found in a state which permits immediate use is copper. In their hunts for useful stones, primitive people found chunks of copper and learned that it was malleable; that is, it could be pounded into various shapes. They found also that they could polish it by rubbing it hard. As they loved to adorn themselves, they made ornaments of this shining metal. Since it was not very hard, however, it was not a good substance for axes and spears. The edge of copper would not keep its sharpness.

In their search among the stones, primitive people also found another metal, tin. After a long time, they discovered that by melting tin and mixing it with copper they could make a hard alloy, called bronze. Then they had a metal that could be hardened and polished and given a keen and lasting edge. It could be used for making tools, weapons, sheets of metal, pots, kettles, and many other useful things. This marked a wonderful advance in manufacture.

The Iron Age

Late in the prehistoric period, primitive people discovered the most wonderful metal of all, iron. This was still harder than bronze and could be worked up almost as easily into weapons, tools, and utensils. When mankind reached this stage it was well on its way toward settled and civilized life.

The Ages Overlap

In trying to picture to ourselves these long stages through which mankind passed in prehistoric times, we must keep some things firmly in mind. First, the ages overlapped even among the same races; that is, they did not pass suddenly from one to the other. Secondly, different races passed through these ages at different times. Thirdly, some races skipped one or more of them. For example, the North American Indians were in the Stone Age when Columbus discovered the New World.

They did not pass slowly upward through the Bronze and Iron Ages. They got tools, weapons, and cooking utensils from the white man, and leaped all at once, so to speak, into the age of iron and steel. So it has been with many other primitive peoples. Even in modern times, however, there have been discovered some races that have advanced no farther in civilization than the cave dwellers of Europe who lived more than five thousand years ago.

LIFE AMONG PRIMITIVE PEOPLES

MEN, THE HUNTERS AND WARRIORS

In this upward struggle, there was a division of labor between the men and the women. Men became the hunters of animals for food and skins and the protectors against enemies. They killed game in the forests and streams. They fought wild beasts and their own savage kind. Thus they became skillful in the arts of the chase and warfare. They made weapons of all kinds. In their leisure hours, they polished and decorated their spear handles and bows. Sometimes they drew, on the walls of their caves, pictures of the animals they had hunted. They became artists after a fashion. Their eyes and ears were sharpened in the search for prey. Their limbs became lithe and supple as they chased the deer. They tamed the dog to help them on the hunt and they learned the mysterious ways of wild animals.

WOMEN AND THE ARTS OF PEACE

On the other hand, primitive women started the arts of peace — industries of all kinds, agriculture, and homemaking. While the men were on the hunt, women studied grains, plants, and fruits. One writer has said: "One cannot, without profound thought, look upon the picture of a long train of Ute women (North American Indians) coming home with their drying baskets full of seeds upon their backs, supported by bands across their foreheads, holding also in one hand a gathering wand and in the other a winnowing and roasting tray. For these women are indeed the forerunners of all farmers and harvesters and threshers and common carriers and millers and cooks. The National Museum at Washington possesses a collection of food plants used by [primitive] women, and in the Royal Kew Gardens in London may be seen an exhibit arranged on the basis of plants. Unwittingly both these museums have erected monuments to the manual labor and skill of [primitive] women."

Primitive women learned a great deal about cooking. They cut up and cured the meat killed by the hunters. They discovered how to parch and roast in pits filled with hot stones. They learned how to grind grain, to bake, and to boil. As this work fell to them, it was doubtless they who invented the first utensils — baskets to carry grain in and pots to cook in. They found out how to store provisions and they tamed the wild cat to protect their stocks from vermin. In their endless wanderings, they learned the qualities of plants. They found that some were good, some were poisonous, and others useful in sickness. They were therefore doctors and chemists, as they collected drugs and ground them for medicine. In our National Museum, there are hundreds of specimens of drugs that primitive women used.

Primitive women were also the first clothiers. They cut and sewed the skins of the animals caught in the hunt and made garments from them. They learned how to make threads from wool and from certain vegetables. They were the first spinners and weavers. As time passed, they became ever more skillful and artistic. They made dyes from the juices of the plants they knew, and they made beads from bright-colored bits of stone. Thus domestic arts began. To primitive women we owe the beginnings of gardening, home music, pottery, sculpture, weaving, and embroidery.

Finally there was the care of the baby. It was woman's great task to feed and care for the children. While the warrior destroyed life in battle, she protected life. While his spirit fed on hatred of his enemies, her spirit was nourished by the love of her little ones. She not only cared for their physical needs. She taught them out of her store of knowledge how to guard against things dangerous to life. The girls she trained in her domestic arts. The boys, as they grew up, were trained by the father in hunting, fishing, and fighting.

The Beginnings of Human Society

Primitive Society

In the earliest days of mankind people lived together in small groups. Their only ties were those of the family. Such a group is called a primitive society. Its members were few. They had for a long time no domestic animal. They had no fixed homes but lived in forests and caves. They wandered about from place to place in small bands hunting for food and shelter. Human beings living in this early stage of society, known as Bushmen, were found in Australia when white men first went there.

Domestic Animals and Tribal Society

Humanity took an immense stride forward when it discovered how to tame the goat, the cow, and the sheep. This knowledge made it possible to have milk, meat, and cloth without the uncertain and exhausting labor of the hunt. We do not know when this remarkable discovery was made; but we do know that it was long before people learned to write any story of their doings. It is thought that the dog or the cat was the first animal to be tamed. That may have been a step toward the taming of goats and other animals caught on the chase and kept alive for food.

After the domestication of animals, life for mankind became more certain and secure than when everything depended upon hunting and fishing. Property began to accumulate. Some men grew rich and powerful as their flocks increased. Great tribes of people gathered around the possessors of huge herds of cattle. There was much work to be done watching and taking care of the animals. Slavery was introduced because the labor of captives became valuable to the captors. So some men were turned from hunting and fishing to join the women in peaceful pursuits. Stores of meat, cheese, skins, and wool were laid up against times of dearth. In short, mankind was lifted one stage above the perilous and uncertain life of the savage.

THE ART OF PLANTING AND REAPING

Later in primitive times, long before the art of writing was discovered, there came a second wonderful discovery; namely, that seeds planted in the ground will take root and produce new supplies of grain. With some ancient peoples that discovery may have preceded the taming of animals, but generally. it was much later. When and where the art of agriculture began, we know not. One ingenious student of primitive life explains it in the following way. Grain grew wild in the forests. Primitive women gathered it and made bread of it by mixing it with water and baking it on hot rocks. In a time of abundance some of the grain was hidden in the ground, and, lo and behold! it was called to life a hundred fold by the spring rains. Once discovered, the process was easy to repeat. So the secret of the seeds was found out. This is, of course, sheer guesswork; yet it may be a correct answer to the riddle. At all events, we know that thousands of years before there were any written records of history the art of planting and reaping was learned.

THE BEGINNINGS OF SETTLED LIFE

This art was destined to make another important change in the affairs of mankind, one even greater than that made by the domestication of animals. While people depended upon hunting and cattle raising for a livelihood, they had to be constantly on the move from one hunting ground or pasture to another. This migratory, or nomadic, life was, in time, completely changed by the discovery of agriculture. When people learned the value of the soil, they began to settle down to till it. Houses took the place of tents. The land was claimed as the property of the tribe or family that settled on it. More and more slaves were captured to till the fields. Scattered bands of savage hunters thus developed into farmers. The nomadic shepherds were driven farther and farther into the hills as the farms spread out in every direction. Nations were founded. A mighty struggle for possession of the earth began.

Unit Two: The Patriarchs

THEME: RELATIONSHIP WITH GOD AND HIS PROMISE

FROM THE CHOSEN PEOPLE
By Charlotte M. Yonge

THE PATRIARCHS

"The God of glory appeared to our father Abraham in Mesopotamia."
—Acts 7:2

Among the sons of Shem (called Hebrews after his descendant Heber, who dwelt in Mesopotamia) was Abram, the good and faithful man, whom God chose out to be the father of the people in whom He was going to set His Light. [God] tried Abram's faith by calling on him to leave his home, and go into a land which he knew not, but which should belong to his children after him—Abram, who had no child at all.

Yet he obeyed and believed, and was led into the beautiful hilly land then held by the sons of Canaan, where he was a stranger, wandering with his flocks and herds and servants from one green pasture to another, without a plot of land to call his own. For showing his faith by thus doing as he was commanded, Abram was rewarded by the promise that in his Seed should all the families of the earth be blessed; his name was changed to Abraham, which means a father of a great multitude; and as a sign that he had entered into a covenant with God, he was commanded to circumcise his children.

[His son] Isaac was to inherit the promise, and it was renewed to him and to his father, when their faith had been proved by their submission to God's command, that Isaac should be offered as a burnt-offering upon Mount Moriah, a sign of the Great Sacrifice long afterwards, when God did indeed provide Himself a Lamb.

When Abraham bought the Cave of Machpelah for a, burial-place, it was in the full certainty that though he was now a stranger in the land, it would be his children's home; and it was there that he and the other patriarchs were buried after their long and faithful pilgrimage.

Isaac's wife, Rebekah, was fetched from Abraham's former home, in Mesopotamia, that he might not be corrupted by marrying a Canaanite. Between his two sons, Esau and Jacob, there was again a choice; for God had prophesied that the elder should serve the younger, and Esau did not value the birthright which would have made him heir to no lands that would enrich himself, and to a far-off honor that he did not understand. So despising the promises of God, he made his right over to his brother for a little food, when he was hungry, and though he repented with tears when it was too late, he could not win back what he had once thrown away.

His revengeful anger when he found how he had been supplanted, made Jacob flee to his mother's family in Mesopotamia, and there dwell for many years, before returning to Canaan with his large household, there to live in the manner that had been ordained for the first heirs of the promise.

Jacob's name was changed to Israel, which meant a prince before God; and his whole family were taken into the covenant, though the three elder sons, for their crimes, forfeited the foremost places, which passed to Judah and Joseph; and Levi was afterwards chosen as the tribe set apart for the priesthood, the number twelve being made up by reckoning Ephraim and Manasseh, the sons of Joseph, as heads of tribes, like their uncles. Long ago, Abraham had been told that his seed should sojourn in Egypt; and when the envious sons of Israel sold their innocent brother Joseph, their sin was bringing about God's high purpose. Joseph was inspired to interpret Pharaoh's dreams, which foretold the famine; and when by-and-by his brothers came to buy the corn that he had laid up, he made himself known, forgave them with all his heart, and sent them to fetch his father to see him once more. Then the whole family of Israel, seventy in number, besides their wives, came and settled in the land of Goshen and were there known by the name of Hebrews, after Heber, the great-grand-son of Shem. There in Goshen, Jacob ended the days of his pilgrimage, desiring his sons to carry his corpse back to the Cave of Machpelah, there to be buried, and await their return when the time of promise should come. He gave his blessing to all his sons, and was inspired to mark out Joseph among them as the one whose children should have the choicest earthly inheritance; but of the fourth son, he said, "The scepter shall not depart from Judah, nor a lawgiver from between his feet, until Shiloh come." Shiloh meant "Him that should be sent" and Judah was thus marked out to be the princely tribe, which was to have the rule until the Seed should come.

FROM BOOK OF THE ANCIENT WORLD FOR YOUNG READERS
By Dorothy Mills

THE LAND OF PALESTINE

Palestine is a very little land, but little lands have been of great importance in history; for example, Palestine, Greece, England, Belgium. The Palestine of the Hebrews was situated between the lands where the great empires of Egypt and Assyria and Babylon flourished. She was the meeting-place, as it were, for travelers and traders going to and from these countries, and in consequence the civilization of these places passed through her, and she was able to learn a great deal from them. But just as in modern times, Belgium, being on one of the high roads between France and Germany has been used over and over again as a battlefield by the European nations, so in ancient times, Palestine, on the high road between Egypt and Babylon was also the battlefield of nations, especially in the plains in the North. The war and commerce of nearly all the ancient world passed through this little land.

The Hebrew inhabitants of Palestine were not sailors; they never used the sea as a highway, but they looked upon it as a boundary, as something that cut them off from other peoples. There were some good harbors in the North, but these did not belong to the Hebrews.

The climate of Palestine is very varied. The top of Mount Hermon is covered with snow, but in the valley of the Jordan, not so very far away, there are tropical plants. In ancient times there was more forestland than now, and there were more olives. In those days, there were terraces "clad with vines." There are two clearly marked seasons in Palestine, the rainy and the dry. The rains fall from October to April, and then from May to October the land is dry. Spring is a most beautiful time, for in few other lands are there more wildflowers. The Hebrews called this time the "coming of flowers" and one of their poets wrote of the spring:

> Lo, the winter is past,
> The rain is over and gone;
> The flowers appear on the earth;
> The time of the singing of birds is come,
> And the voice of the turtle is heard in our land;
> The fig tree ripeneth her green figs,
> And the vines are in blossom,
> They give forth their fragrance.

The Hebrew people who came to this land and lived in it, came originally from beyond the Euphrates River, and the name "Hebrew" means "a dweller on the other side." The Hebrews called themselves the "Sons of Israel," taking their name from one of their ancestors. It is the story of these people that we read about in the Bible.

THE BIBLE

The world owes a great deal to the ancient Egyptians and to the Babylonians, but it owes still more to the Hebrews, for it was they who taught the world the knowledge of God. Politically the Hebrews were of little account in the world, but in the story of how man in learning how to live, has sought to satisfy the searching of his spirit, they stand supreme.

The Bible is the book in which the Hebrews have written their history. The word "Bible" is a Greek word meaning "book," though the word "book" is a wrong one to use, as the Bible is made up of a great many different books, written by many different writers over a long period of years. At one time, it was called the "Divine Library," which is really a much more accurate name. For convenience' sake, these books have been bound together in one volume, but doing this has made it difficult to remember how many different kinds of writing there are in it. When the Hebrews wrote it, they had paragraphs, made their poetry different from their prose, and kept the separate books apart. There were no chapters and verses, these were arranged much later in order to make it easier to find the various passages wanted. In the Bible, there are legends and history, law, poetry, religious teaching, in fact the whole literature of the Hebrew people. The history is written in an especially interesting way, for the writers have put it in a dramatic form, that is, they have made the people about whom they are telling us, do their own talking, as they would in a play, and like all Eastern peoples they use a language full of poetry and imagination.

The Hebrew people were always looking forward to the coming of a period of better conditions in the world, and their writings are very interesting records of progress, from ignorance to fuller knowledge, and from lower to higher ideals. Religion held the most important place in their lives, and the history of the Hebrew people is chiefly the history of how they learned to know the character of God. He was known to them by the Hebrew name Jehovah, and in the beginning they thought of Him as a stern master whose anger had to be appeased. Later He was to them the Lord of Hosts, Who fought for them as their Leader in war. At this time, they believed that other nations had their own gods, but they were different from God, for these gods were not regarded, even by those who believed in them, as entirely free from human frailties, whereas the Lord was a God of absolute righteousness and justice. As the centuries went by, the Hebrews learned that their early conceptions of God were inadequate, and that He was the One God of the whole world. Through their experiences, they learned to know His character and what allegiance to Him meant. They learned that:

> *You have been told, O Mortal, what is good,*
> *and what the Lord requires of you:*
> *Only to do justice and to love goodness,*
> *And to walk humbly with your God.*
> Micah 6:8

FROM BOOK OF THE ANCIENT WORLD FOR YOUNG READERS
By Dorothy Mills

THE LAND OF MESOPOTAMIA

Long ago, when men were first learning how to do things; when they were finding out how to write, how to build and how to make all kinds of things needed in their daily life; when they were first finding out something about nature, about the sun and the moon and the stars, about the rivers and the sea; and when the men of each country were learning that they were not the only people in the world, but that others were living in lands across the deserts and beyond the seas, there were two that were greater and of more importance than the others. These two were Egypt, and Assyria and Babylon.

Assyria and Babylon were the countries that were found along the banks of the Tigris and Euphrates, and to the northern part of these lands the Greeks gave the name "Mesopotamia," which is the Greek of the "land between the rivers." The earliest civilizations developed on the banks of rivers, for the waterways served as roads and made communication easier, it helped to make the land more fertile and so the supply of food was more certain. Of the two rivers in Mesopotamia, the Euphrates has been the more important; its current was not so swift as that of the Tigris, the banks were less steep, and the towns and the villages in its valley were more protected from attacks that might be made by unfriendly peoples from the East.

The traveler who goes to this land today finds in the North a desolate, bare and uncultivated plain, and in the South swamps and marshy districts, full of fever and malaria. In ancient times this dreary land was the garden of the world, and tradition tells us that in one beautiful region was the Garden of Eden. In the winter the climate was so soft and mild, that when Babylon formed a part of the Persian Empire, the Great Kings made Babylon one of their winter residences, in order to escape the cold of their own Persian land. This land between the rivers was rich and fertile. There were great towns full of palaces and temples and busy crowded streets were found on the banks of the rivers. Herodotus, the ancient historian, tells us of the wonderful grain he found growing there; he says: "The leaf of the wheat and barley is as much as three inches in width, and the stalks of the millet are so tall that no one who has never been in that country would believe me, were I to mention their height." Herodotus probably exaggerated, but in those days Babylonia produced so much grain that she supplied nearly all the known world. The land was also rich in palm trees, and fruit abounded. The rivers were full of fish, and waterfowl of all kinds lived in the reeds and rushes by the river banks.

What has happened to change this country? In those ancient times the kings and rulers saw to it that the land was irrigated. They built canals and regulated the floods, and so brought water to those parts of the country that otherwise would have been dry and parched. If all this were done today, Mesopotamia would be just as fertile as it was of old, but the land was ruled for such long years by the Turks, who have neglected everything that was useful, that this rich and fertile country has become a wilderness.

This land is just about as old as Egypt, but the dry and sandy soil of Egypt has preserved the ancient buildings in a way that the soil in Mesopotamia has not done, and so this country is not as rich in monuments of the past. There was not as good stone for building as there was in Egypt, and so the people used sun-dried bricks. Dotted about on the plains are mounds that show us where once there were cities. These cities began by being just a cluster of houses forming a little town, for people wanted to live near each other for safety. Then they would build a temple to some particular god who was supposed to have them in his special care. The chief man in the town would rule them as their king, and would build a palace for himself, and so gradually the town would become larger and the inhabitants would build strong walls around it as a defense against all enemies. The fields were generally outside the walls, though there were gardens within, so that in case of a siege the people would not starve. At first there were a number of these independent towns, but after a while there were some very strong kings who united them, and by gradually extending their power formed mighty kingdoms, which developed into powerful empires. Four great peoples ruled in turn over these lands; they were known as Sumerians, Babylonians, Assyrians, and the Later Babylonians, also known as the Chaldeans.

These peoples were very remarkable: they built great cities, they wrote many books and had large libraries, they knew a great deal about the stars, and the Babylonians were traders and merchants. The Assyrians were a very cruel nation; they waged constant war against their neighbors and were a scourge to the ancient world, until at last they were themselves destroyed.

After the fall of these empires, there followed a time when no one remembered anything more of them. The cities fell into ruin and were slowly covered up by dust and sand, until they looked only like great rubbish heaps. The gardens and fields became waste and desolate, the canals fell into disuse, and every year the desert sands drifted more over the land until everything was hidden. All memories were blotted out and history became silent. Then suddenly out of these dreary wastes, the buried cities reappeared, voices from the past spoke in the midst of the silence, and the life and splendor of these ancient peoples was discovered.

It came about in this way. From time to time explorers from Europe had taken home with them bricks and tablets covered with a strange writing, and the imagination of scholars, who knew what a flourishing place Mesopotamia had once been, began to see what might possibly be hidden under the dreary-looking mounds, and what secrets of the past they might discover, if only they could find more of the engraved bricks and learn to read the strange writing.

At the beginning of the nineteenth century a French consul had been sent to this dreary land. He was interested in the ancient past and had been told that if he would dig and search in the mounds, he would find treasures. Soon after his arrival he employed a great many Arab workmen to dig under one of the mounds, but for some time they found nothing. One day, however, a stranger Arab came wandering by and watched them at work, and on hearing what they wanted to find, he told the Frenchman, that if what he wanted was stones and bricks covered with carving, he would find plenty of them at a mound a few hours' journey away. So they went and began to dig, and what did they find? Not only a great many carved stones and bricks, but what no eye had seen for centuries. They found the lower part of a whole palace, the walls of which were covered with the most wonderful sculptures which represented scenes from Assyrian life: war and feasting and hunting, and at the doors stood strange beasts with heads like men, wings like angels, and bodies like bulls and lions. They worked hard and soon the whole palace and part of the town near it was unearthed. All the rooms could be traced: reception rooms, bedrooms, kitchens; and the walls were decorated with sculptures showing the life of the people who once had lived there.

A few years later an Englishman began to work on another mound. From his boyhood he had loved adventure, he had read the Arabian Nights and every tale of the mysterious East he could find, and now it seemed to him that his boyhood dreams of really finding hidden cities of the past were about to come true. He spent the night before he began to work on the mound in an Arab town, and he has told us of his thoughts as he lay awake waiting for the dawn.

> Hopes long cherished were now to be realized or to end in disappointment. Visions of palaces underground, of gigantic monsters, of sculptured figures, and endless inscriptions floated before me. After forming plan after plan for removing the earth and extricating these treasures, I fancied myself wandering in a maze of chambers from which I could find no outlet. Then, again, all was reburied and I was standing on the grass-covered mound. Exhausted, I was at length sinking into sleep when, hearing the voice of Awad (his Arab host), I rose from my carpet and joined him outside the hovel.

It was morning and work began, and did his hopes come true? He found more than he had dared expect. A great palace was unearthed full of sculpture, and guarding the silent palace were found more winged bulls and lions. As these creatures rose mysteriously out of the ground, the Arabs were in great fear, for it seemed to them that these silent winged beings were spirits rising out of the underworld to do them harm. But their fears vanished when the strange beasts were found to be of stone. They were sent to London, where they now stand at guard over the treasures from these lands that are in the British Museum.

But an even greater discovery was then made, though it did not seem to be such a thrilling one at first. Some rooms were found full of little clay tablets covered with writing. When this writing had been deciphered, it was discovered that these tablets were books, and they were full of stories of the beliefs of the Assyrians and Babylonians about how the world was made, and the stories of their great heroes. There were also books of science telling about the stars, and medicine, and there were a great many letters.

Some of the most interesting of the tablets were those on which was written the story of a Flood, very similar to the Hebrew story in the book of Genesis, and those tablets which have been called the Creation Tablets, because from them we learn how the Babylonians believed the world had been created; and like the Flood story, these, too, in many ways resemble the Hebrew story of the Creation. Marduk was the Babylonian Creator, and the story tells us that

He laid a reed on the face of the waters,
He formed dust and poured it out beside the reed,
That he might cause the gods to dwell in the dwelling of their
   hearts' desire,
He formed mankind;
With him the goddess Aruru created the seed of mankind.
The beasts of the field and living things in the field he formed;
The Tigris and Euphrates he created and established in their place;
Their names he proclaimed in a goodly manner.
The grass, the rush of the marsh, the reed and the forest he created.
The lands, the marshes and the swamps,
The wild cow and her young, the wild calf,
The ewe and her young and the lamb of the fold.

It is from these discoveries that after two thousand years of silence, we have been able to learn about the life of the people who lived along the banks of the Tigris and Euphrates.

FROM OUR OLD WORLD BACKGROUND
By Charles Beard

THE GREAT NATIONS OF ANTIQUITY

After mankind learned to tame animals and till the soil, the number of people on the earth increased. Rich grazing lands were made use of for flocks and herds. Fertile river valleys were laid out into fields for cultivation. Men who had once thought only of hunting and fishing settled down with the women to the arts of peace. Wealth in cattle and grain accumulated.

Then those who had riches became a target for the tribes which kept their old fighting habits. Warriors found it easier to conquer and rob than to watch flocks or till the soil themselves. Warfare on a large scale came to plague the earth's multitudes. Out of warfare sprang powerful military leaders who conquered vast territories inhabited by herdsmen and tillers of the soil. So began the making of kingdoms and empires, wide reaching and long enduring.

ANCIENT DESPOTS

The oldest nations of which we have written records rose in the fertile valleys of the Nile and Euphrates rivers, in the regions generally known as Egypt and Babylonia. There many a kingdom was set up, flourished, and vanished thousands of years before Christ. Indeed, the history of the earliest centuries about which we know anything is little more than a story of one mighty king after another.

First, it seems, warriors from the regions of Babylonia conquered the lands east to the mountains and west to the Mediterranean. They ruled millions of subjects and were, in turn, themselves overthrown.

Then the emperors, or Pharaohs, of Egypt extended their dominion by force of arms from the Sahara to the banks of the Euphrates. They governed their subjects with pomp and ceremony. Then they, too, were beaten in battles. After them came the Persian emperors, who overran all Asia Minor and Egypt and boasted of an empire greater than any the world had yet seen. They also had their day and left behind nothing but a few relics to tell of their riches and power.

One modern scholar fixes the date of the first Egyptian king at more than 5000 years before Christ; another places it at 3400 B.C. The earliest mention of Babylon is at least 3800 B.C. We know that about 2300 B.C. the borders of the kingdom of Babylon reached the shores of the Mediterranean. We know that before the earliest kings of whom we have written records there were hundreds of minor rulers who built up great states and disappeared before new conquerors.

The striking thing about these ancient kings is that they were all despots, or absolute rulers. That the common people, who tilled the fields, wove the cloth, or guarded the herds, should have a voice in their own government was not thought of. The king stood above all. Everything was made to glorify his name. The mighty pyramids of Egypt were the tombs of kings. The ruins of temples that still stand tell of their majesty. The pictures on the crumbling walls, the huge statues that once adorned imperial cities, the songs and ballads that have survived the wreck of ages, all bear witness to the prowess and grandeur of the despot. Artists, architects, and writers vied with one another in praising the names and deeds of their royal masters. Some kings ruled more wisely than others, but practically all of them ruled without regard to the desires of their peoples. They levied taxes at will; they imprisoned or put to death any who incurred their displeasure; they waged war, whenever they liked, to gain territory or to add to their glory. Their strength lay in the ignorance and fear of their subjects; their weakness lay in the fact that their subjects and slaves did not care much whether their rulers were overthrown in battle or not.

Under such a system, the people had no freedom of spirit. They had to flatter the king to secure his favor. They cringed before him to escape his ill will. They said and wrote things to please him. As despotism was the chief mark of the government, so cowardice and cringing were the chief marks of the subjects. Fraud and deceit became common; for by deceit the king's taxes and penalties could be avoided.

JOSEPH THE DREAMER
By Amy Steedman

This is the story of Joseph, the boy who had the strangest and most exciting adventures of any boy who ever lived.

Joseph was but a little lad when his mother died. His father, Jacob, had loved that mother more than any one else in the world, so that when she died leaving Joseph and a baby brother, Benjamin, all the love in the father's heart turned to his two little sons.

The elder brothers were strong, grown-up men, quite able to look after themselves, and no longer needing their father's care; so perhaps it was no wonder that Jacob made a special favorite of the little lad Joseph, and loved him best.

At first the older brothers took no notice of their father's way with the younger boy; but as Joseph grew older they began to feel uneasy and envious. Why should this child be marked out for special favor? Their father took no pains to hide the fact that the boy was the apple of his eye. Even his clothes showed this.

While the brothers wore the ordinary shepherd clothing, Joseph had a beautiful coat of many colors. His father had made it for him of different pieces of colored cloth joined together, and it was so bright and beautiful that everyone who saw him wearing it said, "This must be the son of a great chief!"

But if the coat made them angry, they were more angry still when Joseph began to dream strange dreams, which he always told to them.

As they sat around in the fields watching the sheep, the boy would come running to them, full of excitement, as he begged them to listen to a wonderful dream he had had.

"Hear, I ask you, this dream that I have dreamed!" he cried, sitting down among them. "We were binding sheaves in a field, and lo! my sheaf arose and also stood upright, and, behold, your sheaves stood round about and bowed to my sheaf!"

Another time his dream was about the stars; the sun and moon and eleven stars, he said, had all bowed down before him. This was really more than his brothers could bear. Did he really think he was going to rule over them? Were they to bow down before this boasting boy in his fine coat?

Even his father did not quite approve of these dreams. But Joseph had not really meant to boast. It was the wonder of the dreams that made him repeat them. If he was proud of his coat of many colors, it was only because it was a gift from his father. He was a straightforward good-natured boy, clever and brave, and ready to take his turn in watching the flocks or helping his brothers with their work in the fields.

But it grew day by day more difficult to keep the peace at home, and the only quiet times were when the elder brothers went farther afield to find new pasture for their flocks.

It was at one of these times, when the brothers had been gone for some time, that Jacob called Joseph to him, and bade him go and find his brothers, and bring back news if they were safe and well.

Joseph was now a lad of about seventeen, and this would be the first journey he had taken by himself, so he was eager to show that he was to be trusted, and he set out most cheerfully.

After some days he arrived at Shechem, where his father had told him he would find his brothers. But he could find no signs of them there. Unwilling to go home without news, Joseph wandered about until he met a man who directed him to a place farther on where his brothers might be, and at last he caught sight of their tents in a field far ahead. How lucky he was to find them, he thought to himself, as he hurried forward eager to meet them.

It was a clear day, and the shepherds' keen eyes could see far along the winding road that stretched out across the low hills towards Shechem. Long before Joseph came within hail, his brothers saw his figure in the distance hastening towards them. Perhaps it was the gay color of his coat that first told them who it was, and perhaps it was the coat that reminded them of their hate and envy, and brought back to their memory again those dreams so full of pride.

"Behold, this dreamer comes!" they said one to another. "Come now, therefore, and let us slay him, and cast him into some pit, and we will say, 'Some evil beast has devoured him!' and we shall see what will become of his dreams."

With dark looks of hate they watched the colorful figure coming so joyfully towards them, and only one heart felt any pity for the boy. Reuben, the eldest brother, made up his mind quickly that he would save him if possible. Only he must set to work cunningly, for those other nine brothers were very determined men.

So he began by suggesting that it seemed quite unnecessary to kill the boy themselves when the easiest plan would be just to put him down the pit, which was close at hand, and there leave him to die. (For he thought if he could persuade them to do this he would come back and save Joseph when the others had gone.) Never dreaming of evil, Joseph came on, and now he ran eagerly up to them and began to give them their father's message.

But the rough hands held out to him were not held out in welcome. The brothers seized the boy and savagely tore off his beautiful coat, as if the very sight of it hurt their eyes, and then they hurried him towards the pit which Reuben had pointed out.

Then Joseph knew that they meant to kill him. He knew that if they threw him into one of those deep narrow pits there was no chance of climbing up its steep sides, even if he were not immediately drowned in the water which often gathered at the bottom.

Was he never to see his father and little brother again? Never to spend any more happy days in the fields under the blue sky? It was useless to cry out and beg for pity. Reuben, the eldest brother, who might have helped him, was not there, and the others he knew were merciless.

The pit was reached, and in spite of his cries strong hands pushed him forward and over the edge. Down, down he fell into the blackness, until with a terrible thud he reached the bottom. There was no water to break his fall, for the pit was dry.

Well—that was done! The cruel brothers went off to a little distance and began to eat their midday meal. But scarcely had they begun when they caught sight of a company of travellers passing along the road close by. There was a long train of camels laden with spices, evidently on their way down to Egypt.

Here was a splendid opportunity of making some money out of their evil plan. Instead of leaving Joseph to starve in the pit, they would fetch him out and sell him to these merchants. Most likely they would get a good price for such a strong young slave.

Perhaps when Joseph heard their voices at the pit's mouth, and when they drew him up and lifted him out into the sunshine again, he thought for a moment that they meant to be kind to him after all. But that thought soon vanished.

The Midianite merchants were waiting, the bargain was struck, and very soon a rope was bound round his hands, and he was tied to the saddle of the man who had bought him. He knew now they had only taken him out of the pit to sell him as a slave.

Meanwhile Reuben had been keeping out of sight, waiting to return and rescue his young brother as soon as it was safe to do so. Very cautiously at last he stole back. But, alas! when he reached the pit he found that it was empty. In his distress he forgot his caution, and cared no longer if his brothers guessed what he had meant to do.

"The child is not, and I, where shall I go?" he cried to them in bitter sorrow when he met them.

With angry, sullen looks they told him that Joseph was now far away on his road to Egypt. Reuben must keep their secret. There was but one thing to be done. Joseph's coat lay there, just as they had torn it off his back. They would dip the coat in goat's blood and carry it to their father.

The poor, brightly-colored little coat, all blood-stained and torn, was brought and held up before Jacob's eyes.

"This have we found," said the brothers; "know now whether it be your son's coat or not?"

Did he not, indeed, know that coat of many colors? Had he not matched and joined together each of the pieces? Had not his heart been filled with pride and love as he watched the boy wearing it with such a gallant air?

"It is my son's coat!" he cried with a bitter cry of grief; "an evil beast has devoured him! Joseph is without doubt rent in pieces!"

It might perhaps have seemed better just then for Joseph if he had been dead instead of being carried away into slavery. It was a terrible fate, and he might well have become sullen and hopeless in the strange land of Egypt to which the merchantmen took him.

But instead of being sorry for himself, and thinking only of the unkindness and wickedness of his cruel brothers, he made the best of everything, and set himself to do his new hard work as well as possible. If he was a slave he would, at any rate, be a thoroughly good slave.

And very soon his master, Potiphar, found that this fair-haired, good-looking Hebrew boy was one to be trusted, and, as time went on, he not only gave him his freedom, but made him the chief servant of the house-hold. Then, just when happy days began to dawn for Joseph, misfortune once more overtook him.

His master's wife accused him of doing wrong, and declared he was thoroughly bad. And so all his well-deserved favors were taken from him, and he was put into prison.

Even in prison Joseph's quiet goodness and his wise ways made him a favorite. He was the friend of all the other prisoners, and before long he became the governor's right hand.

Still it was weary work to be shut up in prison, and he longed with all his heart for freedom, and a chance to win a place for himself in the great world. He knew that Pharaoh, the King of

Egypt, was not unfriendly to strangers. If only he could reach his ear all might be well.

At last the chance came. There were two of Pharaoh's servants in the prison—one, the king's cup-bearer, and the other his chief baker, and both these were sorely troubled one night because of the dreams they had dreamt. They were sure these dreams had a meaning, but who was to explain them?

Now Joseph had learned to know a great deal about dreams, and so he listened to these men and told them what he thought their dreams must mean.

The chief baker's dream was a sad one. He had dreamt of three baskets which he carried on his head—baskets filled with the king's food—but the birds had come and eaten up all the food. "Alas!" said Joseph, "the three baskets must mean three days, and in three days the baker must be hanged, and the birds would come and eat his flesh."

But the cup-bearer's dream was a happy one, for he had seen a vine which bore three clusters of grapes, which he had pressed out into the king's cup and presented to Pharaoh. The three clusters of grapes were again three days, said Joseph, and in three days' time the cup-bearer would be once more free and hand the king his golden cup.

"But think of me when it shall be well with you," added Joseph to the cup-bearer, "and show kindness, I beg you, to me, and make mention of me to Pharaoh, and bring me out of this house. For, indeed, I was stolen away out of the land of the Hebrews, and here also have I done nothing that they should put me into the dungeon."

In three days all that Joseph had said came true. The chief baker was hanged, and the chief butler was set free, and stood once more before the king; only he quite forgot the man who had been so kind to him in prison, and for two years never once thought of Joseph.

But at last something happened that reminded him. Once again it was a dream, but this time the dreamer was Pharaoh, the great king. He had sent for all the cleverest men in the land to explain his dreams to him, but no one could find a meaning for them.

Then the cup-bearer suddenly remembered Joseph, and came and told the king all that had happened to him when he was in prison. Surely it would be worth while to try this man. So Pharaoh sent and brought Joseph out of prison, and asked him if it was true that he could tell the meaning of dreams.

There was no pride nor boastfulness in Joseph's answer. Of himself, he said, he could do nothing; but with God's help he would tell the king all that he could.

So Pharaoh told his dreams, and as Joseph listened he knew at once that they had been sent as a warning from God. Seven years of good harvests and plenty of food were coming, and after that seven years of famine, when, if all the food of the good years was eaten up, the people would starve. The warning dreams had been sent so that the corn might be saved up and stored. And it would be a good plan, said Joseph, to find the very wisest and best man in all the land who would undertake to do this.

Pharaoh listened thoughtfully, and soon made up his mind. He felt at once that Joseph was a man to be trusted.

"Forasmuch as God has shown you all this," he said, "there is none so discreet and wise as you are. You shall be over my house, and according to your word shall all my people be ruled. Only in the throne will I be greater than you."

What a wonderful adventure this was for Joseph! One day only a poor unknown prisoner, and the next the lord and ruler over all the land of Egypt—next only to the king in power.

But although Joseph's outside life was changed, he himself remained just the same. He was as keen as ever on doing his best, as brave and fearless in serving God and the king, as wise in ruling as he had been in serving.

So when the years of famine came there were great stores of corn laid up to feed the Egyptians, and not only the people of Egypt, but strangers from other lands came to Joseph, the Ruler, to buy food.

Then it was that one day ten tired, travel-stained men arrived at the city, saying they had come from the far-distant land of Canaan to buy corn for their wives and families, who were starving.

Joseph knew them at once. They were his ten brothers—those brothers whom he had last seen when, as a helpless boy, he had knelt and begged them for mercy. Now they came kneeling to the great ruler, little dreaming that this powerful prince was the young brother they had betrayed and sold into slavery.

And Joseph did not mean to tell them just yet. He pretended to take them for spies, and he spoke roughly to them.

"Your servants are no spies," the brothers answered humbly. "We are the sons of one man, in the land of Canaan, and, behold, the youngest is this day with our father, and one is not."

Even then Joseph pretended that he did not believe them. No, they must first prove their words by bringing their youngest brother to him. They might leave one of their number behind as a hostage, and take corn for their families, and return to fetch their brother. This he said because he longed to see Benjamin again.

The men listened sadly to what the great man said. They must have the corn or their families would starve. And yet how could they leave one of their brothers behind when they knew their father would never allow Benjamin to return with them.

"This is just what we deserve," they said to one another. "We would not listen to Joseph when he begged for mercy, and now this is our punishment."

"Did I not beg you not to hurt the child?" said Reuben.

They did not know, of course, that the great ruler could understand what they were saying in their own language; but as Joseph listened he was obliged to turn away to hide the tears that were in his eyes.

There was nothing for it but to agree to the conditions, so it was decided that Simeon should be left behind, and the order was given that all the sacks should be filled with corn, and that every man's ass should be laden with as much corn as could be carried; only, instead of taking money for the corn, Joseph ordered that it should be secretly hidden in the sacks, each man's money in his sack of corn.

So the men started off on their journey home, and travelling all day came at night to an inn to rest. There one of the men opened his sack to give his ass some food. What, then, was his surprise to find his bundle of money tied up in the mouth of his sack!

The other brothers gathered round and looked on in amazement. Yes, it was quite true. There was the money which was the price of the corn—not a penny of it taken! What could it mean?

But they were still more amazed when at last they came to their journey's end and found, when they opened their sacks, that all their money had been returned. There was a bundle of money in each sack!

It was so strange that they grew uneasy and frightened. Then, too, they were obliged to tell their father that Simeon had been left behind as a hostage, and that the great lord of the country had taken them for spies, and had demanded that Benjamin should return with them before he would believe their story.

But Jacob would not hear of parting with his youngest son. Had he not lost two sons already, first his beloved Joseph, and now Simeon?

"Will you also take Benjamin from me?" he asked. "All these things are against me!"

In vain Reuben promised that he would bring Benjamin safely back. Jacob only shook his head.

"My son shall not go down with you," he said. "His brother is dead, and he is left alone. If mischief befall him by the way in the which you go, then shall you bring down my gray hairs with sorrow to the grave!"

Now that was all very well while the corn lasted; but when the famine still went on, and all the corn was eaten up, there was nothing to be done but to go back to Egypt and try to buy some more.

And it was no use going without Benjamin, for had not the great lord of the country declared, "You shall not see my face except your brother be with you."

So at last Jacob was obliged to let his precious son go with his brothers, although it almost broke his heart to part with him.

Now Joseph had been quite sure that his brothers would return, and when at last they appeared he was overjoyed to see that Benjamin was with them. He ordered a great feast to be made, and invited them all to dine with him; but still he kept his secret, and they did not guess who he was, although they could not help noticing that Benjamin was singled out for special favor.

So their sacks were filled again with corn, and the brothers prepared to set out joyfully on their return journey. Only this time Joseph had ordered his servants to put his silver cup into Benjamin's sack.

The men had not gone far before they were overtaken by the great ruler's servants, who accused them of stealing their lord's silver cup. Of course they indignantly denied this; but when the baggage was searched the cup was found in Benjamin's sack.

Now indeed was their joy turned into blackest sorrow. They must go back at once to try and explain matters to the lord of the land. But would he listen to them?

At first Joseph pretended to be very angry, but as he listened to their tale and heard how they dared not face their father without the beloved youngest son, he saw that they had earned his forgiveness, and he kept up the pretense no longer. Sending all the servants away he held out his hands to his brothers, his eyes blinded with tears.

"I am Joseph, your brother, whom you sold into Egypt," he said. "Now, therefore, be not grieved nor angry with yourselves that you sold me here, for God did send me before you to preserve life."

At first the brothers could scarcely believe their ears. Could this great lord really be their little brother Joseph? And could he really forgive them their cruelty?

Then Joseph put his arm round Benjamin's neck and kissed him, and afterwards kissed each of his other brothers, so that they began to feel that the wonderful story was real and not a mere dream.

There was no fear of famine for them now. Nothing in all the land was too good for the brothers of the great ruler, and before long there were wagons and camels on their way to Canaan to fetch Jacob, the old father, and all the wives and children belonging to the ten brothers. They would all now share in Joseph's good fortune.

So Jacob's sorrow was turned into joy when the news was brought to him that Joseph was alive and was governor over all the land of Egypt.

It sounded almost like a magic tale, and at first Jacob could not believe it; but at last, when he saw the wagons and heard Joseph's own message to him, his heart was filled with joy and thankfulness.

"It is enough," he cried. "Joseph, my son, is yet alive; I will go and see him before I die."

It was a long journey for such an old man; but joy gave him strength to endure it, and at the end Joseph stood waiting to welcome him—Joseph the great ruler, clad in rich robes, living in princely state, whose word was law, and who held the highest honors in the land.

FROM BOOK OF THE ANCIENT WORLD
By Dorothy Mills

HAMMURABI

The most ancient race that lived near the Euphrates was that of the Sumerians. Until a very short time ago, this people seemed to belong to that far-away past that was dim and almost unreal to us. It was known that their language had survived a long time after they themselves had disappeared, for it became the religious language of the Babylonians, and all their legends and stories of their gods, their hymns and prayers were written in Sumerian.

Recently, however, tombs have been found, the contents of which show that the Sumerians had developed a civilization older even than that of Egypt. About 3500-3200 B.C. the period when Memphis was the old capital of Egypt, and Menes was uniting Upper and Lower Egypt into one kingdom, the Sumerians had developed a skill in various arts and crafts that was only attained later by the Egyptians. In the tomb of Queen Shub-Ad was found goldsmith's work, jewellery, pins, combs, exquisite head-dresses of gold inlaid with colored stones, work that could only be the result of a long period of development. Work in other metals, bowls, and goblets, inlaid lyres and harps, mosaic work, carvings in ivory have also been found, all of which for artistic skill and workmanship can stand worthily beside anything made later in Egypt or Babylonia.

From these discoveries, it would seem that though the Sumerians as a distinct race disappeared, the later peoples who followed them inherited their civilization, and what was originally Sumerian developed gradually and almost imperceptibly into early Babylonian.

The kings of these early Babylonians became powerful about four thousand years ago. The greatest of them was called Hammurabi, and he has left us two things which tell us about the life of his time. The first is a collection of letters he wrote, and the second is a large slab of stone on which his laws are inscribed. His letters show us what were some of the duties of a Babylonian king. We can picture him sitting in his palace with his secretary by his side to whom he dictated his letters. The secretary would take a reed stylus out of the holder at his girdle and as the King dictated, he would cover a clay tablet with wedge-shaped writing. Then he would sprinkle a handful of dry powdered clay over the soft wet tablet in order to prevent the clay from sticking to the surface. He would then write the address on the clay and send the letter out to be put in the furnace and baked.

The King had a great many things about which he had to write, for all kind of matters that nowadays would be dealt with by various officials, in those days were directly attended to by the King himself. He may have received a letter saying that there were floods in the river and that the boats were delayed, so he would send a reply ordering the governor of that province to clear the channel and make it navigable again. To another he would send a warning that the taxes were due and that they must be paid promptly; another governor would receive orders to punish three officials who were guilty of bribery, and he would be told quite sharply to see that the royal orders were carried out. Other letters were sent with instructions about sending laborers to certain places, or ordering slaves to be brought before him. Directions were also given for harvesting the royal corn, for sheep-shearing, and for strengthening the walls of the city. Then there were other letters to be written about certain feasts that were to be observed, and about the King's property in the country that must be looked after.

Hammurabi was one of the first of ancient kings who understood that his chief duty was to care for the well-being of his people. He drew up a code of the ancient laws of Babylon, the earliest code as yet known, and had it engraved upon a shaft of stone, at the top of which was a slab of sculpture in which he was represented as receiving the law from the Sun-God. In the prologue to his code of laws Hammurabi described himself as an exalted prince and worshipper of the gods, who had been divinely called to administer justice, to destroy all that was wicked and evil, to prevent the strong from oppressing the weak, to enlighten the land and to further the welfare of the people. He declared that he had brought about plenty and abundance and made the fame of Babylon great, that he was a soldier who had no equal. Hammurabi insisted on justice to the poor in his laws, but his ideas of punishment were the old primitive ones of "an eye for an eye and a tooth for a tooth," and injuries were to be punished by inflicting on the culprit whatever he had inflicted on others. This spirit is shown in the following ways:

> If a man destroy the eye of a man, his eye shall they put out.
>
> If a man knock out the teeth of his equal, his teeth shall be knocked out.
>
> If a doctor has put out the eye, his hands shall be cut off.
>
> If a son strike his father, they shall cut off his fingers.
>
> If a builder build a house for a man and does not make its construction firm, and the house which he has built collapsed, that builder shall be put to death.

FROM BOOK OF THE ANCIENT WORLD
By Dorothy Mills

CUNEIFORM WRITING

Ashurbanipal collected a library, but the books that made up this library did not look in the least like our books, neither were they like the Egyptian papyrus rolls. In ancient days there were two ways of writing: one was to use a brush or a reed and with different colored pigments to paint what was to be written on a soft material that could be rolled: this was the method used by the Egyptians. The other way was to take a tablet of soft clay or wax, and to scratch the writing on it with a sharp-pointed tool, called a stylus; this was what the Assyrians and Babylonians did.

Like the Egyptians, they began by having a picture writing, but even sooner than the Egyptians they began to find it very tiresome to have to draw so many pictures, especially as it was difficult to draw well on clay, and so they dropped off bits here and bits there, until there were only signs left. Assyrian and Babylonian writing is called "cuneiform," a word which means "wedge-shaped," and it is quite easy to see why it has this name. With his papyrus, and his reed pens and paints for ink, the Egyptian scribe could make graceful lines and pictures for his writing, but the Assyrian and Babylonian with his sharp stylus and clay could only make deep cuts and thick wedge-shaped marks, and so the cuneiform writing is not so pretty to look at as the hieroglyphics. The characters were very small, so small that a magnifying glass has to be used in deciphering them. It is possible that Assyrian scribes used magnifying glasses when writing, for a crystal lens was found at Nineveh.

The Egyptian book was made out of a long papyrus roll, the Assyrian or Babylonian book was made up of numbers of small clay tablets. This form of book was another reason why the cuneiform writing became so shortened. A book was a very clumsy thing, and the shorter the words, the fewer the tablets needed. But if clay books are clumsy, these ancient clay books had some good points. Egyptian papyrus was very expensive and took time to make; clay was cheap, and only needed to be pressed into the right shape and it was ready for use. When these tablets had been written on, they were baked, and this made them hard and durable: they could not be burned in the fire, nor hurt in water, and if they were broken, they could be put together again. The result for us is that there are thousands of clay tablets, covered with cuneiform writing which has been deciphered, and books about history, geography, astronomy, letters, stories and poetry have all been found. The clay tablet pages were all numbered, and in this way: if the first tablet of a story began with the words, "In the days of King Sargon," that tablet would be numbered "First tablet of In the days of King Sargon"; the next would be, "Second tablet of In the days of King Sargon," and so on to the end. It was necessary to name the story of its beginning every time, as there was no way of binding the pages together, and if they got lost or mixed up it was like a very difficult puzzle to put them together again. Another custom, which is still to be found in some old English books, was to begin every tablet with the last few words of the preceding tablet. In this way, it was not so difficult to keep the tablet pages in their right order.

Like the Egyptians, the Assyrians and Babylonians had scribes to write for them. When a letter had been written, it would be signed by pressing the seal (which every Assyrian and Babylonian wore on his wrist for the purpose), on the clay, and then it would be baked and a clay envelope would be rolled round it, and the address written on it with the stylus.

The key to the understanding of cuneiform writing was found in Persia, of which the story will be told in its own place.

Unit Three: Egypt and Exodus

THEME: TRUSTING IN DIVINE PROVIDENCE

FROM THE CHOSEN PEOPLE
By Charlotte Yonge

INTRODUCTION TO EGYPT

"When Israel was a child I loved him,
out of Egypt I called my son."
—Hosea, 11:1

The country where the Israelites had taken up their abode, was the valley watered by the great river Nile. There is nothing but desert, wherever this river does not spread itself, for it never rains, and there would be dreadful drought, if every year, when the snow melts upon the mountains far south, where is the source of the stream, it did not become so much swelled as to spread far beyond its banks, and overflow all the flat space round it. Then as soon as the water subsides, the hot sun upon the mud that it has left brings up most beautiful grass, and fine crops of corn with seven or nine ears to one stalk; grand fruits of all kinds, melons, pumpkins, and cucumbers, flax for weaving linen, and everything that a people can desire. Indeed, the water of the river is so delicious, that it is said that those who have once tasted it are always longing to drink it again.

The sons of Mizraim, son of Ham, who first found out this fertile country, were a very clever race, and made the most of the riches of the place. They made dykes and ditches to guide the floodings into their fields and meadows; they cultivated the soil till it was one beautiful garden; they wove their flax into fine linen; and they made bricks of their soft clay, and hewed stone from the hills higher up the river, so that their buildings have been the wonder of all ages since. They had kings to rule them, and priests to guide their worship; but these priests had very wrong and corrupt notions themselves, and let the poor ignorant people believe even greater folly than they did themselves.

They thought that the great God lived among them in the shape of a bull with one spot on his back like an eagle, and one on his tongue like a beetle; and this creature they called Apis, and tended with the utmost care. When he died they all went into mourning, and lamented till a calf like him was found, and was brought home with the greatest honor; and for his sake all cattle were sacred, and no one allowed to kill them. Besides the good Power, they thought there was an evil one as strong as the good, and they worshipped him likewise, to beg him to do them no harm; so the dangerous crocodiles of the Nile were sacred, and it was forbidden to put them to death. They had a dog-god and a cat-goddess, and they honored the beetle because they saw it rolling a ball of earth in which to lay its eggs, and fancied it an emblem of eternity; and thus all these creatures were consecrated, and when they died were rolled up in fine linen and spices, just as the Egyptians embalmed their own dead.

Mummies, as we call these embalmed Egyptian corpses, are often found now, laid up in beautiful tombs, cut out in the rock, and painted in colors still fresh with picture writing, called hieroglyphics, telling in tokens all the history of the person whose body they contained. The kings built tombs for themselves, like mountains, square at the bottom, but each course of stones built within the last till they taper to a point at the top. These are called pyramids, and have within them very small narrow passages, leading to a small chamber, just large enough to hold a king's coffin.

They had enormous idols hewn out of stone. The head of one, which you may see in the British Museum, is far taller than the tallest man, and yet the face is really handsome, and there are multitudes more, both of them and of their temples, still remaining on the banks of the Nile. The children of Israel, being chiefly shepherds, kept apart from the Egyptians at first; but as time went on they learnt some of their habits, and many of them had begun to worship their idols and forget the truth, when their time of affliction came. The King of Egypt, becoming afraid of having so numerous and rich a people settled in his dominions, tried to keep them down by hard bondage and heavy labor. He made them toil at his great buildings, and oppressed them in every possible manner; and when he found that they still throve and increased, he made the cruel decree, that every son who was born to them should be cast into the river.

But man can do nothing against the will of God, and this murderous ordinance proved the very means of causing one of these persecuted Hebrew infants to be brought up in the palace of Pharaoh, and instructed in all the wisdom of the Egyptians, the only people who at that time had any human learning. Even in his early life, Moses seems to have been aware that he was to be sent to put an end to the bondage of his people, for, choosing rather to suffer with them than to live in prosperity with their oppressors, he went out among them and tried to defend them, and to set them at peace with one another; but the time was not yet come, and they thrust him from them, so that he was forced to fly for shelter to the desert, among the Midianite descendants of Abraham. After he had spent forty years there as a shepherd, God appeared to him, and then first revealed Himself as YHWH, the Name proclaiming His eternal self-existence, I AM THAT I AM, a Name so holy, that the translators of our Bible have abstained from repeating it where it occurs, but have put the Name, the LORD, in capital letters in its stead. Moses was then sent to Egypt to lead out the Israelites on their way back to the land so long promised to their fore-fathers; and when Pharaoh obstinately refused to let them go, the dreadful plagues and wonders that were sent on the country were such as to show that their gods were no gods; since their river, the glory of their land, became a loathsome stream of blood, creeping things came and went at the bidding of the Lord, and their adored cattle perished before their eyes. At last, on the night of the Passover, in each of the houses unmarked by the blood of the Lamb, there was a great cry over the death of the first-born son; and where the sign of faith was seen, there was a mysterious obedient festival held by families prepared for a strange new journey. Then the hard heart yielded to terror, and Israel went out of Egypt as a nation. They had come in as seventy men, they went out as six hundred thousand, and their enemies, following after them, sank like lead in the mighty waters of that arm of the Red Sea, which had divided to let the chosen pass through.

FROM BOOK OF THE ANCIENT WORLD
By Dorothy Mills

THE HISTORY OF ANCIENT EGYPT

THE LAND OF EGYPT

Egypt is one of the most interesting countries in the world. Its records are among the oldest, and it has had a long and wonderful history. This book is going to tell the story of those faraway days, thousands of years ago, in that interesting country, and we shall be able to learn how people lived then, how their houses were built and how they dressed, how they worked and traded and fought, how they amused themselves, and how they worshipped in their temples. In museums there are still to be seen many articles used by the Egyptians, things they had in their houses, jewelry, ornaments, weapons, and toys with which the children played. There are few other countries in the world able to show us such ancient things as Egypt, and these things are not only interesting because they are old, but because they are the beginnings of many things that we use today: the first paper, the first writing, the first book, the first statue all came from Egypt.

Now in every land, the shape of the country, the surroundings and the climate have had a great deal to do with the history of the people who lived there, and this is especially true of Egypt. If you look at a map, you will see that Egypt is a long and narrow country along the banks of the river Nile. Someone once described the shape of Egypt as being like a lily, the Nile being the long and crooked stem, and the Delta the flower. The Nile is about three thousand miles long, a little longer than the width across the Atlantic Ocean between Europe and America. Its source is in Victoria Nyanza in Central Africa, and it is known then as the White Nile; about thirteen hundred and fifty miles from the sea it is joined by the Blue Nile, and a hundred and forty miles further on by the Atbara; after this junction the river flows on to the sea as a single stream, the Nile itself.

Egypt is very narrow compared to its length, it consists of the valley of the river and nothing more. Between the Nile and the Red Sea are the Arabian Mountains; they are wild and desolate and no Egyptian ever made them his home, but the region was used as a stone quarry, and there the Egyptians went to procure the great stones for their huge buildings. It was a dreary land, where famine and thirst and death reigned. Slaves were sent to work in the quarries, and many never returned. West of the Nile are the Libyan Mountains, just as desolate as the mountains in the east, and beyond these the land slopes down to the Desert of Sahara. The land of Egypt is, therefore, simply the strip of land lying on either bank of the Nile, about seven hundred miles in length, with desolate, lifeless mountains on each side as soon as the river valley is left behind. The width of the valley varies from ten to thirty miles; sometimes the mountains come so close to the river that there are only a few miles of fertile land on the bank. There is very little rain in Egypt, hardly any at all in upper Egypt. The sky is a beautiful blue, and the sun is always bright, so Egypt can be pictured as a bright shining river, with green banks, cliffs sloping up to the grey mountains, and brilliant undimmed sunshine over all.

An ancient Greek historian once said that "Egypt was the gift of the Nile." This saying is quite literally true, for it is the Nile that makes the country fertile. Perhaps you have already been wondering how anything could grow in a country where it seldom or never rained? But in the mountains from which the Blue Nile and the Atbara come, there is a rainy season beginning about April. The rain comes down so heavily that the rivers rise and become very much swollen. The snows melt and all these waters rush into the main body of the stream, bringing with them rich deposits of thick black mud. As the river flows on towards the sea, it overflows its banks, covering the soil with the thick, rich mud. This inundation begins in Egypt about the end of June, and the river goes on rising until the middle of September, when it remains stationary for two or three weeks and then rises again, reaching its greatest height in October. Then it begins to sink gradually, until by the following June it reaches its normal level before the rising begins again. To the ancient Egyptians this was a most extraordinary thing, which they could not explain in any way, and they said that the Nile was "an incomprehensible mystery." In modern times great canals and embankments have been built, so that when the overflowing begins, the water irrigates a large surface of land, making it rich and fertile, and the towns and villages are reached by roads over the embankments, the canals being built so that the water is carried to the places that need it most.

The course of the Nile is interrupted six times by Cataracts[1]. These Cataracts are not great waterfalls like Niagara, but they are found in rocky regions where the rocks are so hard that the river is unable to wear down a channel as in the other parts of its bed, and so it winds in and out amongst great rocks that seriously interfere with navigation. In ancient times, when men knew less about engineering, the Nile was navigable only as far as the First Cataract. The part of the country from this First Cataract to Memphis was known as Upper

---

[1] waterfalls

Egypt (the kings of which wore a White Crown), and the part from Memphis to the sea was called Lower Egypt (the kings wearing a Red Crown). These ancient Egyptians called their land "Kam," a word meaning black or dark-colored, from the color of the soil.

In the days when the Nile was still digging a bed for itself through the rocky soil, the northern part of the country was entirely under water. The Mediterranean Sea reached nearly as far as where Cairo now stands, making a wide bay. The water, however, was very shallow, and as the river brought down its thick deposits of mud, the bay gradually filled up, until it became a swampy, but very fertile soil. In places the water remained deep, and this resulted in the Nile branching into several arms and entering the sea by a number of mouths. At one time there were seven, but in modern times the water has been drained off and now there are only two. This formation is known as the Delta. The name was given to it by the Greeks, who saw it in the shape of their capital letter D, which is made in the form of a triangle and is called Delta. (Since then all river mouths which branch out in this way have been known by the same name.)

The climate of Egypt is almost the most perfect in the world. The desert air is pure and dry, so that the heat is rarely oppressive, and there is no humidity. The nights are always cool, even in the heat of summer, and in winter they are surprisingly cold.

The shape of the land and its climate have influenced the history of Egypt. Because of the length and narrowness of the country, communication between the various towns and villages scattered along the banks of the Nile was difficult. So instead of having one government, they developed independent governments of their own, and there were a number of small city states instead of one strong one. But, on the other hand, as soon as the people began to learn how to irrigate, they found that it was necessary to join together in some form of government, and to organize an ordered way of living together. We shall soon see that the Egyptian buildings were very huge; the people were probably influenced by the flat stretches of land along the river banks, and wanted to build something in contrast to them. The surrounding mountains also influenced the ideas of the earliest Egyptians about the rest of the world; we shall see what these ideas were in another chapter.

EARLIEST EGYPT

It is not known with any certainty where the ancient Egyptians came from, but it is believed that long ago, before history began, they came from Asia and made homes for themselves along the banks of the Nile. They probably brought their domestic animals with them: the ox and cow, the sheep, the goat and the dog. The domestic animals that were native to Egypt were the ass and the cat; the wild animals were the crocodile, the hippopotamus and the snake.

The very earliest Egyptians soon forgot about the land from which they came, and as any kind of communication with the world beyond the mountains was almost impossible in those days, the Egyptians grew to believe that their land of Egypt was in the center of the world; it was a sacred place to them, and all who lived there were thought of as noble and fine. Most sacred of all was the Nile, for though they did not understand what caused the yearly overflowing of the river and inundation of the fields, they knew that it was the Nile that made their land fertile, so that their crops grew in such rich abundance. They believed that the earth was flat, and of a long oval shape, with the Nile flowing from end to end; they thought that high mountains surrounded the whole land, and that beyond the mountains all round the world flowed the Heavenly River. No one had ever seen this wonderful river, but the Egyptians were quite certain it existed, and that a beautiful Heavenly Boat in which the Sun-God sat, sailed round the world on the river once every twenty-four hours. These very early Egyptians believed that the setting of the sun only meant that the Heavenly Boat was hidden for a time behind one of the highest mountains.

The Egyptians were always longing to know where the Nile began. The Cataracts made it impossible for them to sail very far up, and its source was a matter of great mystery to them. They concluded finally that it must be a part of the Heavenly River, and that it entered the land of Egypt through a cleft in the mountains somewhere in the far away South. There, in an underground cavern, they pictured to themselves the Nile-god, kneeling on the rocky floor, with a sacred vessel in each hand, out of which streamed the life-giving waters of the Nile.

For long centuries explorers were continually trying to find the source, but the difficulties in the way of navigation were so great, that it was not until comparatively recent times that it was discovered. It was in 1862 that the English explorer J. H. Speke reached the place in Central Africa where the White Nile flows out from Victoria Nyanza.

We know very little about these ancient Egyptians. The first records of them tell us something of what they were like; they were dark-haired and slender; the men wore a skin thrown over the shoulder with sometimes a short white linen kilt, and the women wore long, straight garments reaching down to their feet They lived in mud houses, and they knew how to make the finest pottery of that age. They were probably farmers, hunters, and fishermen. But the most interesting thing that we know about this period is that in the year 4241 B.C. a calendar was introduced. This is the first fixed date in the history of the world of which we are certain. Before this time the Egyptians had reckoned by the moon (the word moon means "the measurer of time"), but the length of each moon varied from twenty-nine to thirty days. When they made this new calendar, they made twelve months of thirty days each, but as they found out that this way of counting was not accurate at the end of the year, instead of giving some months thirty-one days and having a leap year once every four years as we do, they celebrated the extra days as feasts and holidays at the end of every year. Then they wanted some way of counting the years; for about seven hundred years they gave a special name to each, taking the name from some particular event that had happened in that year, but this did not prove convenient, so later they numbered the years of each king's reign, and spoke of the first or second or third year of the reign of a certain king. Naming a year after an important event may not have been a very convenient method for the ancient

Egyptians, but it has given us a very valuable historical record of the chronology of those early days.

The men of this far away time worked very hard to make their country prosperous; they deepened the bed of the Nile, and built canals and ditches so that as much as possible of the land might be irrigated and made fertile; they turned the marshy swamps of the Delta into good land for crops and pasture, and they also learned a number of arts and crafts. They did not live in large towns, but in small communities all along the river bank, each of which had its own laws and customs, its temple and priests and warriors. They were quite independent of each other, though they were all looked upon as belonging to either Upper or Lower Egypt. In each little settlement it was the priests who had the most leisure to make plans for good government, and so they took the lead in everything. Unfortunately these little towns were frequently jealous of each other, and were often at war.

As soon as these early Egyptians began to learn that there were other countries in the world besides their own, they found out that Egypt was in a very good position in the middle of what was then known of the world. They were rich, for gold and ivory could be had in the upper parts of the Nile, the Red Sea gave them coral, and the mines of Sinai were rich in turquoise and copper. All that was needed was a man who realized the value of these natural resources, who had imagination to see what a great country Egypt might become, and who would himself be capable of seizing an opportunity when it arose. At last there was such a strong man, and he made himself overlord of all Egypt, becoming King of the whole country, uniting the White and the Red Crowns of Upper and Lower Egypt. According to tradition this king was Menes, and he probably lived about 3400 B.C. He built the city of Memphis, the oldest city in the world, and this was the capital of Egypt for about fifteen hundred years. Menes, with his young daughter, whose name Bener-ab meant "Sweetheart" beside him, was buried at Abydos, which became the city of tombs, and as the Egyptians placed in their tombs all kinds of things they thought the dead person might want in the next world, such as, toilet articles, ointment, food, drink, weapons, and many other things, we have been able to find out the kinds of things they used. But even with these we do not know very much about those remote times. We do know, however, that the kings claimed to be descended from the gods, so they were treated with great reverence; they seem to have been mighty hunters, and to have lived for those times in some magnificence, for finely wrought furniture, beautiful bowls, ornaments and carvings of this time have been found.

It was from these beginnings that the Egyptians went on to develop the powerful and civilized state that Egypt became.

EGYPTIAN BOOKS AND WRITING

The art which has had more influence in the world than almost any other, is that of writing and of making books. The Egyptians were the first people who made paper, and they were also the first who thought of making a book, but their books were different from ours.

When the Egyptian wanted to make paper, he took the stem of the papyrus plant (a reed-like plant that grew in the Nile), put it into thin slices lengthwise, laid the strips on a board in a row and placed similar strips crosswise on them. The surfaces were then joined by a kind of glue, pressed and dried, and the paper was made. The pieces of paper were of different widths, six, eleven, twelve and fourteen inches wide, and they varied in length from a few inches to as much as a hundred and thirty feet. If the Egyptian wanted many pages for his book, he did not cut the pages into sheets and bind them together as we do, but he took the long strips and fastened them together at the ends and rolled them up; the longer his book, the bigger grew the roll.

Not everyone knew how to write, but there were scribes whose business it was to do writing for all sorts of people. Today very busy people sometimes have secretaries to write for them, because they have more to do than they can do themselves; in ancient Egypt they had scribes to write for them, because they often did not know how to write themselves. The scribe wrote with a pen cut out of reed, and he kept his pens and ink or paint on a palette. This was a piece of wood from five or six to twenty inches long, with oblong places cut out for the reeds, and shallow holes for the ink. Most of the ordinary writing was done in black, but sometimes red and other colors were employed. Some scribes tried to be very realistic and used red for the sun, yellow for the moon, green for trees and plants, but this method was not always very successful, as there was only a limited number of colors, and so sometimes the objects were not very true to nature.

Egyptian writing is called "hieroglyphics," from two Greek words which mean "sacred" and "to engrave." So "hieroglyphics" really mean "sacred engraved signs." This name was given by the Greeks who could not read the writing and who thought that only the priests could write, and that as so much of the writing was on tombs and temples, it must be all about religious subjects. But Egyptian books covered a great many subjects: we have poetry, tales of adventure and magic, mathematics and medicine, as well as religious teaching and hymns.

Egyptian writing is a picture writing, that is to say, that instead of having an alphabet of letters which spell words, little pictures were drawn of everything that was written about, and these pictures were generally arranged in columns. In the earliest days, pictures were enough, but as time went on, the Egyptians wanted to write about many things which were difficult to represent by means of pictures, so then they began to use certain signs for different words, or for the different syllables of one word, but all these signs were still pictures of birds and animals and leaves and other objects, so that Egyptian hieroglyphics look like long columns of quaint drawings which are very pretty.

As long as the Egyptians had not very much to write about, or only wanted to decorate their temples and tombs and obelisks, this picture writing did very well, for though it took a long time to do, it was very ornamental, but when it came to writing books or keeping business records, these hieroglyphics were a slow and complicated way of writing. So by degrees the pictures and signs were changed, little bits of the picture being cut off here and there in order to write more quickly, until at last the writing had completely changed from the old hieroglyphic form. This new kind of writing was called "hieratic," and was used chiefly for writing on papyrus, the hieroglyphic form being still used for engraving on stone. After a time even this changed, and nothing seemed left of the original picture form but some lines and dots and dashes. This kind of writing was called "demotic," which means "popular," and the Egyptians used it until they gave up writing by means of signs and pictures and began to use an alphabet.

For a long time no one could read the Egyptian writing; learned men tried to find a key, but they never succeeded. But a little over a hundred years ago, some engineers were fortifying Rosetta, a place near the mouth of the Nile, and as they were digging deep into the soil, they found a slab of stone engraved with writing. This was the Rosetta Stone. It is covered with three kinds of writing, hieroglyphics at the top, and Greek at the bottom. In the Greek text there were found to be two proper names, King Ptolemaios and Queen Cleopatra. In the hieroglyphics there were groups of signs enclosed in a kind of shield (called a "cartouche"), an arrangement which had often been found in the inscriptions on the monuments. It was suggested that these were perhaps proper names. This gave a clue to the writing; if the single signs in the enclosed groups answered to the Greek letters in the names, then the key to most of the Egyptian writing would be found. Scholars worked at it, and though not immediately successful, after many attempts and much study and comparing of other signs and names and inscriptions, it was found possible to read the Egyptian writing. The scholar whose name will always be associated with the decipherment of the Egyptian hieroglyphics was a Frenchman, Champollion.

The Rosetta Stone is now in the British Museum. A large part of the top and a piece of the side is broken away, but when what was left was deciphered, it was found to be a decree drawn up by the priests of Memphis in honor of their King Ptolemaios, praising him and giving an account of his benefactions and saying that as a reward "the gods have given him health, victory, might and all other good things, the crown to remain with him and his children for ever."

EGYPTIAN BUILDINGS: THE TOMBS

The Ancient Egyptians wrote no books of history such as we write today; but they left the records of their life inscribed upon the walls of their principal buildings, more especially upon the tombs. The Egyptians believed that the soul of a man, the spirit that did not die when the body died, called by the Egyptians the "Ka," would return and visit his body after his death, and that if he wished to live for ever with the gods in heaven, his body must be preserved. But it would have been vain to preserve the bodies of the dead, unless secure hiding places could be provided for them. The tombs had to be guarded against the attacks of thieves and of wild animals, and to be placed beyond the reach of the overflowing waters of the Nile. In very ancient times the graves were dug deep in the sandy or rocky soil at the edge of the desert, but soon the beliefs of the Egyptians about the life of the soul after death, made them build more permanent tombs. They called their dwelling-places "inns," because they expected to remain in them but a short time, but their tombs they called "eternal dwelling places," because in these they would live forever.

These Egyptian tombs were built of stone and consisted of several chambers above ground, and a deep underground pit which led to a vault where the coffin was placed. It is from these chambers that we have learned so much about the daily life of the Egyptians, for the walls were covered with paintings showing what had been the daily life of the person buried beneath. There are pictures of men hunting, fishing and doing every kind of farm work; craftsmen in the towns can be seen weaving, making pottery, glass or beads; scribes are writing, slaves are working, and every other kind of occupation is shown. In one chamber were placed images or statues of the dead person, and sometimes this chamber was walled up so that no one could enter, and only a narrow slit in the wall was left, through which the statue could be seen. One chamber was called the "Offering Chamber," in which there was always a false door, and in front of this door was the table on which the offerings of cakes, fruit, bread, vegetables, flowers and other things were placed. These were for the spirit when he visited the tomb.

The Egyptians also believed that things the dead person had used on earth would be useful to his spirit in the next world, and so they placed in the tomb all kinds of articles used by people in their daily life: the bow and arrows of the hunter; the spear and dagger of the warrior; the palette and colors of the artist; dices and counters used in games; children's dolls and toys; combs, mirrors, hairpins and fans belonging to ladies; jars, vases, bottles of all kinds; chairs, tables, couches, stools, boxes, ornaments and jewelry, such as beads, necklaces, rings and bracelets. Quantities of these things have been found and can now be seen in the great museums of the world. The pictures on the walls are still there; and thus it is that the tombs form a very important part of the history book of Egypt.

THE PYRAMIDS

"All the kings of the nations lie in glory,
each in his own tomb."
— Isaiah 14:8

Not far from Cairo, on the edge of the desert stand the Pyramids, the oldest monuments constructed by human hands in the world. They were already ancient to the men of periods that we call ancient, and there they stand, silent and awe-inspiring, as they have stood for more than four thousand years.

The pyramids were the tombs of the kings. When a new king ascended the throne, he at once began to build his pyramid. He chose the site and had the ground levelled, and then he sent one of the principal nobles of his court on a special mission to the quarries, and the greater the speed with which he procured the necessary blocks of stone, the greater was the favor shown him on his return by the King. But the largest of the pyramids took a very long time to build, for the stone had to be brought from the quarries over the desert, and before this could be done a roadway had to be built. The roadway for the Great Pyramid of King Khufu took ten years to build, and a hundred thousand men at a time worked at it; every three months they were changed, and altogether four million men were employed just to build the roadway. On the Pyramid itself, which took twenty years to build, seven million men were employed. Every year the King lived, more layers were added to his Pyramid. A chamber was built at the very beginning for the coffin of the King, and as the pyramid grew larger, more chambers were added, and these were probably used for members of the royal family. A pyramid did not have an offering chamber as did the ordinary tomb, but attached to each pyramid was a temple, which took the place of the different chambers in other tombs.

The Great Pyramid is a solid mass of stone blocks, each fitted exactly to the one next to it. Two million three hundred thousand blocks of limestone were used, each of which weighed about as much as an ordinary wagon-load of coal, and it has been calculated that a wall might be built around France with the stones used. The sides of the Great Pyramid are 755 feet long, and the Pyramid itself is a little less than 500 feet high, that is to say, it is about thirty feet higher than St. Peter's, Rome, about a hundred and twenty feet higher than St. Paul's Cathedral in London, about two hundred feet higher than the Capitol in Washington. All the pyramids are not as high as this one, and some of them were never finished, as some kings did not live long enough to make their tombs as huge and imposing as they would have liked, and others were not rich enough, for it was very costly to build a pyramid. The Egyptians had no cranes or machinery for lifting the enormous stones used in their buildings, and for a long time the mechanical means they used were not satisfactorily explained. It is thought now, however, that they constructed great slanting ascents of sand and rock, up which they pushed the blocks of stone. These ascents would grow higher and higher as the building progressed, and when it was completed, they would be leveled to the ground.

Khufu called his Pyramid "Khut," a word which means "Glory," and from what we know of the way in which these immense royal tombs were built, we can guess something of the character of the kings who ordered their erection. Only men of overweening pride and ambition, of selfish indifference to the sufferings of the slaves who toiled at their tasks for long years, could have insisted on the building of monuments which, as far as we can see, were for no other purpose than the glory and renown of the king himself. But if the pyramids speak to us of the ruthless ambition and splendor of the kings, they also speak to us of the greatness of the architects who designed them. The fame of kings and conquerors, who have added to the greatness and wealth of their land, has sometimes been allowed to overshadow that of the thinker, whose work endures long after the wealth and might of the conqueror have passed away. The empire of the ancient Pharaohs has long since disappeared, but the work of their architects has lasted, and the art and science first conceived by them have left imperishable marks upon the world. There is in Egypt a pyramid, several centuries older than the Great Pyramid of Khufu. The man who planned it, a man possessed of skill and imagination equal to that of any modern engineer, was Imhotep, the first great architect in history.

Near the Great Pyramid is the Sphinx, that strangely mysterious statue, with a lion's body and a human head, that has kept silent watch by the pyramids for centuries. The ancient Greek traveller who visited Egypt, described it as a strange being who was always asking questions that none could answer, and propounding riddles which had no solution. The head is probably that of a king, but no one knows with certainty whom it was meant to represent. Traditions and legends have grown up round it, and to the modern world it has become the symbol of unexplained mystery: problems that our skill cannot solve, questions that our ingenuity cannot answer, mysteries that baffle us, we call riddles of the Sphinx.

THE TEMPLES

In all countries some of the greatest buildings have been cathedrals and churches, and this was true of Egypt, for the Egyptians were a very religious people and they built great temples in which to worship their gods. These temples were built with the same idea as the tombs, that they were to last forever, and though the desert sands in drifting over them for centuries, have spoiled much of the ancient magnificence, their great decorated columns and statues are still there, and we can form a very good idea of their size and appearance in the days when their courts and holy places were thronged with worshippers.

Egyptian temples were not all the same size, but they were generally built on the same plan. A temple was approached by an avenue of sphinxes. These sphinxes in the avenues to the temples had the bodies of lions, but they generally had the heads of some other animal, instead of that of a man like the Great Sphinx. These led up to the gate, which was made of cedar wood and overlaid with beaten bronze or silver. On each side of the gate were two high towers, and this entrance was called a Pylon. In front of the entrance stood an obelisk, and both it and the towers were covered with Egyptian writing and pictures describing the deeds of the Pharaoh who had built the temple, and generally there were great statues of him sitting beside the obelisk. These statues were so enormous that it is difficult to understand how any beings were strong enough to have brought the great stones from the quarries, to have carved them, and then set them up in their places.

The gate opened into a court, which had a colonnade running round it, and in the center was another obelisk covered with carvings telling of the generosity of the Pharaoh who had built the temple, and this obelisk was often studded with precious stones. Another gateway opposite the first led into a hall of columns, out of which opened the holiest place of all in the temple. This was a smaller and lower chamber, and the only light that ever entered it was that from the lamp carried by the priest, who was the only person allowed inside. The doors of cedar, covered with gold, were always locked, and inside was the shrine and statue of the god to whom the temple was dedicated. The statue was made of wood, and the duties of the priest were to paint his face afresh, and to give him new garments (the old ones were carefully put away, and were used to wrap round the mummies of those who had given great and rich gifts to the temple). The priest had also to set food, wine, water and flowers before the god, and on very great festivals, the statue was placed in a beautiful boat and carried on the shoulders of the priests in a gorgeous procession round the city.

The space behind the temple was occupied by great storehouses, full of grain and fruits and wine, and the houses of the priests. A god was one of the greatest of Egyptian landowners. Besides the temple, he had farms and fields, he owned boats which traded up and down the Nile, and he even had his own army. All this brought great wealth to the god and to the temple where he was worshipped, and it needed very large numbers of priests to attend to all the business connected with so rich and important a personage. This made the priests very powerful in Egypt, and even the Pharaoh himself stood in awe of them.

The greatest Egyptian temple was at Thebes, known today as Karnak, because the ancient city of Thebes has disappeared and the village near the temple is called Karnak. Like many of the great cathedrals in Europe, this temple was not all built at once or by one person. Twenty-one different kings helped to build it during a period of about eighteen hundred years. It contained several courts and halls and chambers, which were entered by no less than six Pylons, and its great hall was the largest in any temple. Twelve enormous pillars formed the nave, and smaller ones made aisles and held up the roof on each side. The great pillars in the middle were so large that it would require six men with outstretched arms to span them, and a hundred men could stand with safety on the capital of each. All the pillars and walls glowed with color, red and blue and green, and they were covered with pictures and writing describing the god worshipped there. At Karnak there was the god Amon. He was the Sun-God, and in earliest times we was the god who belonged especially to Thebes (every town had its own particular god), but he grew more and more important in the belief of the Egyptians, until he became recognized as their chief god, and all Egyptians paid him honor in his great temple at Thebes.

THE EGYPTIAN GODS AND HEAVEN: PRIMITIVE BELIEFS ABOUT THE GODS

In very primitive times, man was so much occupied in learning how to satisfy the practical needs of his body, that he had but little time to devote to anything else. He was afraid of nature, because he could not control her. But by degrees he began to realize that some power must be in control, that the sun did not shine, nor the wind blow, nor the rain water the earth of themselves, but that these things were ordered by some power greater than man. That one power could govern the world was far too great an idea for his understanding, and so he began to associate each power of nature both good and bad with a different god. Animals were included in this worship, because they too, showed the characteristics of god-like powers; at first they were worshipped as types of these powers, but in time they came to be regarded as gods themselves, and hence it came about that the gods were frequently given animal forms. It was also believed that the gods sometimes visited the earth in the form of animals, a belief which easily led to the worship of the animals themselves. Beside these nature gods, there were supposed to be others whose special care it was to watch over the interests of a particular group of people. At first each family had its own guardian spirit, later this spirit grew more important and he became the god of the tribe, then of the city and lastly of the state. Each great nation of the ancient world had its own national god.

EGYPTIAN RELIGION

The great god of Egypt was the Sun. The Egyptians worshipped him under the name of Ra or Amon-Ra. They looked upon him as the source of life and goodness and righteousness, lord over all the gods and the special protector of kings. They thought of him as "compassionate to those that fear him and as hearing those that cry unto him." They said he would "protect the weak against the strong, that he knew those who knew him, rewarded those who served him, and protected those who followed him."

It was Ra, the Sun-God who sailed in his golden boat across the sky, and in all the paintings of him, he is made to wear the sun-disk, a symbol of the goodness of the sun. But the sun could also destroy and scorch, and because he had this power, the Egyptians also gave him the asp as a symbol of his destructive power. The greatest of the temples at Thebes, was built in honor of Amon-Ra.

Thoth was the god of intelligence and wisdom. He was supposed to have invented writing, to have taught men mathematics and other sciences and arts, especially music and sculpture, and also how to measure the flood of the Nile, and to study the movements of the moon and the stars.

Hathor was the goddess of the sky, the Queen of Heaven, and she was frequently given the head of a cow as her symbol. She had a gentle and kindly nature, and she was especially loved and worshipped by women, who called her the "Lady of the Heavens," and the "Queen of Beauty and of Love."

Egyptian gods are nearly always represented as carrying a Key of Life in their hands, a symbol which belonged to them alone.

Like most Eastern peoples, the Egyptians were superstitious, and they believed that amulets and charms would keep evil luck away from them. The scarab, a kind of beetle on which was engraved an inscription or the name of a king, was one of such charms, and a great many of them have been found in the tombs.

The Egyptians paid respect to animals and, as we have seen, they frequently gave their gods partly animal forms. The bird ibis, the cat and the crocodile were all held sacred, and some were embalmed and buried in burying places of their own. The crocodile was looked upon as the evil power in nature. The cat was so sacred, that to kill one, even unintentionally, meant instant death to the offender. But the most sacred animal of all was the Bull Apis, who was considered as representing the Nile. Only an animal of a certain color and with certain marks could be an Apis, and there could only be one at a time in all Egypt. He lived at Memphis, in a splendid stable to which was attached a temple; he was waited on by his own special priests and at certain festivals was shown to the people in a stately procession. When the Apis died, there was mourning in all the land, and the priests had to search until another bull with the right markings was found, when there was great joy and public rejoicing and holiday everywhere.

The Egyptians worshipped a great many gods, and this made their religion very complicated, because they feared that neglect of any god would bring some kind of suffering or loss upon them, either in this world or the next. They paid great respect to the gods in their temples, they sang very beautiful hymns in their honor and they sought to please them by rich gifts and sacrifices. Herodotus, the Greek historian who has told us so much about the Egyptians said of them: "The Egyptians are very religious, surpassing all men in the honors they pay to the gods."

The Egyptians were a people of high ideals, but there was a very material side to their religion, for they believed that sin could be paid for by offerings and sacrifices, and though great importance was attached to the character of a man, it was because they believed that his prosperity either on earth or in a future life would be hurt by his wrongdoing.

THE EGYPTIAN HEAVEN AND THE JUDGMENT OF THE DEAD

The most important religious teaching of the Egyptians was that which concerned their belief in a future life. When an Egyptian died, his body was made into a mummy. This was done because of the Egyptian belief that the happiness of a spirit in heaven depended on the preservation of his body in the tomb. To ensure this the body was embalmed, and when that had been carefully done, it was wrapped in linen which had been soaked in resins and sweet-smelling spices. As each part of the body was wrapped up, the priests recited prayers and uttered charms which were to help the dead man to get safely to heaven.

There were three methods employed in making a mummy which varied in expense. Only the rich could afford the most elaborate method and the larger tombs, but the priests assured the poor, that if certain words were repeated over the bodies of their dead, and that if the earthly life had been righteous, all would go well with the soul at last. All Egyptians, however, believed that the greater the care with which the burial ceremonies had been completed, the surer was the soul of future happiness.

When the mummy was ready, it was placed in the first coffin which was made in the shape of the body and which had a gilded face, and sometimes it was decorated still further with beads and precious stones. This case was then put into another coffin, which was covered both inside and out with pictures and hieroglyphics. The inner case was always turned over, so that the body lay on its side with the face turned towards the eye panel, a panel on the outer coffin on which two eyes were painted, in order that the dead body might "behold the Lord of the Horizon, when he sails across the heavens." The coffin was then ready to be placed in the tomb, and the Egyptian believed that the soul started on its way to heaven.

The Egyptians thought that heaven was a wonderful land far away in the West; they called it the "Fields of Bulrushes," or the "Fields of Content." It was a land of corn and plenty, of trees and streams. Arrived there, the soul led a very pleasant life of ease; he could sow and reap, sail in his boat, sit under the shade of the trees, eat and drink, and play games with his companions. The rich noblemen who had always had slaves to work for them on earth, wanted their slaves in heaven. In order to be sure of having plenty, they placed little statues in their tombs and they engraved on them the answer each was to make when his master called him. The master is supposed to have said to his slaves: "O ye figures, be ye ever watchful to work to plough and sow the fields, to fill with water the canals, and to carry sand from the east to the west," and each little figure was to answer his master: "Here am I, ready when thou callest." The old Egyptian word for an answer was "Ushabti," and so these figures are called Ushabti or Answerers.

But the soul did not reach heaven immediately after death, there was a long and perilous journey to be taken along difficult and dangerous roads, that were haunted by serpents and dragons, demons and other terrors. But the Egyptians believed that certain charms, if properly recited would drive them all away. These magic charms and spells were collected by the Egyptians in a book, which we call the "Book of the Dead," but which they called the "Book of the Entrance into Light," for they said that souls did not "depart as those who are dead, but they depart a those who are living." These charms were beautifully written on papyri, and a copy of the book or parts of it were buried with the dead, in order that the soul might have them on its journey, but many of the charms had already been taught the Egyptians during their lifetime.

The first part of this perilous journey led the soul to the gates of the palace of Osiris, who was King of the Underworld, and in whose palace was the Hall of Truth where the souls were judged. The Egyptians were the first of the ancient peoples who believed that happiness in heaven depended on the character of a person while on earth, and before reaching the Egyptian heaven the soul had to be carefully judged. At the entrance to the palace of Osiris, the soul recited this prayer: "Grant that I may come unto you; I who have not lied, nor borne false witness, but who feed on truth, I who have given bread to the hungry and drink to him that was athirst and who have clothed the naked with garments. My mouth is pure; my two hands are pure." These words may be compared with the familiar words in the New Testament: "For I was hungry and you gave me food, I was thirsty and you gave me drink, a stranger and you welcomed me, naked and you clothed me, ill and you cared for me, in prison and you visited me." These two sayings seem to set the same standard for character, but in reality are very different, for the principle underlying those of the Egyptian was that good deeds are performed for the sake of the reward. But it must be remembered that the Egyptian standard was one of nearly two thousand years before that of the New Testament.

When the gates of the palace of Osiris were opened, the soul entered the great Hall of Truth. All round the hall sat forty-two judges, each of whom had power to punish a particular sin, and close at hand was a pair of scales, beside which stood the god Thoth, ready to see that everything was done justly and fairly, and to mark down on his tablets the result of the judgement. The soul first made a long statement to the judges, saying that he had not committed the sins they could punish; but that was not enough, for he might not be speaking the truth; so his heart was taken and placed on one of the scales, whilst a feather, the Egyptian symbol for truth, was placed on the other. Whilst this was being done, the soul cried out to his heart not to testify against him, and he said: "My heart of my being! Make no stand against me when testifying, and make no failure in respect of me before the Master of the Balance." If the heart was not of the right weight, it proved that the man was false, and his heart was thrown to a dreadful and horrible monster, called the "Eater of the Dead," who sat behind the scales waiting to devour the hearts of the wicked; he had the head of a crocodile, the body of a lion and the hindquarters of a hippopotamus. But if the heart weighed right, Thoth declared to the judges that all was well, and then Horus, the son of Osiris, led the soul into the presence of his father, who declared that as he was just, he was fit to go to heaven.

The Egyptians believed that Osiris had been made King of the Underworld by the gods. They thought that long ago he had been a good King of Egypt, and that he and his wife Isis were very happy. Osiris was supposed to have taught his people agriculture and to have given them good laws, and Isis to have shown them how to make bread, and she was said to have been very skilful in healing all manner of sickness. But Set, the brother of Osiris, was wicked and jealous of him and he conspired against him. He invited Osiris to a feast at his house, and after the feast he showed to his guests a beautiful chest. He persuaded Osiris to lie down in it, and as soon as he was in, Set and his conspirators shut down the lid and fastened it and carried it to the Nile. They threw it into the river, and it was quickly washed away. Isis was in despair, and broken-hearted she searched for the chest until she found it, where it had been washed up on the river bank. She hid it and went to find her son Horus, in order that he might avenge his father. But before they returned, Set found the body, and cut it in pieces and scattered them in every direction. But even so, the faithful Isis searched again until she found them, and reverently buried them. Horus, however, challenged Set to fight and he defeated him. Thereupon the gods assembled and declared Osiris innocent of all the crimes of which Set had accused him, and they raised Osiris from the dead and made him King of the Underworld and Judge of the Dead.

LIFE IN TOWN AND COUNTRY: EGYPTIAN DRESS

The Egyptians generally used linen for their clothing, and in the earliest times this was thick and coarse, but later a very fine kind was woven that was so slight as to be almost transparent and like silk. For many centuries Egypt was a great and powerful country, and so the fashions of dress changed just as they have done at all times, but the Egyptians were a very conservative people and when a fashion changed, the older one continued to be worn at the same time as the new one.

Egyptian dress began by being very simple, but as the centuries went by, it grew more elaborate. In the earliest times the men wore a short white kilt, such as can be seen on the facades of many tombs. Such portraits show the full dress of an Egyptian nobleman: a white kilt, sandals, a wig of long straight hair and a short false beard, a long staff in the hand, and round the neck a flat bead collar. The women wore long straight garments that reached from the breast to the ankles; they were generally held up by straps over the shoulders and tied at the waist with a girdle. It is said that the ancient Egyptian women were very good-looking; they liked to adorn themselves and wore bead collars and necklaces, bracelets and anklets. The women either wore wigs, or arranged their own hair so that it hung loose to the shoulder with a side-lock hanging down on each side of the face, and a colored ribbon or a wreath of flowers was often tied round the head across the brow. Sometimes the women braided their hair in a number of braids, and in order to make it appear that they had more hair than was really the case, they braided locks of goats' hair with their own.

As time went on, these simple garments became more elaborate. Both men and women began to wear fuller skirts and robes, and the last fashion seems to have been to wear draperies. The men still kept to the kilt, but it was fuller, and when they wanted to dress in a more elaborate costume, they added such things as sashes, and magnificent bead collars, so wide that they covered the shoulders, and armlets and bracelets. The women at this time kept their narrow, close-fitting dress, but over this they wore a long loose mantle of fine pleated linen.

Fashion in color rarely changed in Egypt, and the garments were nearly always white, though sometimes other colors were used, green being a favorite, and beautiful designs in colors were used as embroideries.

In the earliest days the Egyptians wore nothing on their feet, but later they wore sandals. These were made of papyrus, palm-fiber or leather, but they had always to be taken off in the presence of the King. Kings, Queens, and members of the royal family wore various kinds of head-dresses. On state occasions soldiers wore gold collars, which were given them as a reward of bravery.

The heat of the Egyptian sun and the hot winds from the south made it necessary for the Egyptians to take great care of their skin. They rubbed oil all over their bodies, and they smeared ointment on their eyelids; this was done once a day, and many women painted their eyebrows and added a thick line under each eye. A black paint called kohl was used for this, and the kohl pot and the ointment vase were very important articles on the dressing table of an Egyptian lady. They used copper mirrors, which were polished until they shone as glass. The women also rouged their cheeks and lips, and they all stained their fingernails a reddish yellow with the juice of a plant called henna.

Children generally went bare, and so did the peasants when they were at work.

THE EGYPTIAN HOUSE

Egyptian houses were lightly built. Tombs and pyramids and temples were constructed to last forever, but the houses were looked upon as only temporary dwelling places of those who lived in them, and were always so built that they could easily be changed should later dwellers in them wish it. The houses were built of sun-dried brick and wood and were bright and cheerful. Most of the larger houses had gardens, and both houses and garden were surrounded by a high wall. Inside the gate was a courtyard round which were quarters for the slaves, shelters for the chariots and horses, and storerooms; a doorway at the further end led into the garden, which was always planted with trees and shrubs, fruit and flowers, and where there were pools of water and shady arbors, where people could sit protected from the hot sun. There is an old Egyptian story written on papyrus about 1300 B.C. called *The Tale of the Garden of Flowers*, which tells us some of the things, both familiar and unfamiliar, which grew in an Egyptian garden:

> She led me, hand in hand, and we went into her garden to converse
>   together.
> There she made me taste of excellent honey.
> The rushes of the garden were verdant, and all its bushes
>   flourishing.
> There were currant trees and cherries redder than the ruby.
> The ripe peaches of the garden resembled bronze,
> And the groves had the luster of the stone "nachem."
> The "menni" unshelled like coconuts they brought to us,
> Its shade was fresh and airy.

Egyptians of all classes were fond of flowers and they gave great care to the cultivation of their gardens, so that flowers bloomed in great profusion all the year round.

The King's palace was built on the same plan as other houses, except that it was much larger and contained many halls and courts where the King held great state ceremonies, gave audiences and administered justice. He had a great many rooms for his own private use, and there were separate apartments for the Queen and the women.

The peasant lived in a small mud hut that was thatched. The floors were bare or covered with rushes or mats. The huts were poorly furnished and crowded together. In the cities or near the great temples that were being built, there were barracks for the workmen, which were an immense succession of mud huts, often opening one into the other. The life of the peasants on the large estates in the country was more wholesome, and they did not live in such a crowded fashion.

The rooms of an Egyptian house were beautifully decorated with paintings on the walls, ceilings and floor. The ceilings were painted to look like an indoor sky; stars shone out from a blue background, and the capitals of the pillars which supported the roof looked like trees, with the carved foliage on the capital and gaily painted birds flitting about beneath. In the same way the floor was painted to represent the green of the marshes, and the water of the pools, with fish and waterfowl hidden in the reeds.

The ancient Egyptians did not fill their houses with furniture as we do. They had beautifully carved and inlaid chairs, low couches, a few tables and stands, and not much else. Clothing, jewelry, and valuables were generally kept in chests and boxes instead of in cupboards and closets. There were always a number of vases about, and these were often beautifully decorated. The Egyptian loved his home, and everything about it reflected his bright and cheerful character.

EGYPTIAN TRADE WITH OTHER LANDS

The earliest Egyptians, as we have seen, knew nothing of any lands but their own. By degrees, however, their horizon widened and they began to have intercourse with lands far from Egypt. They built ships, and these vessels traded in the Mediterranean and in the Red Sea. Their most famous trading expedition was that to the land of Punt, which took place during the reign of Queen Hatshepsut, who lived about three thousand years ago, at a time when Egypt had become a powerful empire. Hatshepsut was a very remarkable woman. The king, her father, allowed her to take part in the government of the country before his death, a very unusual privilege for a woman, but she was clever and capable and quite equal to the task. She had a magnificent coronation, when all Thebes kept holiday, and the great event was recorded in sculpture. One of the inscriptions describes her in very flattering terms: "To look upon her was more beautiful than anything; her form was like a god, she did everything as a god, her splendor was like a god; her majesty was a maiden, beautiful, blooming."

After the death of her father and half-brother who succeeded him, Hatshepsut reigned for sixteen years alone. Her reign was peaceful and prosperous and one of the chief events of it was the expedition sent to the land of Punt to trade there with the natives. Before her death Hatshepsut built a very beautiful temple, and the walls were adorned with sculpture telling the whole story of this expedition, which she declared to have been commanded by the god Amon. Punt was probably the land known today as Somalia.

Five vessels started out "sailing in the sea, beginning the goodly way towards God's Land, journeying in peace to the land of Punt, according to the command of the Lord of Gods." The voyage was accomplished safely and the Egyptians landed, carrying the things they had brought to use as articles of exchange. The sight of the foreign ships had brought out the natives of Punt, and headed by their chief, they came down to the shore. "Why," they said, "have ye come hither unto this land, which the people know not? Did ye come down upon the ways of heaven, or did ye sail upon the waters, upon the sea of God's Land?" Friendly relations were soon established, and the natives of Punt brought the rarest products of their land, which they exchanged for the articles the Egyptians had brought. The latter had decidedly the best of the bargain, for they gave such things as necklaces, hatchets, daggers and the like in exchange for myrrh trees and incense; ivory, ebony and gold; sweet-scented woods; apes and skins of animals. The natives helped to load the Egyptian ships, which then returned in safety to Egypt.

Some of the chiefs of Punt accompanied them and the return of the expedition caused great excitement in Thebes. Rumors of the extraordinary riches brought back from Punt spread all over the city, and two holidays were celebrated in honor of the event: one on the day when the chiefs of Punt and the rich produce from their land were presented to the Queen, and the other on the day when she made a thank-offering in the temple. "The marvels of Punt" were talked of everywhere. The inscription over the sculpture showing the Queen in the temple, makes the god say to her:

> I have given to thee all lands and all countries, wherein thy heart is glad. I have given to thee all Punt as far as the lands of God's Land... I have led thy army on water and on land to explore the waters of inaccessible channels, and I have reached the myrrh-terraces. It is a glorious region of God's Land; it is indeed my place of delight.

In the Country

Away from the cities, along the banks of the Nile and surrounded by gardens and fields, were the country houses of the Egyptians. These were built on the same plan as the city houses, but the gardens were larger, and most of the great landowners had farms where nearly everything they needed for food, both in the country and in the city, was produced. Their food was varied. We find that even the dead desired in the world to come "ten different kinds of meat, five kinds of poultry, sixteen kinds of bread and cake, six kinds of wine, eleven kinds of fruit, besides all sorts of sweets and many other things."

The poorer people ate coarse bread, onions and other vegetables, and salt. The principal vegetables were: onions, beans, peas, lentils, cucumbers, radishes, watermelons, leeks and garlic.

The richer people ate meat: the flesh of the goat, cow, and ox; geese, pigeons and doves. Milk and cheese were used a great deal, and fruit, such as figs, dates, mulberries and grapes. Beer and different kinds of wine were largely drunk.

All these things came from the estates and farms of the well-to-do Egyptians, and a good part of the time of such a landowner when he was in the country was spent in superintending the work of his estate. The work was done by slaves, with overseers to see that they wasted no time, and when the Egyptian noble came to the country, the overseers would report to him on the condition of his estate. The cattle and other livestock were passed in review before him, and he would be given information as to the work in his fields and orchards.

When this business had been attended to, the Egyptian would go off fishing, hunting or sailing along the Nile. The river was the great highway in Egypt, and an Egyptian would own several kinds of boats: travelling, fishing and pleasure boats. If he were going off on an expedition for several days, a kitchen boat would accompany the travelling boat, as none of the vessels were very large and there was not much space for cooking in the travelling boat itself. The boats gave the river a very gay appearance for they were brightly painted, and the sails of boats belonging to great nobles were often richly embroidered.

Hunting was another favorite amusement; some animals were hunted for food, others for the sport or for the sake of their skins, and the Egyptians often went out in light papyrus skiffs to hunt the waterfowl and animals found in the reeds by the river bank.

The Egyptians liked good food, but their manners at meal times would seem strange to us today. They had no plates, but used thick pieces of bread in their place, on which they frequently wiped their fingers after the meal. Occasionally they used spoons, but not always and most of the food was eaten with the fingers. The chief meal of the day was eaten about sunset, and the Egyptians loved making occasions for feasts. All the same, they believed in teaching the young to be moderate in eating and drinking, and the following instructions were given to them:

> If thou art sitting in company hate the food which thou likest; restrain thy appetite, for greediness savoreth of the beasts. Since one cup of water will quench the thirst, and a mouthful of vegetables establish the heart, and one kind of good food is as good as a large quantity, the man who permitteth his appetite to guide him is an abomination.

But it was not considered polite for the guest to leave anything uneaten. "When thou art seated among the guests of a great man, accept what he giveth thee gracefully. Look before thee, nor stare at the food, nor look at it often; he who departeth from this rule is a boorish fellow."

In the cool of the evening, the Egyptians would spend some time in their gardens, or on the roofs of the houses, and these hours were often enlivened by musicians, who came with harps and lyres and played until the stars shone out in the deep blue of the Egyptian sky, and it was time for rest.

CHILDREN IN ANCIENT EGYPT

For the first three years a child was always with his mother, and she carried him about with her, generally on her back, wherever she went. If she were the wife of a great lord, she would, however, leave her children to be cared for by her women. After these first years, the children ran about, wearing no clothes as a rule, except perhaps a girdle round the waist, and during this time they seem to have had a great many toys to play with: balls made of papyrus or of leather, or stuffed with chopped straw, and dolls of all kinds, clay dolls, wooden dolls, dolls with hair made of beads, and dolls without any hair at all; they also had toy animals of every description. In the British Museum there is a small wooden cat with crystal eyes, and a movable jaw and metal teeth, which must have been a great treasure to some Egyptian child.

The children of the peasants probably never went to school, and no girls seem to have been taught reading or writing, but the well-to-do boys were sent to school, or as the Egyptians said, they became "writers in the house of books." The first thing a boy was taught in school was to write, and Egyptian writing is very difficult to do well, but the boys worked hard and they practised their writing by copying out sayings of their wise men. Some of the most ancient of these wise Sayings or "Maxims" were written by Ptah-hotep, who lived in Memphis about 3500 B.C. He was one of the teachers of a royal prince, and the King attached great importance to the learning of such Maxims. "Instruct thou my son," he said, "in the words of wisdom of olden time. It is instruction of this kind alone that formeth the character of the sons of noblemen, and the youth who hearkeneth to such instruction will acquire a right understanding and the faculty of judging justly, and he will not feel weary of his duties."

Some of the ancient wisdom taught an Egyptian child ran as follows:

> Be diligent at all times. Do more than is commanded. Waste not
> the time wherein thou canst labor.

> The man that uttereth ill-natured words, must not expect to
> receive good-natured deeds.

> Seek silence for thyself

> If thou journeyest on a road made by thy hands each day, thou wilt
> arrive at the place where thou wouldest be.

Besides writing, they learned some arithmetic, addition, subtraction and a clumsy way of multiplying. There exists a papyrus called "directions for knowing all dark things," some of which "dark things" are problems in arithmetic.

Many boys did not learn more than this, but some went on to the colleges of the priests, where they were taught a great deal about their religion, and some astronomy. One of the chief colleges was at Heliopolis, famous for its school of astronomy. Nothing stands now of those ancient college buildings, all that is left is an obelisk, which has stood in the same spot for four thousand years, pointing to the sky which was studied there by sages of old.

Lessons at school began early in the morning, and lasted until noon, when the boys "left the school with cries of joy," and had their lunch which was brought to the school by their mothers, and which usually consisted of three bread cakes and two jugs of beer. Egyptian boys were frequently punished, chiefly by being flogged. An Egyptian saying was that "a boy's ears are on his back." They were punished for being lazy, late or inattentive, and once an exceedingly naughty boy was locked up for three months in a room in a temple. Egyptian boys seem to have taken their punishments with a good grace and as a matter of course, for they were a cheerful people, and their lives do not seem to have been made gloomy by this severity towards them in their youth. One boy wrote in later years to his teacher: "I was with thee back and thy instructions went into my ear." We do not know whether they had much or any homework, but they seem to have had plenty of time for games and expeditions out into the country when their fathers went hunting or fishing.

One thing was taught every Egyptian child with the very greatest care, and that was courtesy and respect to all who were older than he. He might never sit down whilst some-one older was standing: "Sit not down when another is standing up, if he be older than thou, even if thy rank in life be higher than his," and at all times his manners were expected to be very good. His parents were the chief people to whom he was to show courtesy, and especially his mother, for few nations have shown more love and honor and respect to their mothers than the Egyptians. Here is some advice an Egyptian once gave his son:

> Thou shalt never forget what thy mother hath done for thee. She bare thee and nourished thee in all manner of ways. She nursed thee for three years. She brought thee up, and when thou didst enter the school and wast instructed in the writings, she came daily to thy master with bread and beer from her house. If thou forgettest her, she might blame thee; she might lift up her hands to God, and He would hear her complaint.

There was much family affection amongst the Egyptians, and on the tomb walls are often found such sayings as: "I was one beloved of his father, praised of his mother, whom his brothers and sisters loved."

THE PHARAOH

In the earliest times the land of Egypt was supposed to have been ruled by the gods, who lived on earth and mixed with the people. But at length they decided to leave the earth and return to heaven, and Horus, the last King who was also a god, appointed his son, whose mother had been an Egyptian maiden, to succeed him as king. This king was, therefore, supposed to be half-god and half-man, and so it came about that the Egyptians continued to worship their kings as divine, and their statues were placed beside those of the gods. This supposed divine origin of the kings helps us to understand why the Egyptians made their statues so enormous. These kings were not men like themselves, they were related to the gods, they were the all-powerful rulers and conquerors, who were to be not only obeyed, but feared and worshipped.

The king in Egypt was known as the Pharaoh. The name Pharaoh is the equivalent of our word "king," though the real meaning of the Egyptian word is "Great House." Great honor and reverence were always paid the Pharaoh. The highest nobles prostrated themselves on the ground when they came into his presence, pretending that they were blinded by his glory. It was a very great honor to be allowed to carry the king's chair or his sandals, and on an inscription in one of the tombs, it is recorded of the noble buried there, that he had been of such great importance and distinction, that the Pharaoh had not only allowed him to kiss the ground under his feet but the royal foot itself! Court etiquette was very elaborate, and every want of the Pharaoh was in the charge of some official. The kings were well educated, and as princes had often had experience in state service of various kinds.

The Pharaoh of three thousand years ago was a very busy man, for at that time the Egyptians ruled over a large empire. His work would begin early in the morning. First of all, certain officials would bring him letters and documents to read or sign. Perhaps news would have come from one of the generals who were leading the army against an enemy, and the Pharaoh would have to decide what commands to send him, for he had absolute power, and though he might ask the advice of his ministers, he was not obliged to take it, and whatever might be his word, it became law. There would also be reports from the official sent to superintend the work of bringing the stone from the quarries for the great buildings started by the Pharaoh; or merchants on the royal ships sailing up the Nile as far as they could go, would report on the treasures they were bringing back.

When all this business was over, it would be time for the Pharaoh to give audience to those who wished to see him. This occupied a long time, for there were always a great many people to see him, and it took each one some time to get to what he really wanted to say, as everyone who spoke to the Pharaoh had to begin by making him a flattering little speech, telling him how great and powerful he was, none like him in the world, the joy of his people, and a god in his glory dazzling all those who came near him.

The Pharaoh would also spend a great deal of his time in the temple, and on great occasions it was he who offered the sacrifices to the god in place of the priests, for he was half-god himself, and so he had the right to approach the god in his shrine.

Two of the greatest Pharaohs were Thutmose III and Ramses II. Thutmose III reigned immediately after Queen Hatshepsut, and he was one of the most renowned conquerors in history. The record of his campaigns is inscribed on the walls of Karnak and a Hymn of Victory celebrates his deeds. Long after his death, his name was engraved on countless scarabs as a charm to protect the wearer against evil. He erected a number of obelisks, but none of them are now in the land of the Pharaoh; they are scattered, and are to be found not only in the Old but also in the New World; one of them stands on the banks of the Thames in London, where it is known as Cleopatra's Needle, and another is in New York.

Ramses II was another great warrior who waged war against the Hittites, in which he showed great daring and courage. He was one of the builders of Egypt both of cities and temples, and huge statues of him have been found. It was probably Ramses II who made the

Hebrew slaves work for him in the building of his new treasure cities, and who oppressed them so cruelly.

When a Pharaoh returned in triumph from war, a holiday would be proclaimed. A great procession would wend its way to the temple. Priests with garlands and flowers headed it, then would follow the army, with the Pharaoh in the center, standing upright in his chariot, and as he passed, the people would prostrate themselves on the ground before him. The prisoners formed part of the procession; they marched tied together with ropes, and sometimes the king would drive a number of them before him. The entrance gates to the temple would be gaily decorated with flags and banners, and the long procession would enter. Trumpet blasts then summoned the soldiers to approach the altar, on which they laid twigs of olive as symbols of peace. A stately service would then follow, and at its conclusion the king drove back to his palace. Once again the people thronging the streets would bow low as, standing upright in his chariot and paying little heed to the adoration of the crowd, he passed on his way. In his own eyes, and in those of his people, he was the Pharaoh, the Son of the Sun, the mightiest man of earth.

A REFORMER KING

Not quite a hundred years after the death of the warrior Thutmose III, a young Pharaoh came to the throne. His name was Amenhotep IV. This King was an original and independent thinker, but he shut his mind to everything that concerned his country, except that which concerned its religious beliefs. He announced that all the gods were false, and that there was only one God, who dwelt above the sky and who looked down upon the earth through the sun, from which he took his name, the Sun-God or Aton. This was the same Sun-God who was worshipped at Heliopolis, but his worship was now purified and no animals were offered as sacrifices. The King ordered all temples to other gods to be closed, and wherever the names of gods were found inscribed on the walls of the temples or on obelisks, they were to be erased. He had a special hatred for Amon the god of Thebes, and as his own name, Amenhotep, included that of the god, he changed it to Ikhnaton, which means "Aton is satisfied." It was not enough for him to close the temples, Thebes itself became hateful to him, and he built a new city out near the desert, where the village of Tell-el-Amarna now stands, which was henceforth to be the capital.

The religion of Akhnaton was a very pure and beautiful one. He believed that there was only one God, who was a father to men of all races, and his faith came nearer to that of the great Hebrew prophets than any other faith of the ancient world. But Ikhnaton was young and intolerant, and the gods of Egypt had been worshipped for centuries. It is never possible to force men into a new belief and the priests were a very powerful body of men who could not be defied. It was probably their hostility, which decided the King to leave Thebes. The nobles who had supported his predecessors, who had fought for them and with them, and helped to make them great Pharaohs, saw dissatisfaction arising all over Egypt. Revolts occurred against the king, and when he died, because he had neglected his duties as Pharaoh, he left Egypt weak and torn by strife.

The new city was soon forsaken by the Pharaohs who followed Ikhnaton; they returned to the old capital and the old gods. His palace was deserted and was never rebuilt. Three thousand years went by, and an old peasant woman who lived at Tell-el-Amarna was one day turning over the sand, looking for antiquities for which European travelers were so constantly asking. Little did she imagine that she was wandering over the spot where once a King had dwelt. But she discovered there a large number of clay tablets, which were found to be the correspondence written in cuneiform script, of the chief rulers in Egypt and Western Asia in the time of Ikhnaton, and his predecessor. These letters tell the story of how the reformer king's neglect of his kingdom had wrought dissatisfaction everywhere, and they give us an excellent picture of the state of Egypt and the countries with which she came into closest contact during his reign.

Akhnaton failed in what he tried to do because of his intolerance and lack of sympathy with those who disagreed with him, and his figure, as we look back to it is a lonely one, but his name stands out across the centuries as that of the first thinker who tried to break through the rigid conventions of the past in his search for truth.

AKHNATON'S HYMN TO THE SUN-GOD

> Thy dawning is beautiful in the horizon of heaven,
> O living Aton, beginning of Life!
> When thou risest in the eastern horizon of heaven,
> Thou fillest every land with thy beauty;
> For thou art beautiful, great, glittering, high over the earth;
> Thy rays, they encompass the lands, even all thou hast made.
> Thou art Re, and thou hast carried them all away captive;
> Thou bindest them by thy love.
> Though thou art afar, thy rays are on earth;
> Though thou art on high, thy footprints are the day.

Egypt was said to be the "gift of the Nile" and the Egyptians knew this to be true. It was an "incomprehensible mystery" to them, and they believed that there must be a special god who cared for the river, and so it was that they worshipped him as Hapi (or Apis), the sacred Bull, the giver of all good things. They sang to him:

> Hail to thee, Hapi who descendest upon earth, and givest life unto Egypt. Thou who art hidden in the unknown,—whose waters spread upon the fields which the Sun-God hath created. Who givest life to all that are athirst. Thou, the Creator of corn, the maker

of barley—do thy waters cease to flow, then are all mankind in
misery; and when thou wanest in heaven, the gods themselves and
all living things perish.

And so we must leave these ancient Egyptians. Their history does not end here, but their
civilization had reached the point where it was influencing the ancient world, and was to be
an influence to nations not then born. The Egyptians themselves could not advance further,
because their minds were bound by chains to the past, but they had sown the seed from
which greater things were to develop. We know many things today that they did not know,
but every day we use things that were first thought of by them: our calendars may be more
correct, our books and paper more convenient, our paintings and sculpture more full of
grace and imagination, but we owe the beginnings of all these things to the ancient dwellers
on the banks of the Nile.

MOSES AND THE EXODUS FROM EGYPT

The Pharaoh who "knew not Joseph" was probably Ramses II, and he employed the Hebrews in work on his great buildings. They had been increasing in numbers and he was
afraid of their growing power, so he issued a decree that all their baby boys were to be killed.
One woman, however, saved her son by hiding him in a bulrush cradle by the river bank,
where she hoped that no one would find him. But the Pharaoh's daughter coming down to
the river with her maidens, found the little cradle with the Hebrew baby in it, and she took
the child back with her to the palace and adopted him. She called him Moses, a name which
means "taken from the water"; in this way it came about that Moses was brought up in the
palace of the Pharaoh, where he learned all that an Egyptian prince would have been taught.

As he grew up, Moses used to visit the Hebrew slaves, and he was much interested in all
that concerned them. One day his sense of justice and anger were aroused at seeing one of
the Egyptian overseers beating a Hebrew, and in impetuous haste he killed the Egyptian.
In the eyes of the law this was a great crime, and Moses was obliged to flee from the palace,
as otherwise his life would probably have been in danger. Up to this time Moses had been
living as an Egyptian, but this act put him definitely on the side of the Hebrew slaves, and
now, out in the desert, whither he had fled, he was able to think quietly over the condition
of his kinsmen, and there were grew up in his mind the resolve to free them from their
oppressors, and to lead them back to the land which had been promised to their ancestor
Abraham.

Moses, accompanied by his brother Aaron, returned to the city and entering the presence of the Pharaoh demanded the release of the Hebrews, but their petition was refused.
Egypt was always subject to certain pestilences, and the country was evidently visited by
some at this time; the Hebrew writer described them in great detail and attributed them all
to the refusal of the Pharaoh to let the Hebrew slaves, who were very useful to him, leave

the land. These calamities were known as the Ten Plagues, and finally, after the last, the Pharaoh consented to let the Hebrews go. But as soon as he heard that they were really gone, he repented and pursued after them. He arrived too late, however, for, overtaking them by the shore of the Red Sea, the east wind (which had blown with so much strength that the shallow waters of the sea were forced back, leaving a passage free by which the fugitives could escape) changed, and as the Egyptians with their heavy chariots were attempting to cross by the same passage, they were drowned.

This was a tremendous moment in the history of the Hebrews. Behind them lay Egypt, with its fertile land, its broad river which served as a highway for the nations who traded with Egypt and added to her wealth, its busy cities, its learning,—and slavery. Before them was the desert, silent, desolate, bare, apparently uninhabited,—and freedom. Behind them was the land where mind and spirit were bound by tradition, before them lay the silent places, but where was to be found freedom for mind and spirit.

The Hebrews were now able to continue their way secure against further attempts on the part of the Egyptians to pursue them. There were some thousands of them (we do not know the exact number) and they travelled as caravans still travel across the desert. A leader generally goes in front carrying a long pole on the top of which is a brazier filled with smoking coals. During the day the smoke can be seen at a great distance, so that the caravan can tell where the leader is and the direction in which it must travel. At night the glowing coals in the brazier serve the same purpose, and make it possible for travellers to take long night journeys over the desert in order to reach the oases without undue delay. Long years afterwards, when the history of this escape from Egypt was being written, it all seemed so miraculous to the Hebrew writer, that he described the journey over the trackless desert as guided by "the Lord who went before them, by day in a pillar of a cloud to lead them the way; and by night in a pillar of fire, to give them light; to go by day and night."

THE BABE IN THE BULRUSHES

By Amy Steedman

Many long years had passed since the days when Joseph's brothers and their families had settled in the land of Egypt. They were a great nation in numbers now, but the Egyptians still ruled over them, and used them as servants. The Pharaoh who had been so kind to the shepherds from Canaan was dead long ago, and the new kings, or Pharaohs as they were called, hated foreigners, and began to treat the Israelites very harshly. There were too many of them, they said; it was dangerous to have so many strong, powerful slaves. They must be kept down, and made to work from morning till night, and be beaten if they did not work fast enough.

That was very hard for the poor people; but worse was to come. An order was issued one day which spread sorrow through all the land of Goshen, where the Israelites lived. Every baby boy that was born was to be thrown into the river. Girl babies might be allowed to live, for they would be useful as slaves, but boys might grow up to fight for their country, and so they must be destroyed.

In one little house, not far from the great river Nile, a woman sat holding her tiny baby in her arms, while the tears ran down her cheeks. He was such a beautiful baby, so strong and fair and healthy; but the king's order was that he was to be thrown into the river, where the cruel, hungry crocodiles were waiting to snap up everything they could find for a meal. Jochebed, the poor mother, held her baby closer in her arms. No, she could not obey the king's order. She would try and hide the baby for a little while, at any rate.

It was easy to hide a baby while he was still tiny and slept most of the day; but when he grew bigger it was much more difficult. His sister Miriam did her best to help her mother; but any day, now that the baby was three months old, he might be discovered, and something must be done at once.

So Jochebed thought of a plan, and prayed to God that He would help her to carry it out. At the edge of the river there grew tall bulrushes, which, when cut down and dried, could be made into many useful things. Taking some of these bulrushes, she wove them into a little cradle with a cover to it, just like a little ark, and this she covered with a kind of pitch, so that not a drop of water could come through. Inside the cradle she made a soft bed, and laid the baby there while he was fast asleep, and set the ark afloat in the water where the bulrushes were growing. She knew that presently the great princess, Pharaoh's daughter, would come down to bathe in the river, and would notice the queer little ark floating there.

Very soon the royal procession came winding down from the palace towards the river, as the princess in her gorgeous robes made her way to bathe in the pool of the lotus flowers. But at the edge of the river she stopped. What was that among the bulrushes? It was no lotus flower, but a strange-looking covered basket, and she ordered her maidens to bring it to her.

The little ark was lifted out of the water and carried to the princess. There was surely something alive inside, and the princess was full of curiosity as she leaned down and lifted the cover to look in. Then she started back in amazement. The dearest little baby she had ever seen lay there, all rosy and fresh after his sleep, gazing up at her with wide-open eyes. The maidens crowded round, and the sight of all those strange faces was more than the baby could bear. He puckered up his face and began to cry.

The princess loved babies, and she had none of her own. That little wailing cry went to her heart. She guessed at once that this was one of the Hebrew babies which had been ordered to be destroyed, and she made up her mind that this beautiful boy should at least be saved.

All this time Miriam had been watching from her hiding-place close by, and with anxious, beating heart she came forward now. Could she help the princess? she asked. Should she run and find some Hebrew woman who might look after the baby?

Perhaps the princess guessed that the baby's mother would not be far off, and she must have smiled a little when a nurse was so quickly found. But she took no notice of that.

"Take this child away," she said, when Jochebed stood humbly before her, "and nurse it for me, and I will give thee thy wages."

It was merely as a nurse that the mother was hired. The great princess meant to adopt the baby as her own. But he was safe, and Jochebed's heart was full of gratitude to God as she took her little son into her arms again.

As long as he needed a nurse the baby was left to be looked after by his mother in the little house by the river-side. The princess called him Moses, which means "drawn out," because he had been drawn out of the water, and she had made up her mind that as soon as he was old enough he should come to live with her at the palace, and be brought up as a prince. He would be treated just as if he was really her son.

But his poor mother had him for those first precious years while he was still a little boy, and she did not waste one minute of that time in her training of him. She taught him about God, and told him all the wonderful stories about his own country, so that he should never forget that he belonged to God's people, even when he should become a prince in the Egyptian palace. Just as a gardener sows seeds in a garden which afterwards grow up into beautiful flowers, so she sowed the seeds of truth in the heart of her little son, which long afterwards were to blossom out and bear such wonderful fruit.

Then when Moses was old enough to do without a nurse, she took him to the palace, and "brought him unto Pharaoh's daughter, and he became her son."

But deep down in his heart he never forgot his own people.

It happened one day that he saw one of the Egyptian taskmasters treating one of the poor Israelite slaves with great cruelty, beating him most unmercifully with a long whip. This made Moses so angry that he rushed in to defend the slave, and dealt the taskmaster such a blow that it killed him.

But instead of being grateful the Israelites would not trust him, and began to whisper the tale of how he had killed the Egyptian, so that Moses was obliged to flee for his life, leaving behind all the riches and honors he had enjoyed so long.

A very different kind of life began now for Moses. He journeyed far into the desert and joined company there with an Arab tribe, and wandered from place to place feeding their flocks and living the life of a shepherd.

But God had more difficult work for him to do than feeding sheep, and one day when he was in the desert he saw a strange sight. A bush was growing there, and in the middle of the bush a fire was burning, and the strange thing was that although the fire kept on burning fiercely the bush was not burnt at all. It was the Angel of the Lord that was in the midst of the fire, and as Moses drew near God called him by his name, and told him that he was to go back and set his people free from the tyranny of Pharaoh and lead them into the Promised Land.

At first Moses said it was impossible for him to do this. His own people would not trust him, and he was no great speaker; he would certainly fail. But God bade him do his best, and Aaron his brother would speak for him; and above all God would be his helper.

So Moses returned to the land of Egypt and boldly asked Pharaoh to allow the people to go and worship God. Time after time Pharaoh refused, although God sent dreadful plagues to warn him. At last, however, when the angel of death killed all the eldest sons of the Egyptians, Pharaoh was terrified and said the people might go at once and take all their belongings with them.

It was a great company of people that set out, and Moses the great leader guided them on their way. They had many adventures, and braved many dangers and difficulties, but God was always their shield and defense. He delivered them by parting the waters of the Red Sea and allowing them to walk over dry-shod when Pharaoh and his army were pursuing them. And when the pursuers tried to follow them, the waters rolled back, and the whole great army were swept away by the returning tide.

Yet in spite of God's care and goodness towards them, these Israelites were often ungrateful, and complained bitterly when they suffered any want. And it was always Moses whom they blamed.

Moses was very patient with them; but once he was so angry that he was tempted to disobey God's direction, and as a punishment God told him that though he should see the Promised Land from afar he would never enter it himself.

There on the mountain top he stood, gazing into the far distance, where the Land of Canaan, that fair land flowing with milk and honey, lay stretched out before him. Then he bowed his head to God's will. The murmuring people never saw their great leader again. He "was not, for God took him."

Unit Four: Desert Wanderings

THEME: OBEDIENCE

FROM ANECDOTES AND EXAMPLES
ILLUSTRATING THE CATHOLIC CATECHISM
By Rev. Francis Spirago

*They who lived before the Son of God became man could be saved
by believing in a Redeemer to come, and by keeping the Commandments.*

THE FRUIT OF THE PROMISED LAND

Moses, while still with the Israelites in the desert, sent two spies to view the Promised Land. On their return from their tour of investigation, they brought back in proof of the land's richness an immense bunch of grapes strung on a pole and so carried between them, one preceding, the other following. That cluster of grapes represents Christ on the cross; and he that went before personifies the saints of old, and he that followed typifies those who came after Christ. Thus the virtue of the cross touches each, and Christ's sweetness and refreshing grace are ever ready to their hands, though in this respect the Christian has the advantage. To the men of old, God said, "Go before Me and be perfect," but to His Christian followers Christ Himself has shown the way, and, leading, says, "Come, follow me."

FROM THE CHOSEN PEOPLE
By Charlotte Yonge

THE WILDERNESS

*"Where is the one who brought up out of the sea the shepherd of his flock?
Where is the one who placed in their midst his holy spirit?"*
—Isaiah 63:11

When Moses had led the 600,000 men, with their wives, children, and cattle, beyond the reach of the Egyptians, they were in a small peninsula, between the arms of the Red Sea, with the wild desolate peaks of Mount Horeb towering in the midst, and all around grim stony crags, with hardly a spring of water; and though there were here and there slopes of grass, and bushes of hoary-leaved camel-thorn, and long-spined shittim or acacia, nothing bearing fruit for human beings. There were strange howlings and crackings in the mountains, the sun glared back from the arid stones and rocks, and the change seemed frightful after the green meadows and broad river of Egypt.

Frightened and faithless, the Israelites cried out reproachfully to Moses to ask how they should live in this desert place, forgetting that the Pillar of cloud and fire proved that they were under the care of Him who had brought them safely out of the hands of their enemies. In His mercy God bore with their murmurs, fed them with manna from Heaven, and water out of the flinty rock; and gave them the victory over the Edomite tribe of robber Amalekites at Rephidim, where Joshua fought, and Moses, upheld by Aaron and Hur, stretched forth his hands the whole day. Then, fifty days after their coming out of Egypt, He called them round the peak of Sinai to hear His own Voice proclaim the terms of the new Covenant.

The Covenant with Abraham had circumcision for the token faith as the condition, and the blessing to all nations as the promise. This Covenant remained in full force, but in the course of the last four hundred years, sin had grown so much that the old standard, handed down from the patriarchs, had been forgotten, and men would not have known what was right, nor how far they fell from it, without a written Law. This Law, in ten rules, all meeting together in teaching Love to God and man, commanded in fact perfection, without which no man could be fit to stand in the sight of God. He spoke it with His own Mouth, from amid cloud, flame, thunder, and sounding trumpets, on Mount Sinai, while the Israelites watched around in awe and terror, unable to endure the dread of that Presence. The promise of this Covenant was, that if they would keep the Law, they should dwell prosperously in the Promised Land, and be a royal priesthood and peculiar treasure unto God. They answered with one voice, "All the words the Lord hath said will we do;" and Moses made a sacrifice, and sprinkled them with the blood, to consecrate them and confirm their oath. It was the blood of the Old Testament. Then he went up into the darkness of the cloud on the mountain top, there fasting, to talk with God, and to receive the two Tables of Stone written by the Finger of God. This was, as some believe, the first writing in the letters of the alphabet ever known in the world, and the Books of Moses were the earliest ever composed, and set down with the pen upon parchment.

Those Laws were too strict for man in his fallen state. Keep them he could not; breaking them, he became too much polluted to be fit for mercy. Even while living in sight of the cloud on the Mountain, where Moses was known to be talking with God, the Israelites lost faith, and set up a golden calf in memory of the Egyptian symbol of divinity, making it their leader instead of Moses. Such a transgression of their newly-made promise so utterly forfeited their whole right to the covenant, that Moses destroyed the precious tables, the token of the mutual engagement, and God threatened to sweep them off in a moment and to fulfill His oaths to their forefather in the children of Moses alone. Then Moses, having purified the camp by slaying the worst offenders, stood between the rest and the wrath of God, mediating for them until he obtained mercy for them, and a renewal of the Covenant. Twice he spent forty days in that awful Presence, where glorious visions were revealed to him; the Courts of Heaven itself, to be copied by him, by Divine guidance, in the Ark and Tabernacle, where his brother Aaron, and his seed after him, were to minister as Priests, setting forth to the eye how there was a Holy Place, whence men were separated by sin, and how it could only be entered by a High Priest, after a sacrifice of atonement. Every ordinance of this service was a shadow of good things to come, and was therefore strictly enjoined on Israel, as part of the conditions of the Covenant, guiding their faith onwards by this acted prophecy; and therewith God, as King of His people, put forth other commands, some relating to their daily habits, others to their government as a nation, all tending to keep them separate from other nations. For transgressions of such laws as these, or for infirmities of human nature, regarded as stains, cleansing sacrifices were permitted. For offences against the Ten Commandments, there was no means of purchasing remission; no animal's, nay, no man's life could equal such a cost; there was nothing for it but to try to dwell on the hope, held out to Adam and Abraham, and betokened by the sacrifices and the priesthood, of some fuller expiation yet to come; some means of not only obtaining pardon, but of being worthy of mercy.

The Israelites could not even be roused to look for the present temporal promise, and hankered after the fine soil and rich fruits of Egypt, rather than the beautiful land of hill and valley that lay before them; and when their spies reported it to be full of hill forts, held by Canaanites of giant stature, a cowardly cry of despair broke out, that they would return to Egypt. Only two of the whole host, besides Moses, were ready to trust to Him who had delivered them from Pharaoh, and had led them through the sea. Therefore those two alone of the grown-up men were allowed to set foot in the Promised Land. Till all the rest should have fallen in the wilderness, and a better race have been trained up, God would not help them to take possession. In their willfulness they tried to advance, and were defeated, and thus were obliged to endure their forty years' desert wandering.

Even Moses had his patience worn out by their fretful faithlessness, and committed an act of disobedience, for which he was sentenced not to enter the land, but to die on the borders after one sight of the promise of his fathers. Under him, however, began the work of conquest; the rich pasture lands of Gilead and Basan were subdued, and the tribes of Reuben and Gad, and half the tribe of Manasseh, were permitted to take these as their inheritance, though beyond the proper boundary, the Jordan. The Moabites took alarm, though these, as descended from Abraham's nephew Lot, were to be left unharmed; and their king, Balak, sent, as it appears, even to Mesopotamia for Balaam, a true prophet, though a guilty man, in hopes that he would bring down the curse of God on them. Balaam, greedy of reward, forced, as it were, consent from God to go to Balak, though warned that his words would not be in his own power. As he stood on the hill top with Balak, vainly endeavoring to curse, a glorious stream of blessing flowed from his lips, revealing, not only the fate of all the tribes around, even for a thousand years, but proclaiming the Sceptre and Star that should rise out of Jacob to execute vengeance on his foes. But finding himself unable to curse Israel, the miserable prophet devised a surer means of harming them: he sent tempters among them to cause them to corrupt themselves, and so effectual was this invention, that the greater part of the tribe of Simeon were ensnared, and a great plague was sent in chastisement. It was checked by the zeal of the young priest, Phineas, under whose avenging hand so many of the guilty tribe fell, that their numbers never recovered the blow. Then after a prayer of atonement, a great battle was fought, and the wretched Balaam was among the slain.

The forty years were over, Moses' time was come, and he gave his last summing up of the Covenant, and sung his prophetic song. His authority was to pass to his servant, the faithful spy, bearing the prophetic name of Joshua; and he was led by God to the top of Mount Nebo, whence he might see in its length and breadth, the pleasant land, the free hills, the green valleys watered by streams, the wooded banks of Jordan, the pale blue expanse of the Mediterranean joining with the sky to the west; and to the north, the snowy hills of Hermon, which sent their rain and dew on all the goodly mountain land. It had been the hope of that old man's hundred and twenty years, and he looked forth on it with his eye not dim, nor his natural force abated; but God had better things for him in Heaven, and there upon the mountain top he died alone, and God buried him in the sepulchre whereof no man knoweth. None was like to him in the Old Covenant, who stood between God and the Israelites, but he left a promise that a Prophet should be raised up like unto himself.

FROM BOOK OF THE ANCIENT WORLD
By Dorothy Mills

The Land and People of Phoenicia

The land of Phoenicia was the strip of fertile land on the east of the Mediterranean. It was about two hundred miles long, and at its widest, only thirty-five miles across, in places it was only half that width. It faced West towards the setting sun, the direction in which adventurous spirits have always turned. It was a very fertile land, and the name "Phoenicia" means "the region of palms"; grain grew there in abundance, and the vine, orange, olive and mulberry trees; the forests were rich in timber for building purposes, especially the cedar of Lebanon, and the coast lines afforded good harbors. The position of Phoenicia was exceedingly good; on the North and East mountain ranges protected her from the armies which so often invaded and harassed the land between Mesopotamia and Egypt, and the sea lay on the West. Phoenicia occupied a unique position in the middle of the world as it was known to ancient peoples.

In this well-favored little land, there lived a remarkable people. In appearance, they were of medium height, with thick hair and broad and often hooked noses. They were vigorous and active, and were a nation of sailors and traders. Their character fitted them for this life. They were not soldiers, though they could defend themselves and their country bravely when need arose, but they did not seek occasions to quarrel, and were more interested in the development of their commerce and wealth than in building up a great empire by means of conquest. They got on well with other nations and were always welcomed by them: the Egyptians traded with them and allowed them to build a temple to their own gods in the Egyptian capital; the Hebrews traded and intermarried with them, and the Phoenicians supplied them with workmen as well as materials; the Assyrians and Babylonians not only traded with them, but protected their caravans, and allowed them a free passage through their empire from the Mediterranean to the Persian Gulf; the Greeks welcomed them in their ports; and the Persians, even after they had conquered them, allowed them to keep their own kings, taxed them lightly, and relied on them to supply ships for their fleets.

The Phoenicians had endless capacity for hard work, and were capable of enduring great hardships, but at the same time they loved luxury and ease, and their cities were centers of very luxurious living. They spoke a language that was very like Hebrew, but they have left no literature behind them, their interests were all active, practical and commercial. They were the greatest traders, miners, manufacturers, sailors and colonizers of their time.

The chief god of Phoenicia was Baal, who was sometimes known by his Canaanite name of Moloch. He was supposed to be the Sun-God, who destroyed by his consuming fire, and who brought the drought and dried up the springs. The Phoenicians believed that they must appease him by offering to him that which was dearest to them, and their principal sacrifice of this kind was that of children. This cruel and brutal side of their religion tended to make the people themselves cruel and brutal and developed the lower side of their nature. They had no belief in a future life, they called death "the time of non-existence," and said that those who died "went down into silence and became mute." The only immortality for which they hoped was to be always remembered on earth.

The Phoenicians came into frequent contact with the Hebrews whose land was so near their own. Jezebel, the daughter of a Phoenician king, married Ahab King of Israel, and through her influence many of the Phoenician religious customs were introduced amongst the Hebrews, though they were always sternly denounced by the Hebrew prophets, especially by Elijah.

But though the Phoenicians were not a people of high ideals, and constantly disregarded the rights of others, especially those of the weak, by their perseverance and their fearless defiance of danger, they became the carriers of a great civilization.

FROM BOOK OF THE ANCIENT WORLD
By Dorothy Mills

WHAT WE OWE TO PHOENICIA

The beginnings of the modern alphabet have been generally attributed to Phoenicia. The Egyptians and Babylonians had a very large number of symbols in their written languages, and though the Phoenicians did not invent the modern alphabet, they reduced the number and complication of the signs used, and introduced twenty-two much simpler ones. As the Phoenicians were the only nation who sailed North and South and East and West in the Mediterranean, and as their trading transactions required some kind of written form, their alphabet was naturally the one first introduced into Europe.

When the Greeks first saw these mysterious looking black marks written on paper, they were rather afraid of them, and thought they were some kind of magic that would bring them bad luck. But they soon not only grew accustomed to the Phoenician alphabet, but adapted it to their own use, improved on it, and handed it on to western Europe, and the letters we use today are descended from it.

Another debt we owe the Phoenicians is the example they have given to all other nations who have carried civilization to the ends of the earth. Their ships were the best of their time, it is true, yet they were only frail boats compared to the great vessels of today; they had no proper maps, or charts, or compass, but their daring, their fearlessness in the face of danger and their perseverance in overcoming difficulties have seldom been surpassed in later times and had never before been seen in their own.

But the Phoenicians left no history of their nation, what we have learned about them has come to us chiefly from other sources, they wrote no poetry, they made no original contributions to art or scientific knowledge, they do not even seem to have had their imagination which would have led explorers of different ideals to find out something of the lands they visited, they interpreted everything in terms of money. There has never been such a completely mercenary nation as Phoenicia. And so, though they were the carriers of a rich civilization from the East to Europe, they were themselves uncivilized, for true civilization consists in believing that there are things worth striving for that cannot be expressed in terms of money, and that the worth of a man's life is not measured by the abundance of the things he possesses.

FROM BOOK OF THE ANCIENT WORLD
By Dorothy Mills

PHOENICIAN CITIES AND INDUSTRIES

The government of Phoenicia was not a strong and central one like that of Egypt or Assyria. The cities were partly independent and were only bound together by a loose kind of confederation, and in case of attack, each had to defend itself. In spite of her protected position and her general friendliness with other nations, Phoenicia was attacked from time to time by the great empires of the period, and she submitted in turn to them all. She preferred to live under the protection of a strong foreign power and to be allowed to pursue her commerce in peace, to making a very stubborn resistance and so risking destruction. After submission had been made, rebellions occurred from time to time, but in the end the Phoenicians generally acknowledged the overlordship of the foreign power, and whatever may have been their feelings, they paid the tribute exacted of them, and then settled down to their former way of living. In this way Phoenicia owed allegiance in turn to Assyria, Babylon, Persia and Alexander the Great, until in the time of the Romans she was at last completely conquered and ceased to exist as a nation.

The chief cities of Phoenicia were Tyre and Sidon. There are practically no remains of the architecture in these cities; the foundations of the buildings were of stone, but the houses themselves seem to have been constructed of wood, and they have therefore, disappeared completely. Tyre was the chief city and the capital. It was strongly fortified and had an excellent harbor in which the fleet could be so well protected, that it was said to be "as if within a house whose doors were bolted."

The Phoenicians did not actually invent anything themselves, but they learnt from the countries with which they traded and in many cases improved upon the models, and they were famous in the ancient world for the manufacture of four things: Purple dye, glass, woven fabrics and fine metalwork. The purple dye came from the murex, a shell fish found all over the Mediterranean, but of a particularly fine quality and in large quantities on the coast of Phoenicia. According to the old Phoenician legend, the murex had been discovered by the god, Melkart, who noticed that his dog's nose always got red after he had been poking amongst the murex shells. As a matter of fact, the dye was probably first discovered by the men of Crete. The coloring matter was a creamy liquid contained in a small sac, yellowish in color, but turning first green and then purple as soon as it was exposed to the light. Large numbers of the murex were required, as three hundred pounds of liquid would only dye fifty pounds of wool. This dyeing industry was carried on chiefly in Tyre, and Tyrian purple speedily became very famous and was everywhere considered a great luxury.

Glass-blowing was the chief industry of Sidon. The Sidonians had probably first learnt the art in Egypt, but they rapidly improved upon the Egyptian methods, and Sidonian glass, vases, bowls, drinking-cups and vessels of all kinds became very celebrated. Sidon was also the chief center for the weaving of beautiful fabrics, first of linen and then of wool, later of silk. The fabrics were not only beautifully woven, but rich in color and embroidery.

Tyrian craftsmen were also famous for the engraving of gems, which they had learnt from Babylonians, and all kinds of fine metal work. In as ancient a time as the days of Homer, the poet spoke of:

> A silver bowl well wrought,
> By Sidon's artist cunningly adorned,
> Born by Phoenicians over the dark blue sea.

The golden bowls, basins, spoons and censers in Solomon's Temple at Jerusalem, as well as all kinds of work in bronze, were the work of men from Tyre. The bronze they used was of a particularly fine quality and their designs were artistic. Beautiful Phoenician jewelry is still in existence, and engraved precious stones of all kinds, the latter being used chiefly as signets or talismans.

With these rich products of their own land to offer in exchange, the Phoenicians went out by land and sea to trade with the whole world. The Hebrew prophet Ezekiel has given a description of the wealth and greatness of Tyre and of the many places with which she traded. He says:

> In the heart of the sea was your territory; your builders perfected
>   your beauty.
> With juniper wood from Senir they built all your decks;
> A cedar from Lebanon they took to make you a mast.
> With oaks of Bashan they fashioned your oars,
> Your bridge, of ivory-inlaid cypress wood from the coasts of
>   Kittim.
> Fine embroidered linen from Egypt became your sail;
> Your awnings were made of purple and scarlet from the coasts of
>   Elishah.
> Inhabitants of Sidon and Arvad were your oarsmen;
> Your own sages, Tyre, were on board, serving as your sailors.
> Every ship and sailor on the sea came to you to carry on trade.
>
> Tarshish traded with you, so great was your wealth,
> Exchanging for your wares silver, iron, tin, and lead.
> Javan, Tubal, and Meshech also traded with you,
> Exchanging slaves and bronze vessels for your merchandise.
> Horses, steeds, and mules from Beth-togarmah were exchanged for
>   your wares.
> Men of Rhodes trafficked with you; many coastlands were your
>   agents;
> Ivory tusks and ebony wood they brought back as your payment.
> Edom traded with you for your many wares: garnets, purple dye,
>   embroidered cloth,
> Fine linen, coral, and rubies they gave you as merchandise.
> Judah and the land of Israel trafficked with you:
> Minnith wheat, grain, honey, oil, and balming they gave you as
>   merchandise.
> Damascus traded with you for your many wares, so great was your
>   wealth, exchanging Helbon wine and Zahar wool.
>
> Dedan traded with you for riding gear. Arabia and the sheikhs of
>   Kedar were your agents, dealing in lambs, rams, and goats.
> The merchants of Sheba and Raamah also traded with you, ex-
>   changing for your wares the very best spices, all kinds of precious
>   stones, and gold.

Haran, Canneh, and Eden, the merchants of Sheba, Asshur, and
   Chilmad, Traded with you, marketing rich garments, purple
   cloth, embroidered fabric, varicolored carpets, and braided
   cords.
The ships of Tarshish sailed for you with your goods; You were full
   and heavily laden in the heart of the sea.

By exporting your goods by sea you satisfied many peoples,
With your great wealth and merchandise you enriched the kings of
   the earth.

(Taken from parts of Ezekiel 27)

FROM BOOK OF THE ANCIENT WORLD
By Dorothy Mills

PHOENICIAN SAILORS AND TRADERS

The earliest Phoenician ships were very small, rowed by from twelve to twenty men, all sitting on one level, and with a large square sail in the middle. Later they used biremes, which were comparatively short boats, with two decks, and with from thirty to fifty rowers. They were well equipped and armed, ordinarily small. The following description of a Phoenician ship was written by Xenophon, a Greek historian who lived in the fourth century B.C., who had himself seen one:

> I think that the best and most perfect arrangement of things which I ever saw was when I went to look at the great Phoenician trading vessel: For I saw the largest amount of naval tackling separately disposed in the smallest stowage possible. For a ship, as you well know, is brought to anchor, and again got under way, by a vast number of wooden implements, and of ropes, and sails the sea by means of a quantity of rigging, and is armed with a number of contrivances against hostile vessels, and carries about with it a large supply of weapons for the crew, and, besides, has all the utensils that a man keeps in his dwelling-house, for each of the messes. In addition, it is loaded with a quantity of merchandise, which the owner carries with him for his own profit. Now all the things which I have mentioned lay in a space not much bigger than a room that would conveniently hold ten beds. And I remarked that they severally lay in such a way that they did not obstruct one another, and did not require anyone to look for them, and yet they

were neither placed at random, nor entangled one with another, so as to consume time when they were suddenly wanted for use. Also I found the captain's assistant, who is called "the look-out man," so well acquainted with the position of all the articles, and with the number of them, that even when at a distance he could tell where everything lay, and how many there were of each sort, just as one who had learned to read could tell the number of letters in the name of Socrates and the proper place for each of them. Moreover, I saw this man in his leisure moments, examining and testing everything that a vessel needs when at sea; so, as I was surprised, I asked him what he was about, whereupon he replied, "Stranger, I am looking to see, in case anything should happen, how everything is arranged in the ship and whether anything is wanting or is inconveniently situated; for when a storm arises at sea, it is not possible either to look for what is wanting, or to put to rights what is arranged awkwardly."

In these little ships the Phoenicians set out on their voyages across unknown seas, to strange shores, often meeting wild and savage natives, in search of new opportunities for trade, for adding to their wealth, or just for pure adventure. They had very real perils to face. The Mediterranean storms come up suddenly and are violent, voyages along the coast are always more dangerous than those in the open sea, there was always danger from pirates, and in addition to these known dangers there were those of the unknown regions into which they sailed. But they went fearlessly on, even between the pillars of Hercules out into the Atlantic, which was supposed to be the abode of monsters with three heads and six arms, and where the flat world came to an end, on to the shores of Britain.

The Phoenicians carried the trade and civilization of the great eastern empires from their own land to the islands of the Aegean, to Greece and Italy, and from Egypt along the coast of North Africa to Gaul and Spain. They took with them their own manufactures, as well as goods brought from Mesopotamia by their caravans, and in the islands of the Aegean and in Greece they exchanged them for bronzes and other works of art; in Cyprus they found boxwood inlaid with ivory; from Egypt came fine linen and embroidery as well as grain; the coasts of North Africa were rich in skins, horns, leather, ivory, ebony, ostrich feathers and gold; Southern Spain gave them silver, iron, tin and lead; and tin came, too, from the far-off Scilly Isles and Cornwall.

But these voyages were not enough for the fearless Phoenician mariners, and it is very probable that they sailed from a Red Sea port round Africa and back through the Straits of Gibraltar into the Mediterranean Sea. The story is told by Herodotus, and was doubted for a long time, but it is quite in character with their other deeds of daring, and there is no reason why it should not be true. Herodotus tells us that the voyage took three years, and that sometimes their food supply gave out, so that they were forced to plough the land and sow seed, and wait until the grain came up before sailing further.

The Phoenicians did not only trade by sea, their caravans also went overland from the Mediterranean to the Persian Gulf, and from Phoenicia overland to Babylon, and across the mountains to Van in Armenia. These land routes gave them honey, oil, and balm from the land of Judah and Israel; precious stones, wine, white wool and linen from Syria; spices and sword-blades from Arabia; carpets, hangings and cloaks from Assyria and Babylon; mules and horses from Armenia; and in Asia they trafficked in slaves.

A Phoenician caravan must have been an imposing sight. It was really like a moving market, and had to be large in order to be safe from robbers. In modern times, goods may be sent from one country to another, without in any way affecting the places through which they pass, but a caravan has to halt from time to time for rest and refreshment, and such stopping-places make markets by the way. The Phoenician sailors who voyaged out into uncharted seas were not the only men of their nation who braved dangers; the first armed merchants who left Tyre to go overland to Babylon faced dangers just as great. They had to cross the deserts with no maps or knowledge of the route, they had to trust to native guides who often misled them, they had to pass through remote and inhospitable regions, and to run risks of attack from hostile tribes roaming over the desert. After a time the journey had been made so often, that the route became known, many of the difficulties were removed and the caravan journey became easier, but only men of fearless determination to succeed could have accomplished what the first Phoenician merchants did.

The journey from Tyre lasted about three months, and when the traders arrived they generally pitched their tents outside the city walls, near water and trees. They could be seen by the watchmen on the towers, and no time would be lost in spreading the news that the caravan had arrived. Early in the morning the Phoenicians would be astir, arranging their goods so that they could be seen to the best advantage, and as soon as the city gates were opened, out would come the inhabitants, dressed as for a holiday, and very quickly bargaining would begin. The most important buyers were the great city merchants who had ordered goods in advance, and who now came to pay for and receive them.

Other caravans went to Armenia, and this road led through a rough mountain land, impossible for camels, and so the merchandise would be loaded on the back of mules and asses as well as on those of men. It was a cold journey, and the Phoenicians wore fur and leather garments. They brought back over the same rough road large numbers of mules and horses in which the Armenian lands were rich.

All this trade and enterprise brought great wealth to Phoenicia, and spread the knowledge of the industries of the East over the whole of the then known world, but the Phoenicians themselves were not a nation of high ideals and though they helped to spread civilization through the world, their intercourse had other consequences not so good. Wealth for themselves was their sole ambition, but they had no worthy aim for the employment of their wealth. In their determination to obtain everything a country could give them, they exhausted the fishing beds and mines, and drained the population of other lands in such a way that they destroyed rather than developed their resources. These methods hindered the development of other countries, for as long as their natural resources lasted, they served only to minister to the wealth of Phoenicia.

FROM: A BOOK OF DISCOVERY: THE HISTORY OF THE WORLD'S EXPLORATION, FROM THE EARLIEST TIMES TO THE FINDING OF THE SOUTH POLE
By Margaret Bertha Synge

EARLY MARINERS

The law of the universe is progress and expansion, and this little old world was soon discovered to be larger than men thought.

Now in Syria—the highway between Babylonia and Egypt—dwelt a tribe of dusky people known as Phoenicians. Some have thought that they were related to our old friends in Somalia, and that long years ago they had migrated north to the seacoast of that part of Syria known as Canaan.

Living on the seashore, washed by the tideless Mediterranean, they soon became skillful sailors. They built ships and ventured forth on the deep; they made their way to the islands of Cyprus and Crete and thence to the islands of Greece, bringing back goods from other countries to barter with their less daring neighbors. They reached Greece itself and cruised along the northern coast of the Great Sea to Italy, along the coast of Spain to the Rock of Gibraltar, and out into the open Atlantic.

How their little sailing boats lived through the storms of that great ocean none may know, for Phoenician records are lost, but we have every reason to believe that they reached the northern coast of France and brought back tin from the islands known to them as the Tin Islands. In their home markets were found all manner of strange things from foreign unknown lands, discovered by these master mariners—the admiration of the ancient world.

"The ships of Tarshish," said the old poet, "did sing of thee in thy market, and thou wast replenished and made very glorious in the midst of the seas; thy rowers have brought thee into great waters; the east wind hath broken thee in the midst of the seas."

All the world knew of the Phoenician seaports, Tyre and Sidon. They were as famous as Memphis and Thebes on the Nile, as magnificent as Nineveh on the Tigris and Babylon on the Euphrates. Men spoke of the "renowned city of Tyre," whose merchants were as princes, whose "traffickers" were among the honorable of the earth. "O thou that art situate at the entry of the sea," cries the poet again, when the greatness of Tyre was passing away, "which art a merchant of the people from many isles.... Thy borders are in the midst of the seas; thy builders have perfected thy beauty. They have made all thy ship-boards of fir trees ... they have taken cedars of Lebanon to make masts for thee. Of the oaks of Basan have they made thy oars.... Fine linen with broidered work from Egypt was that which thou spreadest forth to be thy sail.... The inhabitants of Sidon ... were thy mariners; thy wise men were thy pilots."

As time goes on, early groups round the Euphrates and the Nile continue, but new nations form and grow, new cities arise, new names appear. Centuries of men live and die, ignorant of the great world that lies about them— "Lords of the eastern world that knew no west."

England was yet unknown, America undreamt of, Australia still a desolate island in an unknown sea. The burning eastern sun shone down on to vast stretches of desert-land uninhabited by man, great rivers flowed through dreary swamps unrealized, tempestuous waves beat against their shores, and melancholy winds swept over the face of endless ocean solitudes.

A Book of Discovery: The History of the World's Exploration,
From the Earliest Times to the Finding of the South Pole
By Margaret Bertha Synge

Hanno's "Periplus"

Hanno's "Periplus," or the "Coasting Survey of Hanno," is one of the few Phoenician documents that has lived through the long ages. In it the commander of the expedition himself tells his own story. With an idea of colonizing, he left Carthage—the most famous of the Phoenician colonies—with sixty ships containing an enormous number of men and women.

"When we had set sail," says Hanno shortly, "and passed the pillars (of Hercules) after two days' voyage, we founded the first city. Below this city lay a great plain. Sailing thence westward we came to a promontory of Libya thickly covered with trees. Here we built a temple to the Sea-god and proceeded thence half a day's journey eastward, till we reached a lake lying not far from the sea and filled with abundance of great reeds. Here were feeding elephants and a great number of other wild animals. After we had gone a day's sail beyond the lakes we founded cities near to the sea."

Making friends with the tribes along the coast, they reached the Senegal River. Here they fell in with "savage men clothed with the skins of beasts," who pelted them with stones so that they could not land. Past Cape Verde they reached the mouth of the Gambia, "great and broad and full of crocodiles and river-horses," and thence coasted twelve days to the south and again five days to the south, which brought them to Sierra Leone—the Lion Mountain as it was called long years after by the Portuguese.

Here Hanno and his party landed, but as night approached they saw flames issuing from the island and heard the sound of flutes and cymbals and drums and the noise of confused shouts.

"Great fear then came upon us; we sailed therefore quickly thence much terrified, and passing on for four days found at night a country full of fire. In the middle was a lofty fire, greater than all the rest, so that it seemed to touch the stars. When day came on we found that this was a great mountain which they called the chariot of the gods." They had a last adventure before they turned homewards at what they called the Isle of Gorillas. Here they found a "savage people" (Gorillas) whom they pursued, but were unable to catch. At last they managed to catch three. "But when these, biting and tearing those that led them, would not follow us, we slew them and, flaying off their skins, carried them to Carthage."

Then abruptly this quaint account of the only Phoenician voyage on record stops. "Further," says the commander, "we did not sail, for our food failed us."

FROM THE BOOK OF THE ANCIENT WORLD
By Dorothy Mills

PHOENICIAN COLONIES

As soon as Phoenician merchants had established trade in a place, they planted a colony there. These colonies soon became practically independent, only connected by the same loose ties which bound the Phoenician cities together. From Tyre and Sidon they went first to Egypt, where they established a station at Memphis, and then to the coasts of Asia Minor, whence they could easily reach the islands of the Aegean. They established colonies in the east and south of Cyprus, then they sailed on to Rhodes and the Aegean, though they withdrew when the Greeks came to these regions, as they preferred places where they had no rivals. So they passed to Sicily, and along the coast of North Africa (where Carthage became the greatest of all Phoenician colonies), and on to Spain, and then out into the Atlantic to the Cornish coast.

These Phoenician colonies formed three groups: those in the Eastern Mediterranean and the Aegean; those in the Central Mediterranean, North Africa and Sicily; and those in the Western Mediterranean, chiefly in Spain, and for nearly a thousand years Phoenician enterprise by sea and land, overcoming all difficulties, linked these distant places together.

FROM THE BOOK OF THE ANCIENT WORLD
By Dorothy Mills

A VISIT TO THEBES

It was a sunny day, nearly three thousand years ago, and a Phoenician galley was making its way up the river Nile. It was a boat that had often made the voyage before, for the owner was a merchant, and for a long time he had been bringing the products of articles made in Thebes, the most flourishing city of the Egyptians. He had on board now cedar-wood, but from the forests in Lebanon, used by the Egyptians for the great doors of their temples, some copper and tin from Syria, and beautiful stuffs dyed with rich purple dye known only to the men of Tyre, and he hoped to do a good trade with these things and to take home in exchange grain and linen of which there was none better in the world than that of Egypt. On this voyage he had brought with him his young son, who had never been in Egypt before, and as the boat sailed up the Nile, the boy looked eagerly at the country on the banks, so different from his own home.

The young Hiram had been much interested in the Delta, for his father had told him of the skill with which the Egyptians had drained this swampy region and made it into fertile land, so that they were able to sell the grain and the flax which grew there so abundantly. But they had not been very long in reaching the end of the Delta, and soon a city was seen in the distance. Young Hiram thought this must be Thebes, but he was told that before getting to the end of their journey they would pass Memphis, the oldest city in the world. Hiram begged his father to let the boat stop so that he might go ashore and explore, for in the distance he saw mysterious looking obelisks pointing up to the sky, and great temples, and most wonderful of all, the pyramids, those ancient monuments of which his father had often told him. He would have liked to go and see these things nearer, but his father told him it would take them several days still to reach Thebes, and he must wait for another time to see Memphis.

So on they sailed, until at last the buildings of a great city came in sight, and Hiram was told that they were reaching Thebes. But to his surprise he noticed that on one side of the river most of the houses seemed like temples, and there was a stillness over them, whereas from the other side came the hum of a busy city thronged with people. His father explained to him that on one side was the city of the dead, and that most of the buildings he saw there were the tombs where the Egyptians had been buried for centuries. Amongst the tombs were temples, the walls of which were covered with brightly colored paintings and sculpture, and the sunshine resting on them seemed to fill the air with rich and splendid color.

But the Phoenicians had business on the other side of the river, and Hiram accompanied his father into the city of the living, where they were going to buy things to take back in exchange for their shipload of precious woods, stuffs and metals. The streets were narrow, and Hiram wondered how people could like to live in such gloomy-looking houses, but later on, when his father took him into one of the large houses where a friend of his lived, he saw that the dull side of the houses faced the street, and that once inside the heavy gateway, the courtyard was gay and pleasant, with cheerful rooms opening on to it, and he liked the comfortable Egyptian houses where it was easy to keep cool in the heat of the day. But before they made this visit they went into that part of the city where buying and selling were going on. At first Hiram was quite deafened by the noise, for everyone seemed to be shouting at his neighbor and it was sometimes quite difficult to hear what was being said. For there were no fixed prices in this Egyptian market, and Egyptians liked the excitement of bargaining, so they argued as to how many onions a man ought to have in exchange for a bed, or how many ostrich feathers a beautifully carved chair was worth. A few of the merchants had gold and silver rings which they used as money, but the bargaining about the price went on just the same, no matter what was given in exchange. When gold or silver rings were used, however, they were not counted, but weighed. Hiram had some of these rings, and whilst his father was doing his business, he told Hiram to wander about and buy what he wanted to take home with him as gifts for his family and friends.

The shops were square rooms, open in front, where the goods to be sold were displayed. The owner sat in a convenient spot near them, where he could keep an eye on his belongings and at the same time attract the passer-by, with whom he would bargain as long as the customer had patience. Hiram found a potter at work, and he at once bought a beautifully shaped vase to take to his mother, and nearby he found some rush mats which the basket weaver told him were made from plants growing in the Nile, and he bargained for one of these. His father had sent two slaves with him, so that he was able to carry away his purchases. He wandered round the market and found it difficult to choose what to buy, for the jeweler had most beautiful rings and bracelets and necklaces; lovely glass of every hue was in the glassmaker's shop, but he did not buy any of it, for the Phoenicians were even more celebrated than the Egyptians for their glass, and in one place he found them selling some that had been made in Sidon, but he could not resist bargaining for some lovely turquoise beads for his sister. He was much interested, too, in the writing materials and paper, and in the fine leather harness for the horses. He would most certainly have liked to get some of the furniture, a chair or a stool inlaid with ivory, but he could not buy everything, and he contented himself at the furniture maker's with a little inlaid box that he added to his gifts for his mother. He did not buy any linen, though he looked for a long time at the marvellously fine pieces that were almost like silk, for he knew that his father would bring back large bales of that to sell in Tyre, so he passed on to where the coppersmith was selling finely wrought tools and weapons, and he bought a dagger for his older brother. From there he went to the woodcarver, where he found some wonderful toys for his younger brothers and sisters. He bought a doll and some toy animals and would have bought some other things, but he found that he had no more rings left to give in exchange, and as the sun was now very hot, he found his way back to the quay where the galley was moored. His father had arrived just before him, and Hiram showed him all his purchases. He decided to do no more sightseeing that day, for he was quite tired, but his father promised him that if he went to bed early and rose in the morning with the sun, he would take him to see the great temple, the greatest of its kind in the world. So Hiram went to bed that night dreaming of all the craftsmen he had seen at work in Thebes and of their beautiful wares, and that he had made such wonderful bargains with them, that he was going home laden with rich specimens of all that these skillful Egyptians had made, to be the envy of all his friends in Tyre.

Unit Five:
Conquests and Judges
Theme: Strength through Weakness

From The Catechism in Examples
By Rev. D. Chisholm

Humility as Understood by the Saints

St. Augustine spoke of humility in this way: "Humility is the foundation of all other virtues; there is no virtue more powerful than this one for obtaining God's choicest favors."

It was this virtue of humility that the youthful St. Aloysius endeavored to gain with all the eagerness of his soul. Every day he prayed with fervor to the holy angels to obtain it for him by their intercession, since it had been for them the cause of their victory on the day of trial, and of their present glory and happiness in the Kingdom of Heaven.

St. Thomas of Villanova often said these words: "Humility is the mother of many virtues: of it are born obedience, the fear of God, patience, modesty, and peace."

St. Jane Frances de Chantal had so great a love for humility that she watched with the greatest attention never to allow to pass by any opportunity of practicing that virtue. Writing to St. Francis de Sales on one occasion, she used these words: "O my dearest Father, I beg of you, for the love of God, to help me to humble myself daily more and more!"

St. Francis de Paul continually taught humility. "The most powerful weapon for overcoming Satan is humility," he said.

St. Teresa could not understand why priests used to speak so frequently on the necessity of being humble. "Is it not quite evident," she used to say, "that no one can attribute to himself any good he may do? For without the help of God what good could anyone perform? How can people be so proud as to think of any little good they may have done, since they are so full of every kind of evil dispositions, and since they have committed so many sins against God? Even if I should desire to draw to myself vanity from any good I may have performed solely by the help of God, how in justice could I do it?"

St. Dominic had the custom of casting himself on his knees before the gate of any town in which he went to preach, to beg of Our Lord not to visit the people with any affliction on account of his sins.

St. Philip Neri advised all those whom he directed in Confession to say to themselves, when they had fallen into any fault: "Had I only been humble, I never would have committed this sin."

When the holy penitent Thais had been converted from her sinful life, she would continually call to mind the evil she had committed by her own fault in the days when she had fallen away from the path of virtue. She would, in her humility, consider herself unworthy of even uttering the Holy Name of God, and her great prayer was in these words:

"O Thou Who has created me, have mercy on me."

St. Teresa, again, used to say: "One single day in which a person humbles himself profoundly before God on account of his sins and his own natural weakness brings more grace into his soul than if he had spent many days in prayer.

THE CHOSEN PEOPLE
By Charlotte Yonge

ISRAEL IN CANAAN

"But God being compassionate forgave their sin;
he did not utterly destroy them."
—Psalm 78:38

Joshua led the tribes through the divided waters of the Jordan, and received strength and skill to scatter the heathen before them, conquer the cities, and settle them in their inheritance.

The Land of Canaan was very unlike Egypt, with its flat soil, dry climate, and single river. It was a narrow strip, enclosed between the Mediterranean Sea and the river Jordan, which runs due south down a steep wooded cleft into the Dead Sea, the lowest water in the world, in a sort of pit of its own, with barren desolation all round it, so as to keep in memory the ruin of the cities of the plain. In the north, rise the high mountains of Libanus, a spur from which goes the whole length of the land, and forms two slopes, whence the rivers flow, either westward into the Great Sea, or eastward into the Jordan, Many of these hills are too dry and stony to be cultivated; but the slopes of some have fine grassy pastures, and the soil of the valleys is exceedingly rich, bearing figs, vines, olive trees, and corn in plenty, wherever it is properly tilled. With such hills, rivers, valleys, and pastures, it was truly a good land, and when God's blessing was on it, it was the fairest spot where man could live. When the Israelites entered it, every hill was crowned by a strongly-walled and fortified town, the abode of some little king of one of the seven Canaanite nations who were given into their hands to be utterly destroyed. Though they were commanded to make a complete end of all the people in each place they took, they were forbidden to seize more than they could till, lest the empty ruins should serve as a harbor for wild beasts; but they had their several lots marked out where they might spread when their numbers should need room. As Jacob had promised to Joseph, Ephraim and Manasseh had the richest portion, nearly in the middle, and Shiloh, where the Tabernacle was set up, was in their territory; Judah and Benjamin were in a very wild rocky part to the southwards, between the two seas, with only Simeon beyond them; then came, north of Manasseh, the fine pasture lands of Issachar and Zebulon, and a small border for Asher between Libanus and the sea; while Reuben, Gad, and the rest of Manasseh, were to the east of the Jordan, where they had begged to settle themselves in the meadows of Bashan, and the balmy thickets of Gilead.

Many a fortified town was still held by the Canaanites, in especial Jebus, on Mount Moriah, between Judah and Benjamin; and close to Asher, the two great merchant cities of the Sidonians upon the sea-shore. These were called Tyre and Sidon, and their inhabitants were named Phoenicians, and were the chief sailors and traders of the Old World. From seeing a dog's mouth stained purple after eating a certain shell-fish on their coast, they had learnt how to dye woolen garments of a fine purple or scarlet, which was thought the only color fit for kings, and these were sent out to all the countries round, in exchange for balm and spices from Gilead; corn and linen from Egypt; ivory, pearls, and rubies from India; gold from the beds of rivers in Asia Minor; and silver from Spain, then called Tarshish. Thus, they grew very rich and powerful, and were skillful in all they undertook. The art of writing, which they seem to have caught from the Hebrews, went from them to the Greeks who lived more to the north, in what were called the Isles of the Gentiles.

The Canaanites had a still fouler worship than the people of Egypt. They had many gods, whom they called altogether Baalim, or lords; and goddesses, whom they called Ashtoreth; and they thought that each had some one city or people to defend; and that the Lord Jehovah of the Israelites was just another of these, instead of being the only God of Heaven and earth. Among these there was one great Baal to whom the Phoenicians were devoted, and a special god named Ashtoreth, the moon, or Queen of Heaven. Besides these, there was the planet Saturn, or as they called him, Moloch, of whom they had a huge brazen statue with the hands held a little apart, set up over a furnace; they put poor little children between these brazen hands, and left them to drop into the flames below as an offering to this dreadful god.

Well might such worship be called abomination, and the Israelites be forbidden to hold any dealings with those who followed it. As long as the generation lived who had been bred up in the wilderness, they obeyed, and felt themselves under the rule of God their King, Who made His Will known at Shiloh by the signs on the breastplate of the High Priest, while judges and elders governed in the cities. But afterwards they began to be tempted to make friends with their heathen neighbors, and thus learned to believe in their false deities, and to hanker after the service of some god who made no such strict laws of goodness as those by which they were bound. As certainly as they fell away, so surely, the punishment came, and God stirred up some of these dangerous friends to attack them. Sometimes it was a Canaanite tribe with iron chariots who mightily oppressed them; sometimes the robber shepherds, the Midianites, would burst in and carry off their cattle and their crops, until distress brought the Israelites back to a better mind, and they cried out to the Lord. Then He would raise up a mighty warrior, and give him the victory, so that he became ruler and judge over Israel; but no sooner was he dead, than they would fall back again into idolatry, and receive another chastisement, repent, and be again delivered. This went on for about 400 years, the Israelites growing constantly worse.

RUTH, THE GLEANER
By Amy Steedman

Along the hot, dusty road that led from the country of Moab to the fair land of Judah three women were walking with bowed heads and weary, halting steps. Their sorrowful, heavy eyes took no pleasure in the summer beauty of the harvest fields, the shimmering silver of the olive trees, and the rich promise of the vineyards, which bordered their way. The whole world looked sad to them, seen through a mist of tears.

There behind them, in the land of Moab, each of these women had left green graves, which held all they loved best. Naomi, the eldest, was perhaps the most desolate. Her thoughts went back to the time when she was as young and fair as the two daughters-in-law who walked at her side—when with her husband and her two boys she had trod that very road, seeking a home in a strange country to escape the famine, which threatened them in her own land. Now she was returning to her native town of Bethlehem, a childless, lonely widow.

The younger women, who were the wives of those two dead sons, were very sorrowful too, but for them there might yet be happiness in the world. They still had near and dear relatives and many friends in Moab, which was their native land. They had come far enough now, and it was time for them to return.

"Turn again, my daughters," said Naomi, "and go your way."

Their homes lay behind, and she must journey on alone to the little hill town which she had not seen for so many long years. They had kindly come so far to see her on her way, but they must come no farther.

So the little party halted, and one of the young women, weeping bitterly, kissed her mother-in-law and turned to go back. But the other one, whose name was Ruth, clung to Naomi, and would not leave her.

In vain the elder woman urged her to return, and pointed out that Orpah had gone, that home and friends and happiness awaited her there, while in front was only poverty and loneliness. Ruth only clung the closer as she sobbed out her tender, loving words.

"Entreat me not to leave thee," she said, "or to return from following after thee: for whither thou goest, I will go; and where thou lodgest, I will lodge: thy people shall be my people, and thy God my God. The Lord do so to me, and more also, if aught but death part thee and me."

The tender words brought comfort to the heart of Naomi, as soft rain brings refreshment to the hard, dry earth. After all, she was not quite alone; she still had someone to love and care for. So together they journeyed on again, and at last came to the winding road which led up to the town of Bethlehem, nestling like a white bird upon the long ridge of hills.

Naomi knew every step of the way. It seemed almost like a dream to tread on more that winding road, to pass through the city gates and find her way to the little house she knew so well. Although she had been gone so many years there were still people who remembered her, and these came running out to greet her.

"Is this Naomi?" they asked wonderingly.

They could scarcely believe that this sad, broken-down woman could be the pleasant-faced, happy girl who had gone away with her husband and boys in the year of the great famine. But as they listened to her story they did not wonder that she seemed so old and talked so bitterly. It made them look very kindly upon the beautiful girl who kept so close to her mother-in-law, who had given up everything rather than leave her alone.

Naomi had been quite right when she had told Ruth that poverty lay before them. She had come back quite empty-handed, and it was necessary to find some work at once which would at least provide them with daily bread. Ruth, looking out over the fields where already the barley was being cut, made up her mind to go and work there. The poor were always allowed to follow the reapers and glean the stray ears of corn that fell unnoticed. She might at least gather enough to feed her mother-in-law and herself.

Very happily, then, Ruth set out, and found her way into the harvest field, which belonged to a rich man called Boaz. The reapers treated her kindly when she timidly asked for permission to glean there, and when the master arrived to see how the harvest went, he too noticed her at once, for she was very beautiful.

"Whose damsel is this?" he asked.

There were many people ready to tell him her name, and also to tell him how she had left her land and her people to come with Naomi, her mother-in-law. The story had been repeated all through the town.

Boaz listened with interest. Naomi was his kins-woman, and it was only right that he should help her. He would begin by helping the sweet-faced daughter-in-law who had chanced to come gleaning upon his land. So he went and spoke very kindly to the beautiful Ruth, and told her to come every day to his harvest field and share the reapers' food, and he would see that no one troubled her. He even told the reapers to let some handfuls of corn fall in her way, on purpose, so that there might be plenty for her to glean.

So each day Ruth went back and worked in the harvest fields, and each day as Boaz watched her he grew to love the gentle, loving-hearted woman more and more. And when at last the harvest days were over, he went to Naomi and asked that Ruth might become his wife.

There was no more poverty or hard work now for Ruth or Naomi, no anxious days of wondering how long their flour and oil would last. Boaz was very rich, and nothing was too good for his fair young wife, whom he had first seen humbly gleaning in his harvest field.

Happiness, too, began to steal back into the life of Naomi. Winter and spring passed, and when harvest time came round once more, all the sorrow and bitterness faded from her heart, for God sent a little child to comfort her. A baby son was born to Ruth, and the whole world seemed full of sunshine and happiness as she laid him in his grandmother's arms, and the two loving hearts rejoiced in their happiness, just as they had clung together in their sorrow.

Of course, they dreamed many happy dreams over the little downy head, and planned a splendid future for the baby, as all mothers and grandmothers will do. But even their dreams never touched the golden reality, for they did not know that he was to be the grandfather of King David, that in this same little town of Bethlehem there was to be born of his line a greater King yet, the King of Heaven.

From The Book of the Ancient World
By Dorothy Mills

The Land of the Hittites

When Abraham entered Canaan, he found it occupied by a number of different tribes, amongst whom were some who were spoken of by the Hebrew writer as the "children of Heth." These people were also known as Hittites and they seem to have been on very friendly terms with Abraham, for when Sarah, his wife died, they offered to give him a piece of land in which was a cave to serve as her burying-place. Abraham refused to take the land as a gift, but paid four hundred shekels of silver for it, and the land became his. Sarah was buried there, and it became the burial place of the patriarchs. When Jacob lay dying in Egypt, he charged his sons to take him back to the land of Canaan to bury him in the cave that had been bought from the children of Heth, for, he said, "There they buried Abraham and Sarah his wife; there they buried Isaac and Rebekah his wife; and there I buried Leah," and his sons did as he asked.

Long years after, when Moses sent the twelve spies to report on the land of Canaan, they came back and spoke of the Hittites as "dwelling in the mountains," and later still when Joshua led the Hebrews to the conquest of Canaan, the Hittites are again spoken of as occupying a large part of the land. So these people seem to have been firmly settled in parts of Canaan when the Hebrews arrived. Who were they, and whence had they come?

If you look at a map of the ancient world, you will see in the West, Egypt and the fertile valley of the Nile, in the East, Babylon and Assyria in the Tigris-Euphrates valleys, and between them the strip of land, also fertile, occupied partly by the Hebrews and partly by some other smaller nations. To the North of these lands are the Taurus Mountains. Now to the peoples in the rich, warm valleys beneath, these mountains were an almost insuperable barrier. They were high and difficult to cross, the air was cold and the snow was strange and frightening to the dwellers in the warm plains in the South. So it came about that the people who lived in the North were almost unknown to the Egyptians and Babylonians. The latter knew that a strange, fierce people dwelt there, who seemed afraid of nothing. They came down from their mysterious land in the North, over the cold and snowy mountain passes, strongly armed, to destroy cities and slay the inhabitants (once they actually took Babylon), and then back they would go to their own land with their booty and prisoners. The men of ancient times called these people Khatti, we call them Hittites, and their home was in Asia Minor. The interior of this peninsula is a high table-land, very dry and much of it desert. Mountains surround it in most directions, and the valleys are fertile.

It was in this country, north of the Taurus Mountains, that the Hittites lived. They were a mountain people, and the sea played no part in their lives, but shepherds and hunters found all that they needed, and the mineral wealth of their land gave them opportunities for trade. Iron was found in the North, and the Hittites were the first people who distributed iron to the ancient world.

FROM THE BOOK OF THE ANCIENT WORLD
By Dorothy Mills

THE HITTITE PEOPLE AND THEIR CITIES

We know very little indeed about the Hittites, and our ignorance is chiefly due to the fact that we cannot yet read their writing. They seem to have borrowed forms of writing from both the Egyptians and the Babylonians, and clay tablet dictionaries have been found, showing that the Hittites learned both how to write and spell in the cuneiform script, but the Hittite hieroglyphic writing has not yet been deciphered.

A great deal of Hittite sculpture exists, and so we know what the people looked like. The Armenians of today probably resemble them a good deal. They had short, heavy figures, long, prominent noses with markedly receding foreheads and short chins. Because of the mountains which the rest of the civilized world rarely crossed, the Hittites were able to develop in their own way and to become a very strong empire. They were probably originally a group of tribes who found it to their advantage to join together both for purposes of defence and for warlike aggression. In the height of their power they seem to have controlled the whole of Eastern Asia Minor and the North of Syria, and great trade routes passed through their land. To the west of Asia Minor was the Aegean Sea, dotted with islands, where another ancient civilization flourished. Aegean wares of ancient civilization flourished. Aegean wares of various kinds have been found in far inland regions, and in those distant days, before anyone had ever dreamed of such things as trains, or cars, or the telephone or other quick means of communication that are so common today, it was the Hittites who probably formed the link between the peoples of the Aegean and those of Mesopotamia.

One of the earliest important cities of the Hittites was Boghaz-keui in the North of Asia Minor, and it would be difficult to imagine a city more unlike Thebes or Babylon. Those cities were on the banks of broad and shining rivers, surrounded by fertile plains, too hot, perhaps in the summer, but warm and pleasant in the winter. The Hittite city, on the contrary, was like a great fortress up in the mountains; in the winter, bitterly cold and looking out upon a snowy landscape, in the summer however, enjoying a clear, invigorating, healthy atmosphere. Boghaz-keui was the only large city in the early days, the other towns were probably villages, which served as markets for the country people, though they were in all likelihood fortified, so that in time of war they could serve as places of refuge for the neighboring people and their flocks.

Boghaz-keui became a great city about the fourteenth century B.C., some centuries after the Pyramids were built. A great Hittite conqueror founded it and he himself became known as the Great King of the Hittites. The town was built on a hill and commanded one of the mountain passes; it was strongly fortified with great walls and had towers at intervals. Had any daring explorer from the southern lands reached Boghaz-keui, he would have taken back strange tales of this mysterious fortress city up in the hills. The chief gate was guarded by huge carved lions, with open mouths, showing great teeth, and with their tongues hanging out, most terrifying apparitions to strangers. Inside the town the foundations of five large buildings, probably palaces and temples, have been discovered. The royal palace was built around a central court, out of which opened a great many rooms, leading one into the other. The great buildings were guarded by huge animals like the winged bulls of Assyria, but the Hittites were not as artistic or as skillful in their sculpture as the Assyrians. In one of the rooms of the palace at Boghaz-keui were found a great many clay tablets; the room was evidently the Foreign Office or State Department of the empire, and some of these tablets can be read. In those days Babylonian was the diplomatic language in use all over the ancient world, just as French was for a long time in Europe, and so most of the diplomatic correspondence between the Kings of the Hittites and their neighbors was written in the Babylonian language and in the cuneiform script. We know practically nothing at all about the learning of the Hittites, but it is evident that the scribes were thoroughly instructed in the Babylonian language and script.

The emblem of the Hittites was an eagle, sometimes one-, sometimes two-headed, and so able to look in two directions at once, thus keeping double watch over the place he guarded, and a great relief of one exists sculptured near the gateway of one of their cities. It is thought that this device was borrowed in the 13th century A.D. by the Turks and was then introduced into Europe by the Crusaders. This eagle became the emblem of the Teutonic Empire in the fourteenth century, thus linking modern times with the strange mysterious Hittite people of ancient days.

In one of the Hittite invasions of the South, the Babylonians were much mystified over a strange animal the Hittites brought with them. Not knowing what it was, they called it the "animal of the mountains." This unknown animal was the horse, which was known to the Hittites earlier than to either the Egyptians or the Babylonians, and some of the earliest sculptured representations of the horse are Hittite. The Hittite armies made use of large numbers of war chariots. There were always three men in a Hittite war chariot: the driver, the shield bearer, and the warrior himself.

Boghaz-keui had been the capital of the old Hittite power, but in later times it became less important. The Hittites had extended their empire and a new Hittite power arose, of which Carchemish, south of the mountains, became the chief city. It was a very rich and important trading center on the highway from Mesopotamia to both the West and the North, and it is still an important center, and is one of the stopping places on the modern railway to Baghdad.

We can only guess at the Hittite religion from the sculptures that have been found. They evidently had a great many gods, special gods who watched over the cities, others who were gods of mountains and rivers, of heaven and earth. Sometimes they seem to have thought that the mysterious and unknown powers of their gods would frighten away any intruders who came with hostile intentions, and there exists a sculptured relief of a god sitting between two fierce lions, whom he holds back, ready to let loose to spring at any doubtful stranger who might be approaching the city of which he was the guardian.

FROM THE BOOK OF THE ANCIENT WORLD
By Dorothy Mills

THE HITTITES AND THEIR NEIGHBORS

As we have seen, the mountains formed a barrier between the Hittites and the rest of the ancient world, but it was one-sided barrier, which prevented the peoples of the South from penetrating into Asia Minor, but which did not prevent the Hittites from coming into the lands of their southern neighbors, and the Hittites undoubtedly knew a great deal more about the Egyptians and Babylonians than the peoples of these lands knew about the Hittites. Even Assurbanipal, King of Assyria, sent back word to the King of Lydia in Asia Minor who had appealed to him for help, that neither he nor his father had ever heard of the place. Of course this may have been an expression of scorn on the part of the ruler of a great and powerful country for a place which he held to be unimportant, but in any case it points to a general ignorance on the part of the Assyrians of the lands beyond the mountains.

The Hittites probably knew the Egyptians at a very early date, but their first real connection with any of their neighbors seems to have been the raid already mentioned into Babylon, which happened some eighteen hundred years before Christ. They carried off the statue of the Babylonian god Marduk, which they seem to have kept for about three hundred years. The the Babylonians sent an embassy to ask for its return. One can picture the ambassadors setting out on what must have seemed to them a perilous journey into a strange and unknown land. But they were willing to face the dangers not only of what they thought was a barbarous land, but also of a fierce and unfriendly people, in order to recover their god. One rather wonders why they waited three hundred years, but they went in the end and received back the image, and Marduk was restored to his home.

We have already seen that the Hittites were in Canaan in the days of Abraham, and they are frequently referred to in the Old Testament. Sometimes they lived on friendly terms with the Hebrews who intermarried with them. Esau married a Hittite maiden, but his parents did not like his marriage, and we are told that it was a "grief of mind unto Isaac and Rebekah." As the power of the Hebrews grew in Canaan, that of the Hittites declined, and they seem to have become in some measure subject to the Hebrews who exacted tribute from them.

But the chief contact of the Hittites with the world beyond the mountains was that with Egypt in the reign of Ramses II, the Pharaoh of the Oppression. Just before this time the Hittites, under a young, energetic and ambitious king, had much extended their territory and their power, and they had become a force to be reckoned with. Under this king they made a treaty with Egypt by which they kept the places south of the mountains which they had conquered. It was, however, when Ramses II was the Pharaoh that the Hittites and Egyptians faced each other in a great trial of strength. They met in battle at Kadesh. Ramses was young, vigorous, and brave, and a great soldier, but at first the battle seemed to be going in favor of the Hittites; his daring and good generalship, however, saved the day for him, and he claimed that in a great victory he had defeated the Hittites and destroyed the flower of their army. This was probably an exaggeration of what actually took place, but Ramses commemorated his victory in magnificent sculpture and in a great poem, in which he gives an account of how nearly he had lost the day, which was saved for him by the help of the god Amon. He says:

> My warriors and my chariots had deserted me; not one of them stood by me. Then I prayed, where art thou, my father Amon? And Amon heard me and came at my prayer. He stretched out his hand to me and I shouted for joy... I was changed. I became like a god... like a god in his strength, I slew the hosts of the enemy: not one escaped me. Alone I did it.

Following the battle of Kadesh a treaty was made between Ramses and the Hittite King. Egyptian ambassadors went to Boghaz-keui, and in consultation with the Hittite King and his ministers, a treaty was drawn up and inscribed on a silver tablet and brought back to Egypt, where it was presented to Ramses for his approval. When it had received his assent, Egyptian scribes made another copy of it on another silver tablet, which was sent back to the Hittite King. Babylonian being the diplomatic language, the treaty was written in Babylonian and in the cuneiform script. The scribes in both countries at once made new copies; in Egypt they were inscribed on stone and placed in the temples; away off in the Hittite land, the copies were made on clay tablets. Until quite recently the Egyptian copies were the only ones known to be in existence, but in 1906, in the heart of Asia Minor, more than a thousand miles away from Egypt, two tablets in Babylonian script were discovered and they were found to be notes about the ancient treaty in words corresponding almost exactly to the form already known in Egypt.

The treaty begins:

> Ramses the great King, King of Egypt, has made himself in a treaty upon a silver tablet with the great King, King of the land Hatti, his brother, from this day to give good peace and good brotherhood between us forever; and he is a brother to me and at peace with me, and I am a brother to him and at peace with him forever. And we have made brotherhood, peace and goodwill more than the brotherhood and peace of former times, which was between Egypt and Hatti.

Then follow clauses in which mutual help is promised if either of the kings is in danger from an enemy, and a promise that the enemies of either shall not find a refuge in the land of the other.

The gods of Egypt and of the Hittites were called as witnesses to the treaty which concluded:

> As to these words which are upon this tablet of silver of the land of Hatti and of the land of Egypt as to him who shall not keep them, a thousand gods of the land of Hatti and a thousand gods of the land of Egypt shall destroy his house, his land and his servants. But he who shall keep these words which are on this tablet of silver be they Hatti or be they Egyptians, and who do not neglect them, a thousand gods of the land of Hatti and a thousand gods of the land of Egypt will cause him to be healthy and to live together with his houses and his land and his servants.

One would think that a treaty with such an ending would be kept, for it would surely have been somewhat dangerous to have incurred the wrath of a thousand gods in each country.

A few years after the treaty had been signed, a Hittite princess came to Egypt to be the bride of Ramses. The Egyptians gave her a name which meant, "The princess who seeth the beauties of Ra." The marriage was made the occasion of a state visit of the Hittite King to Egypt. As a rule in those days foreign kings only visited each other's lands when they were bent on war, so this peaceful visit was not only a great event, but almost the only one of its kind known in the history of the ancient world. The King and his daughter were accompanied by a large number of tributary kings, chiefs and other vassals, and they were laden with gifts of gold and silver. To the great surprise of the Egyptians they came in the winter, and the Egyptians thought they must indeed be a strange people who braved the dangers of snow and frost and ice for the sake of not delaying their journey.

The Hittites and the Egyptians were now on very friendly terms, and when the Hittite King and his attendants were about to leave Egypt, Ramses made them a parting speech which was later inscribed on stone to be preserved, in which he wished them a pleasant journey, unhindered by snow or ice. But such a journey was far too great an undertaking for Ramses to make a return visit, especially as he probably thought it quite unnecessary to show the Hittite King such honor, as in spite of his friendliness and his bride, he considered himself very superior to the king of the distant land beyond the mountains, as in truth he was. But when a little later he heard that the sister of the Hittite queen was sick and supposed to be possessed by a devil, he permitted the image of Khonsu, an Egyptian god, to be sent to her. This god was famous for his wonderful power of expelling evil spirits, and in great and magnificent state he was sent to the land of the Hittites, where he was said to have cured the suffering princess. A god with such powers was too valuable to be lost, however, and so the Hittites kept him for nearly four years. But at that time the Hittite King had a dream in which he saw the god fly out of his shrine towards Egypt; so rather than risk incurring the wrath of the god, the Hittites sent him home by ambassadors laden with rich and costly gifts.

The Hittites came once more in contact with Egypt, when Ramses wanted some iron and asked for it. But he was told that there was none available at the moment, but it should be sent as soon as it could be procured, and in the meantime they sent him an iron sword blade as a gift.

After this the Hittite power began to diminish, and it grew weaker and weaker, until at last in the eighth century B.C. Carchemish fell before the Assyrian King who made it one of his provinces. The Hittite empire disappeared, but the people as a race remained.

The period of the Hittite empire was a stirring time in history. Egypt and Babylon were the centers of civilizations that even then were ancient, and between them in Asia Minor was the younger Hittite civilization, not as great as the others, and to us today still very shadowy and mysterious, but it was there and of a widespread influence. The Hebrews were entering Palestine and were coming into contact with it. About the same time other great events were taking place, which made the period one of growth and interest. New colonizers were in the South of Palestine, and in the North of Asia Minor, Troy was being attacked by the Greeks. It was a great period in the history of the ancient world, full of stirring events and hero deeds, nonetheless real because so little known. But the shadows that have hidden them for so long are slowly being dispersed, for archaeologists have had imagination to see beneath the desolate mounds in those distant lands, and their spades are revealing the life of these dim and mysterious ancient peoples and are gradually making them real and alive to us.

Unit Six:
Royal Kingdom
Theme: The Dangers of Pride

FROM THE CATECHISM IN EXAMPLES
By Rev. D. Chisholm

THE DANGER OF PRIDE

Pride is the first in order of the Capital Sins.

Pride is an inordinate love of our own worth or excellence. It was the cause of the fall of the angels in Heaven, and also the cause of the fall of our first parents in Paradise, and is now the cause of the daily loss of innumerable souls. My child, be careful to avoid this sin above all others, for it is the most dangerous sin that you can commit.

THE FALL OF THE ANGELS

When God in the beginning created the angels, He bestowed on them, as He afterwards bestowed on man, the gift of free-will. He created them for Heaven, but He desired that they should merit it by acknowledging Him as their Supreme Lord and Master, and by submission to Him as their Creator, to Whom they owed all that they possessed.

Although the Scripture does not relate the history of the fall of Lucifer, the chief of the rebel angels, and of those who followed him in his rebellion against God, it clearly shows us that pride was the cause of their fall.

"How you have fallen from the heavens, O Morning Star, son of the dawn! How you have been cut down to the earth, you who conquered nations! In your heart you said: "I will scale the heavens; Above the stars of God I will set up my throne; I will take my seat on the Mount of Assembly, on the heights of Zaphon. I will ascend above the tops of the clouds; I will be like the Most High!" No! Down to Sheol you will be brought to the depths of the pit!" (Isa. 14:12-15).

The fall of our first parents in Paradise was also due to pride. They desired, like Lucifer, to be like God.

O my child, pride was the first great sin, and the one which destroyed the beauty of so many of the angels, and brought so much evil upon mankind. Watch over your heart carefully, and banish there from every thought which might lead you into the danger of committing it.

From The Chosen People
By Charlotte Yonge

The Philistines

In this time, the Israelites' chief enemies were the Philistines, in the borders of Simeon and Judah, near the sea. These were not Canaanites, but had once dwelt in Egypt, and then, after living for a time in Cyprus, had come and settled in Gaza and Ashkelon, and three other very strong cities on the coast, where they worshipped a fish-god, called Dagon. They had no king, but were ruled by lords of their five cities, and made terrible inroads upon all the country round; until at last the Israelites, in their self-will, fancied they could turn them to flight by causing the Ark to be carried out to battle by the two corrupt young priests, sons of Eli, whose doom had already been pronounced—that they should both die in one day. They were slain, when the Ark was taken by the enemies, and their aged father fell back and broke his neck in the shock of the tidings. The glory had departed; and though God proved His might by shattering Dagon's image before the Ark, and plaguing the Philistines wherever they carried it, till they were forced to send it home in a manner which again showed the Divine Hand, yet it never returned to Shiloh; God deserted the place where His Name had not been kept holy; the token of the Covenant seemed to be lost; the Philistines ruled over the broken and miserable Israelites, and there was only one promise to comfort them—that the Lord would raise up unto Himself a faithful Priest. Already there was growing up at Shiloh the young Levite, Samuel, dedicated by his mother, and bred up by Eli. He is counted as first of the prophets, that long stream of inspired men, who constantly preached righteousness, and to whom occasionally future events were made known. He was also last of the Judges, or heaven-sent deliverers. As soon as he grew up, he rallied the Israelites, restored the true worship, as far as could be with the Ark in concealment, and sent them out to battle. They defeated the Philistines, and under Samuel, again became a free nation.

Samuel, The Little Server
By Amy Steedman

It was some years after Ruth's son had been born in Bethlehem that another mother was made glad by the precious gift of a little son. This mother's name was Hannah, and her baby was a special joy to her because she had so longed to have a son and had prayed so earnestly to God for this great gift.

There was no doubt about the baby's name. He was called "Samuel," which means "God has heard."

For had not God listened to his mother's prayers and given her her heart's desire?

Hannah held her baby close in her arms. He was her very own, and yet he belonged also to God. She had promised, if her prayer was heard, that she would lend him to God, to serve Him in His Holy Temple.

Only for a little while could she keep the baby all to herself. The months passed and then the years, and Samuel grew old enough to run about and take care of himself, needing no longer to be carried in his mother's arms. Then the time came that she should take him to Eli, the priest of God, and leave him to be brought up in the Temple and taught to be a servant of God.

Perhaps at first Samuel cried for his mother, for he was only a very little boy, and must have felt strange and lonely without her; but he very soon grew happy again, and learnt to love the old priest and the new life. It was his mother who suffered most. She missed him so sorely, and mothers do not forget as quickly as children do. But although she had lent him to God, he was still hers too; and every year she went back to see him, and through the long months in between, her fingers were busy making him a little coat of a beautiful blue stuff, sewed with a border of exquisite embroidery, blue and purple and scarlet, that was like a wreath of pomegranates. Just as certain as his birthday came round his mother came and brought with her his little coat, and as he grew bigger every year the coat was bigger too.

Now, as soon as Samuel was old enough he went with Eli, the old priest, into God's house to learn how to help in God's service. Just as we sometimes see now a very little boy helping the priest at God's altar, so Samuel was like a little server as he helped Eli, and he too wore a linen surplice, or ephod as it was called.

Although he was such a little boy, Samuel already showed that he was straightforward, brave, and obedient, a boy who could be trusted. He did his work faithfully, and when Eli began to grow feeble and his sight became dim, the little server was ready with his clear sight and eager footsteps to be both eyes and feet to the old priest.

But besides growing old and feeble, Eli was also growing more and more unhappy day by day. His two sons were wicked and disobedient, and, what was worse, they were teaching God's people to be wicked too. Eli would not punish them as they deserved, so at last the time came when God took the punishment into His own hands. Only He would warn Eli before-hand, for the old priest was His servant.

So one night God's message came, spoken by God's own voice—spoken not to the great priest, but to the humble little server.

It was evening time. All the work of the day was over, and Eli had gone to rest. The lamp in the temple was burning dimly, sometimes flickering as if it would go out altogether, and leave the holy place in darkness. Samuel, tired with his day's service, was fast asleep, when suddenly he woke up, startled and attentive. Someone had called his name: "Samuel, Samuel."

"Here am I," answered the boy at once. Perhaps the old priest was ill, and wanted him. Hastily Samuel slipped out of bed, and ran to Eli. But the old man was lying there quite calmly, and when Samuel asked why he had called, he answered quietly, "I called not; lie down again."

It was very strange; but perhaps he had been dreaming, so Samuel went back and crept into bed, and very soon was once more fast asleep. Then again the voice came: "Samuel." This time Samuel was sure it was no dream, and he ran to Eli and cried to him, "Here am I, you called me."

"I called not, my son," said Eli. "Lie down again."

But when it happened a third time, and the little white figure stood by the priest's bed, declaring positively, "You called me," Eli suddenly realized that perhaps it was God whose voice the boy had heard.

"Go, lie down," he said gently to the bewildered child, "and it shall be if He calls you that you shalt say, 'Speak, Lord, for your servant is listening.'"

One great lesson Samuel had learned, and that was to do exactly what he was told, never questioning. So now he went back to bed without another word.

Did Eli mean that it was the Lord who had called him? The great God who was so wonderful, whose Ark was in the Holy Place behind the veil of blue and purple and scarlet, guarded by cherubim? He had only seemed like a far-off name to Samuel. Could it really be God's own voice that had called Samuel? If that was so, then the great unknown God must all the time have known the little servant in His house.

Then again the voice sounded: "Samuel, Samuel."

This time Samuel was listening with all his might, and obediently his answer rang out fearlessly and clearly—

"Speak, Lord, for your servant is listening."

God knew that His little servant was fit to be trusted with a message, although it was a terrible one; and He told Samuel that a dreadful punishment was to fall upon the old priest Eli and his wicked sons, and so awful would it be that even the ears of the people who heard about it should tingle.

There was no more sleep for Samuel that night. God's voice rang in his ears; his heart was filled with the thought that Eli would ask him what God had said, and he would have to tell him that dreadful message.

At last the morning light began to steal in, and it was time to open the doors of God's house. The little server in his linen ephod was at his post as usual, but today his shining morning face was clouded and troubled, and there must have been a look of awe in his clear eyes.

The call he dreaded came all too soon, and for the first time the sound of Eli's voice was unwelcome in his ears.

"Samuel, my son," called the old man.

Immediately Samuel went and stood at his side, "Here am I," he said.

"What is it that the Lord said to you?" asked Eli. His eyes were very dim, but he felt sure that the boy had a troubled and fearful look. "I ask you not to hide it from me: God do so to you, and more also, if you hide anything from me of all the things that He said to you."

The very worst must be told, and Samuel knew he must hide nothing now. He repeated God's message word for word, and Eli bowed his head as he listened. The poor old priest had been a weak father, but he was a faithful servant, and knew that God was just.

"It is the Lord," he said: "let Him do what seems Him good."

From that day all things were different to Samuel, and year by year as he grew older he learned more and more to love and serve the God who had spoken to him and trusted him. So also as the years went by the people who worshipped at the Temple began to know that the little child who had been such a faithful server was chosen for a post of great honor— that he had been called, indeed, to be a prophet of the Lord.

FROM THE CHOSEN PEOPLE
By Charlotte Yonge

THE KINGDOM OF ALL ISRAEL

"Like the choice fat of sacred offerings, so was David in Israel...with his every deed he offered thanks to God most high, in words of praise...The Lord forgave him his sins and exalted his strength forever; He conferred on him the rights of royalty and established his throne in Israel."
—Sirach 47:2,8,11

When Samuel grew old, the Israelites would not trust to God to choose a fresh guardian for them, but cried out for a king to keep them together and lead them to war like other nations. Their entreaty was granted, and Saul the son of Kish, of the small but fierce tribe of Benjamin, was appointed by God, and anointed like a priest by Samuel, on the understanding that he was not to rule by his own will, like the princes around, but as God's chief officer, to enforce His laws and carry out His bidding.

This Saul would not do. When, instead of lurking in caves, with no weapons save their tools for farming, the Israelites, under his leading, gradually became free and warlike; and his son Jonathan and uncle Abner were able generals, he fancied he could go his own way, he took on him to offer sacrifice, as the heathen kings did; and when sent forth to destroy all belonging to the Amalekites, he spared the king and the choicest of the spoil. For this he was sentenced not to be the founder of a line of kings, and the doom filled him with wrath against the priesthood, while an evil spirit was permitted to trouble his soul, Samuel's last great act was to anoint the youngest son of Jesse the Bethlehemite, the great grandchild of the loving Moabitess, Ruth, the same whom God had marked beside his sheepfolds as the man after His own Heart, the future father of the sceptered line of Judah, and of the "Root and Offspring of David, the bright and morning Star."

Fair and young, full of inspired song, and of gallant courage, the youth David was favored as the minstrel able to drive the evil spirit from Saul, the champion who had slain the giant of Gath. He was the king's son-in-law, the prince's bosom friend; but, as the hopes of Israel became set on him, Saul began to hate him as if he were a supplanter, though Jonathan submitted to the Will that deprived himself of a throne, and loved his friend as faithfully as ever. At last, by Jonathan's counsel, David fled from court, and Saul in his rage at thinking him aided by the priests, slew all who fell into his hands, thus cutting off his own last link with Heaven. A trusty band of brave men gathered round David, but he remained a loyal outlaw, and always abstained from any act against his sovereign, even though Saul twice lay at his mercy. Patiently he waited, and the time came at last. The Philistines overran the country, and chased Saul even to the mountain strongholds of Gilboa, where the miserable man, deserted by God, tried to learn his fate through evil spirits, and only met the certainty of his doom. In the next day's battle his true-hearted son met a soldier's death; but Saul, when wounded by the archers, tried in vain to put an end to his own life, and was, after a reign of forty years, at last slain by an Amalekite, who brought his crown to David, and was executed by him for having profanely slain the Lord's anointed.

For seven years David reigned only in his own tribe of Judah, while the brave Abner kept the rest of the kingdom for Saul's son, Ishbosheth, until, taking offence because Ishbosheth refused to give him one of Saul's widows to wife, he offered to come to terms with David, but in leaving the place of meeting, he was treacherously killed by David's overbearing nephew, Joab, in revenge for the death of a brother whom he had slain in single combat. Ishbosheth was soon after murdered by two of his own servants, and David becoming sole king, ruled prudently with all his power, and with anxious heed to the will of his true King. He was a great conqueror, and was the first to win for Israel her great city on Mount Moriah. It had once been called Salem, or peace, when the mysterious priest-king, Melchizedek, reigned there in Abraham's time, but since it had been held by the Jebusites, and called Jebus. When David took it, he named it Jerusalem, or the vision of peace, fortified it, built a palace there, and brought there with songs and solemn dances, the long-hidden Ark, so that it might be the place where God's Name was set, the center of worship; and well was the spot fitted for the purpose. It was a hill girdled round by other hills, and so strong by nature, that when built round with towers and walls, an enemy could hardly have taken it. David longed to raise a solid home for the Ark, but this was not a work permitted to a man of war and bloodshed, and he could only collect materials, and restore the priests to their offices, giving them his own glorious Book of Psalms, full of praise, prayer, and entreaty, to be sung for ever before the Lord, by courses of Levites relieving one another, that so the voice of praise might never die out.

David likewise made the Philistines, Moabites, Ammonites, and Edomites pay him tribute, and became the most powerful king in the East, receiving the fulfillment of the promises to Abraham; but even he was far from guiltless. He was a man of strong passions, though of a tender heart, and erred greatly, both from hastiness and weakness, but never without repentance, and his Psalms of contrition have ever since been the treasure of the penitent. Chastisement visited his sins, and was meekly borne, but bereavement and rebellion, care, sorrow, and disappointment, severely tried the Sweet Psalmist of Israel, shepherd, prophet, soldier, and king, until in his seventieth year, he went to his rest, after having been king for forty years, he was assured that his seed should endure forever.

All promises of temporal splendor were accomplished in his peaceful son, Solomon, who asked to be the wisest, and therefore was likewise made the richest, most prosperous, and most peaceful of kings. No enemy rose against him, but all the nations sought his friendship; and Zidon for once had her merchandise hallowed by its being offered to build and adorn the Temple, Solomon's great work. The spot chosen for it was that of Isaac's sacrifice, where was the threshing-floor bought by David from Araunah, but to give farther room, he leveled the head of the mountain, throwing it into the valley; and thus forming an even space where, silently built of huge stone, quarried at a distance, arose the courts, for strangers, women, men, and priests, surrounded by cloisters, supporting galleries of rooms for the lodging of the priests and Levites, many hundreds in number. The main building was of white marble, and the Holy of Holies was overlaid even to the roof outside with plates of gold, flashing back the sunshine. Even this was but a poor token of the Shechinah, that glorious light which descended at Solomon's prayer of consecration, and filled the Sanctuary with the visible token of God's Presence to be seen by the High Priest once a year.

That consecration was the happiest moment of the history of Israel, What followed was mournful. Even David had been like the kings of other eastern nations in the multitude of his wives, and Solomon went far beyond him, bringing in heathen women, who won him into paying homage to their idols, and outraging God by building temples to Moloch and Ashtoreth; though as a prophet he had been inspired to speak in his Proverbs of Christ in His Church as the Holy Wisdom of God. A warning was sent that the power which had corrupted him should not continue in his family, and that the kingdom should be divided, but he only grew more tyrannical, and when the Ephraimite warrior, Jeroboam, was marked by the prophet Ahijah as the destined chief of the new kingdom, Solomon persecuted him, and drove him to take refuge with the great Shishak, King of Egypt, where he seems to have learnt the idolatries from which Israel had been so slowly weaned. Sick at heart, Solomon in his old age, wrote the saddest book in the Bible; and though his first writing, the Canticles, had been a joyful prophetic song of the love between the Lord and His Church, his last was a mournful lamentation over the vanity and emptiness of the world, and full of scorn of all that earth can give.

DAVID THE SHEPHERD BOY
By Amy Steedman

Up among the hills, perched like the nest of a bird on one of the long low ridges, lies the little town of Bethlehem. It was but a small town at the time this story begins, and there was nothing about it to make it at all famous. It lay out of the beaten track, and anyone wanting to visit it must climb the long winding road that led from the plain beneath, through olive groves and sheep fields, up to the city gate—a steep, difficult road, leading nowhere but to the little town itself.

It was in these fields on the slope of the hills that David, the shepherd boy of Bethlehem, spent his days watching his father's flocks. That father, whose name was Jesse, was one of the chief men of the town, and David was the youngest of all his sons.

There were seven big brothers at home, and it was no wonder Jesse was proud of his sons. They were tall, splendid young men, all of them doing men's work now, and taking very little notice of the youngest, who was still only a small boy, chiefly useful in looking after the sheep.

But though David was but little thought of, no one could say that he did not do his work well. There was not a more careful or watchful shepherd on all the hills around Bethlehem. He knew each one of his sheep, and never allowed one to stray. He always led them to the best pasture, and found the coolest and freshest water for them to drink. Then, too, he was as brave as a lion, and if any wild beast came lurking round hoping to snatch a lamb away, David was up at once and would attack the fiercest beast single-handed. Nothing could ever do any harm to his flock.

Now it happened that one day while David was, as usual, out in the fields that a sudden stir of excitement awoke in the little town of Bethlehem. Men gathered round the city gate, and with anxious, fearful eyes looked down the long white road that led up from the plain below. And yet there seemed nothing there to make them look so terrified and anxious. Only an old feeble man was slowly climbing up towards the town. He was driving a heifer before him, and carrying what looked like a horn in his hand.

But the people whispered together that the old man was none other than Samuel, the prophet of the Lord, who carried God's messages. He must be bringing a message to them, and who knew if it was good or evil. They tried with uneasy minds to remember if they had been doing anything wrong of late as they watched the old man drawing nearer and nearer. Then at last the chief men of the town went out to meet him.

"Do you come in peace?" they asked anxiously.

The old man lifted his head and looked at them kindly as he echoed their words.

"Peaceably," he answered at once; "I have come to sacrifice to the Lord."

A great sigh of relief went up from the people. The visit was a mark of God's favor and not of His displeasure.

It was true, indeed, that Samuel had come to offer sacrifice, but he had come also on a secret errand about which no man knew but himself. God had bidden him take his horn of oil and anoint one of the sons of Jesse to be king over His people instead of Saul, the present king, who had displeased Him. But it was to be done secretly. Saul must not hear of it, or his vengeance would be swift.

It was in Jesse's house that the feast of the sacrifice was prepared, and Samuel ordered that all the sons of the house should pass before him as they went to attend the sacrifice.

The first to come was Eliab, Jesse's eldest son, and when Samuel saw him he felt sure that this was the man who was to be anointed king. He was a splendid young man, tall and strong and handsome, looking almost as kingly as Saul himself.

"Surely this is he," murmured Samuel to himself. But God's answer came quickly. No, this was not the man. Samuel saw only the outward signs of strength and beauty, but God saw deeper into the heart.

So the eldest son passed on, and one by one the six brothers followed, all sons that a father might well be proud of. But God sent no sign to show that any of them was the chosen king.

Samuel was puzzled. What could it mean? Then he turned again to Jesse.

"Are all your children here?" he asked.

Surprised at the question, Jesse suddenly remembered the little lad, his youngest son, who was out in the fields tending the sheep. Was it possible that Samuel had any use for him?

"Send and fetch him," ordered Samuel instantly, "for we will not sit down till he comes here."

So a messenger was sent in haste to bring David; and presently he came hurrying in, and as soon as Samuel saw him he knew his search was ended.

He was only a little shepherd lad with the breath of the hills about him, his golden hair tossed by the wind, his fair face flushed, and his sunburned hand holding his shepherd's crook. But there was no doubt that God had chosen him.

"Arise and anoint him, for this is he," said God's voice in Samuel's heart.

Slowly, then, the old man rose and held the oil aloft and poured it upon the boy's bowed head, while the rest of the company looked silently on.

They were puzzled to know what it all meant. Perhaps the elder brothers were envious, and wondered why this mere child should be singled out for special favor. But no one dared to question God's messenger.

Nothing further happened just then. Samuel returned as he had come by the winding white road, and before long his visit was forgotten as the people settled to their work again.

Only David, out in the fields, thought more and more about what had happened, and grew more and more certain that it had been a call from God to do some special work for Him. The wonder of it filled his mind, but it never interfered with his work.

There was little time for idle dreaming in the boy's life. He was as watchful as ever in his care for his sheep and as courageous as ever in guarding them from prowling beasts. Even in his leisure time he was busy too, and there was not one of the sunny hours of daylight that he wasted.

He loved music, and he taught himself to play on the harp, practicing so carefully and patiently that his fingers grew most wonderfully skillful. Then he made songs to go to the music, some of the most beautiful songs that ever have been made in all the world. Almost every child today knows his beautiful song about the Good Shepherd: "The Lord is my shepherd, I shall not want."

There was another thing, too, that he learned to do with the same care and patient perseverance, and that was to use his shepherd's sling. There was no boy in all Bethlehem who could shoot as straight as he could. He never missed his mark.

It was no great thing, perhaps, to make music and aim straight, but it was a great thing to do what lay nearest his hand with all his might. Perhaps someday God would make use of his singing or have some work for a boy who had a quick eye and a sure aim. Who could tell?

So David learned to do his very best, and before very long God's call came to him.

Saul, the King of Israel, sat day after day in his darkened tent ill and full of misery. No one dared to go near him, and his servants whispered together, "It is an evil spirit from the Lord that troubles him."

Then someone suggested that perhaps music might help to cheer him and drive the evil spirit from him.

"Let our lord now command your servants to seek out a man who is a cunning player on a harp," they said to the king, "and it shall come to pass that, when the evil spirit from God is upon thee, he shall play with his hand, and you shall be well."

Saul listened to their words, and hope crept into his heart.

"Provide me now a man that can play well, and bring him to me," he said eagerly.

Now the fame of David's playing and singing had spread even beyond Bethlehem. "We must send for David, the son of Jesse," said the king's servants at once. He was the very person they wanted. Not only could he sing and play, but he was a good boy, brave and fearless, and best of all, as the servants said, "The Lord is with him."

So the shepherd boy was brought to the king's darkened tent, ready to do his bidding. Sitting there in the dim light, he drew such magic music from his harp's strings, and sang such sweet songs, that the very song of the birds seemed to be filling the tent. The king, as he listened, seemed to feel the breath of the mountain fields, to hear the call of the sheepfold and the murmur of the dancing streams. It acted like a charm. The black misery was lifted from his heart, and the evil spirit was put to flight by the song of the shepherd boy.

It was no wonder, then, that the king, for a time at least, loved the boy with his bright face and sunny hair, and wanted to keep him as his armor-bearer. But perhaps, as Saul grew well and had no further need of the music, David was no longer wanted, and so he went back again to the Bethlehem fields to look after his sheep.

God had made use of David's skill in music, and before very long another call came to him. This time the need was for one who could aim straight, who had a quick eye and a steady hand.

War had broken out. The fierce Philistines had come up with their great armies to try and conquer the land. Every man in Israel who could fight was called up to protect his country. Already David's three elder brothers had joined Saul's army, which was preparing to fight the enemy.

On either side of a narrow valley, divided by a stream which ran along over smooth stones, the two armies faced each other. There they were encamped, like wild beasts ready to fly at each other's throats. At any moment the fight might begin, and that stream be stained red with blood. Only the Philistines were far the strongest, and the Israelites had but little chance of victory.

This valley was seven or eight miles distant from the little town of Bethlehem, and Jesse waited anxiously, day after day, for news of his three sons. At last he could bear the anxiety no longer, and he determined to send David to the camp to carry food to his brothers and bring back news how they fared.

So, very early one morning, David set out on his errand. He had carefully put his sheep under the care of another shepherd, and he took with him parched corn and loaves of bread for his brothers, as well as ten cheeses which his father was sending to the officers under whom they served.

It was not long before the boy came within sight of the valley, and his heart began to beat with excitement, for he saw that he had arrived just as something was about to happen. The armies were drawn up in battle array, and suddenly a great shout went up from both sides. It was the battle-cry of the two armies which sounded in his ears.

There was no time now to carry food and gifts, so David quickly left his load at the entrance to the camp and hurried on to search for his brothers. He had learned to find his way about a camp, where for a short time he had been Saul's armor-bearer. So now he went swiftly among the soldiers, until at last he found his brothers. "Were they well?" he eagerly asked them; "and what were they doing?"

But even while he spoke there was a stir among the Philistines, and all eyes were turned to watch, all ears were strained to hear the enemy's challenge, which rang out clearly across the narrow valley.

Out of the rank of the Philistines, there had stepped a man so tall and strong that he appeared to be a giant. He was more than nine feet high, and the armor which he wore was so solid and heavy that it would have crushed any ordinary man to the earth.

This was Goliath, the great champion of the Philistines. Every morning and every evening he strode proudly out and defied the Israelites, bidding them find a champion who would come and fight with him. Once again his challenge rang out on the clear air,—

"Choose a man for yourself, and let him come down to me. If he be able to fight with me and to kill me, then will we be your servants; but if I prevail against him and kill him, then you will be our servants and serve us. I defy the armies of Israel this day. Give me a man that we may fight together."

A great silence fell after the champion had shouted his last words of defiance. There was no answer from the Israelites. No man had courage enough to dream of accepting the challenge.

David looked round him in amazement, and his cheeks burned with shame. What were the people doing to allow this boasting heathen Philistine to defy the armies of the living God? Eagerly he turned to the men around him and began to ask them what it meant. The soldiers answered him shortly. No, there was no one who dared to go forth and fight Goliath. The king had promised great rewards to any man who would kill the giant. But no one had dared to try.

David's elder brothers heard his questions, and seeing how amazed he was, they began to grow angry. Did he mean to reproach them? Perhaps he thought of offering himself to fight the champion. It was time that this shepherd boy should be put in his proper place. So his eldest brother turned to him with a sneer.

"Why have you come here?" he asked. "And with whom have you left those few sheep in the wilderness? I know your pride and the naughtiness of your heart, for you have come down so that you might see the battle."

It could not have been very easy to bear this taunt. But David had learned to conquer himself before he set out to conquer giants. So he answered quietly instead of flashing back an angry reply.

"What have I done?" he asked. "May I not ask a harmless question?"

There were many questions he still wished to ask, and presently the soldiers began to repeat his words one to another, until at last the report was spread that someone had been found ready and willing to answer the challenge of the giant Philistine. And of course the news soon reached the king's ear. Saul sent immediately and ordered that the shepherd lad should be brought to him. He had quite forgotten about the boy who had charmed away his black moods with the magic music of his harp. And David had grown and changed since those days.

So now, when David stood before the king, Saul had no idea who he was, and his one thought, as he looked at the slender youth, was that it was madness to think of such a mere boy going out to give battle to the great giant.

"You are not able to go against this Philistine," he said; "for you are only a youth, and he a man of war from his youth."

But David answered eagerly. He did not boast, but spoke steadily and wisely. True, he had not been trained as a soldier, but his courage and his strength had both been already proved. And he went on to tell the king that while he kept his father's sheep he had often to defend them from wild beasts. Once he had fought with a lion and a bear single-handed and had killed them both.

It was not in his own strength that he trusted. "The Lord that delivered me out of the paw of the lion and out of the paw of the bear, He will deliver me out of the hand of this Philistine," he ended triumphantly.

Faith in God was David's sure defense; and Saul as he listened bowed his head in shame, for it was the faith which he himself had lost. It was this faith, he knew, which might win the victory. It was an echo of the confidence he had once felt when his whole trust had been in God, and he recognized the true ring of the boy's courage.

"Go," he said, "and the Lord be with you."

Then the king was eager to put his own armor on David, and he bade the soldiers arm him with the royal sword and put a brass helmet on his head. But David was not accustomed to wear heavy armor, and had never been trained to use a sword. No, he would do his best with the only weapon he thoroughly understood.

So putting on once more his shepherd's coat, he took his sling in his hand, and as he crossed the brook at the foot of the valley he filled his shepherd's bag with smooth stones and fitted one of them to his sling. Then with springing steps he began to climb the opposite side.

The rage of Goliath was great when he saw the slender, fair-haired boy, without either armor or sword, coming so boldly to meet him.

"Am I a dog," he shouted, "that you come to me with staves?"

"I come to you in the name of the Lord of Hosts, the God of the armies of Israel, whom you have defied," rang out the clear answer. "The Lord saves not with sword and spear; for the battle is the Lord's, and He will give you into our hands."

The great giant lifted his spear, ready with one blow to end this unequal fight. But David did not wait to come within reach of the spear. Before Goliath came near, the boy stopped suddenly and sent a stone whizzing through the air straight at the giant's head. The stone sank into Goliath's forehead, and the great figure reeled and fell with a mighty crash to the earth. Instantly David seized his sword and cut off his head.

So God's people were saved, and so again God made use of the shepherd boy's training and skill, this time to win a great victory for His people.

The fair-haired shepherd boy had done his duty faithfully in the fields on the hillside at home, where he was but little thought of. He had always tried to do his best, whether he was keeping the sheep, practicing with his sling, or learning to play the harp. And now, suddenly, the great opportunity had come and found him ready.

He had entered the camp an unnoticed country lad, carrying provisions to his brothers. Now every soldier in the camp was shouting his name; the king was ready to shower rewards and honors upon him. He was the hero of the hour.

The pleasant days in the Bethlehem fields were now over for David. There was no thought of allowing him to return to his work. No, the king declared he must remain as a soldier in the army, ready to defend his king and country. Though he was still a mere boy he was placed in command and set over the men of war.

It was much more difficult work than looking after sheep, and as time went on and dangers and difficulties beset him on every side, David must often have longed for the old quiet days on the hillside. His path was rough and dangerous now, and sad to say his feet often slipped and he wandered far astray, but always he held fast to his faith in God, and found his way back to the straight path.

As the years went by Samuel's promise was at last fulfilled, and David was made king over God's chosen people. David had often forgotten God, but God had never forgotten him.

What a change it was from the days when he wandered about the fields in his sheepskin coat, often sleeping out under the stars, possessing only his harp and his shepherd's sling.

Now he wore royal robes, and there was a crown of pure gold upon his head. Instead of the starry sky for a roof, he now lived in a palace of cedar wood.

And he knew surely that it was God who had taken care of him; that it was God who had set the crown of gold upon his head, the seal to the promise made in that long ago day when the old prophet had poured the anointing oil upon the head of the wandering shepherd boy.

Looking back, he saw that he had made many mistakes, that his soul was stained with many sins; but he knew, too, that God would listen when he prayed, "Wash me, and I shall be whiter than snow."

As a little shepherd lad he had cared far more for his sheep than his own safety. He had always been ready to risk his life for them. So now, when he became king, his people were just as precious to him as his sheep had been. He cared for them with all his heart. He was prepared to suffer himself rather than any hurt should come near them.

So perhaps he was, after all, not unworthy to stand as a type of the great King, "great David's greater Son," the little Baby who was to be born in the town of Bethlehem, the Good Shepherd who was to lay down His life for His sheep.

From Fifty Famous People
By James Baldwin

The King and the Bees

One day King Solomon was sitting on his throne, and his great men were standing around him.

Suddenly the door was thrown open and the Queen of Sheba came in.

"O King," she said, "in my own country, far, far away, I have heard much about your power and glory, but much more about your wisdom. Men have told me that there is no riddle so cunning that you cannot solve it. Is this true?"

"It is as you say, O Queen," answered Solomon.

"Well, I have here a puzzle which I think will test your wisdom. Shall I show it to you?"

"Most certainly, O Queen."

Then she held up in each hand a beautiful wreath of flowers. The wreaths were so nearly alike that none of those who were with the king could point out any difference.

"One of these wreaths." said the queen, "is made of flowers plucked from your garden. The other is made of artificial flowers, shaped and colored by a skillful artist. Now, tell me, O King, which is the true, and which is the false?"

The king, for once, was puzzled. He stroked his chin. He looked at the wreaths from every side. He frowned. He bit his lips.

"Which is the true?" the queen again asked.

Still the king did not answer.

"I have heard that you are the wisest man in the world," she said, "and surely this simple thing ought not to puzzle you."

The king moved uneasily on his golden throne. His officers and great men shook their heads. Some would have smiled, if they had dared.

"Look at the flowers carefully," said the queen, "and let us have your answer."

Then the king remembered something. He remembered that close by his window there

121

was a climbing vine filled with beautiful sweet flowers. He remembered that he had seen many bees flying among these flowers and gathering honey from them.

So he said, "Open the window!"

It was opened. The queen was standing quite near to it with the two wreaths still in her hands. All eyes were turned to see why the king had said, "Open the window."

The next moment two bees flew eagerly in. Then came another and another. All flew to the flowers in the queen's right hand. Not one of the bees so much as looked at those in her left hand.

"O Queen of Sheba, the bees have given you my answer," then said Solomon.

And the queen said, "You are wise, King Solomon. You gather knowledge from the little things which common men pass by unnoticed."

King Solomon lived three thousand years ago. He built a great temple in Jerusalem, and was famous for his wisdom.

Unit Seven: The Divided Kingdom

Theme: Sacrifice Made with a Right Heart

From The Book of the Ancient World
By Dorothy Mills

The Divided Kingdom:

The Kingdom of Israel

It was the Hebrew custom that a King could not consider himself firmly established on the throne, until he had been acknowledged king by his subjects. It was not sufficient that he should be the son or the choice of the former king, he must also be the choice of the people. Solomon was followed by his son Rehoboam, but before the tribes in the north would recognize him as King, they asked him to promise that he would change his father's policy of heavy taxation and forced labor. If he would do this, they assured him of their loyal support. The old and experienced men in the country, men who had known and loved his grandfather David, advised the young king to listen to these requests and to grant them. But Rehoboam, who knew nothing of the real conditions in the country, and would not have cared much if he had known them, turned away from these wise counselors, and listened instead to the foolish advice of the young men who had grown up with him, and he not only absolutely refused to lighten any of the burdens his father had laid on the people, but he declared his intention of making them yet heavier if he thought fit. The result of this stupid answer was a rebellion against him in the North. The rebellion was successful, and the northern tribes separated from the southern and made themselves into an independent kingdom, known as the Kingdom of Israel, and the leader of the rebellion became the first King.

The division of the kingdom was a very important event in Hebrew history. It practically wrecked the work of Saul and David, for instead of one strong little kingdom, there were now two weaker ones, constantly defending their land from foreign foes, and often fighting each other, until at last they fell before the might of Assyria and Babylon and ceased to exist as independent nations.

The northern kingdom was more prosperous than the southern. Samaria was the capital and under some capable kings it became a flourishing city. Trade increased with Damascus and over the great roads to Egypt. Towns grew larger, and better houses were built, but it was the rich who prospered, and their prosperity was gained at the expense of the poor, who labored and paid heavy taxes that the rich might live in luxury. Intercourse with neighboring countries brought an introduction of the worship of false gods into Israel, and all kinds of idolatry were practiced by the people.

This period of prosperity was followed by a series of revolutions which so weakened the country, that when an Assyrian army swept down upon it, Samaria was taken and the people carried off into exile.

THE KINGDOM OF JUDAH

When the northern tribes rebelled and established the Kingdom of Israel, Rehoboam was left as King of Judah, with Jerusalem as his capital. The Kingdom of Judah was never as prosperous as that of Israel. It was a more hilly land and not so easily accessible, the inhabitants were shepherds rather than traders, and Jerusalem was the only large town.

The times were very bloodthirsty, and there was little peace in the land. The foreign power that was a constant menace to both kingdoms was Assyria. During the reign of Hezekiah, Sennacherib, King of Assyria, invaded Judah. He burnt the fields and captured several small towns and would doubtless have besieged Jerusalem, but Hezekiah bought him off by sending him tribute of gold. He was obliged to strip the Temple of much of its ornament in order to do this, but it saved Jerusalem. It was only for a time, however, for soon after Sennacherib came again, and this time he besieged Jerusalem. But the Assyrians did not remain long in the land, and they left the country without continuing the war. The Hebrew historian tells us that "the angel of the Lord smote them," and we have also the traditional account of what happened told in more detail by the Greek historian Herodotus. He tells us "that there came in the night a multitude of field mice, which devoured all the quivers and bowstrings of the enemy and all the thongs by which they managed their shields. Next morning they commenced their flight and great multitudes fell, as they had no arms with which to defend themselves.

The history of Judah then became the story of a struggle on the part of the nation to keep its national existence. Assyria and Babylon on one side and Egypt on the other were all eager to possess it, and the people were sore beset. Sometimes they would have been willing to make an alliance with the foreign power, but the prophet-statesmen always opposed such a policy, and warned them of what would be the consequences: they would lose their freedom and their national traditions. They also feared the influence of the foreign worship of false gods on the Hebrews. Contact with other nations had already caused the purity of the ancient Hebrew worship to become very mixed up with the beliefs of the Egyptians and the Phoenicians, especially with the latter. Commerce had increased and the occupations of the people were changing. There were fewer shepherds and the old hardy simplicity had disappeared. Luxury and soft living had so weakened the character of the people, that a time came when the Syrians were able to send armies without much opposition into the heart of the country, and once Jerusalem was actually sacked by the Egyptians.

After a brief period of prosperity, the Kingdom of Judah grew steadily weaker, until Nebuchadnezzar, King of Babylon, invaded the land, besieged Jerusalem, captured it, burnt the city, the palaces and the Temple, broke down the walls, carried off the gold and silver treasures from the Temple and the King's palace, and took nearly all the people as captives to Babylon.

From The Book of the Ancient World
By Dorothy Mills

The Hebrew Prophets: Elijah and Amos

The first great change in the history of the Hebrews took place after their conquest of Canaan, when from being nomad tribes they became a settled agricultural people. The second change took place when their town life developed, and when to the life of the husbandmen they added that of the merchant and trader. This town life was more fully developed in the northern kingdom of Israel, but Judah also came under its influence. During this period there were a number of great teachers of the people, who were known as Prophets.

The name "prophet" is usually only given now to one who foretells the future, but the title as it was given to the Hebrew prophets means a great deal more than this. The real meaning of the word "prophet," is "one who speaks on behalf of another," and the Hebrew prophets spoke to the people on behalf of the Lord. They made known to them the will and character of Jehovah; they explained as far as they understood, what the various events of their history meant, and what the nation might expect as a result; they gave them their religious teaching; they pointed out their dangers, and warned them against forgetting the Lord and giving way to idolatry like the nations round them. As the Hebrews grew in wealth and developed a higher civilization, the temptations beset them that beset all wealthy and civilized communities: the rich wanted to grow richer, and so the poor were oppressed; money was spent on self-gratification instead of for the good of the whole community.

The early simple relationship of the Hebrews to the Lord had now disappeared, and they no longer thought of Him as their God who took a close personal interest in their affairs. They worshipped Him with great ceremonies in the Temple, but He was far away from them, they did not *know* Him. Their strength was in their prosperity, not in their religion. One of their wise men once said; "Where there is no vision the people perish," and it was at a time when they were in danger of perishing for lack of a vision that the great Hebrew prophets arose, who placed one before them. We know very little about the lives of the prophets themselves, for in the records that have been left us, the work and service of a prophet for the people have been considered of greater importance than the life of the man himself. But their personality shines through their words, and though we may know but little of the events of their lives we have a clear picture of their character.

The prophets were great patriots as well as great religious teachers, and they took a very important part in the life of the nation. Their eyes were on the future, and they awoke in the people a desire for better conditions than those of their very troubled present. They set up ideals of righteousness and justice not only for Israel but for the world, but they were not dreamers of idle dreams, they were practical men, well-informed as to the conditions of their day, but they believed that such things as those they preached were possible, and part of their work was to make the people share their belief, for unfaltering faith in the ultimate triumph of an idea is a great factor in bringing about its fulfillment.

The forerunner of the great prophets was Elijah. Nothing is known of his early life. He appeared from the desert, dressed in the rough mantle of a shepherd and carrying a shepherd's staff. He lived during the reign of King Ahab of Israel who had married a Phoenician princess, and they introduced into Israel the worship of the Phoenician god Baal. Suddenly Elijah appeared in their midst, denouncing their idolatry. He was a very striking figure, and his early life in the desert had taught him to bear hardships easily, and had accustomed him to take long journeys on foot, and he used to appear and disappear and then appear again before the King and the people with unexpected and startling rapidity, which makes his story very dramatic. Elijah was very stern and uncompromising. To him, as to Moses, the Lord was the God of the Hebrews, and every inclination to idolatry was to be stamped out, but he had no objection to other nations worshipping other gods, so long as Israel remained faithful. To him, the Lord was the Lord of Hosts, Who would punish all wickedness, but Who would save Israel and triumph over the gods of the heathen.

We know very little of what Elijah did between his sudden appearances: once he was hiding from the angry King by a brook, and ravens brought him food; another time he visited a poor widow who shared her scanty fare with him; then he had a great contest on Mount Carmel with the prophets of Baal, but his victory over them so angered the Queen that he had to hide again, and lonely and discouraged he wished that he might die. As he hid in a cave, a great and strong wind arose that rent the mountains and broke the rocks in pieces, and the earth trembled beneath on earthquake and fire, and then there was silence, and in the silence Elijah heard God speaking to him, in a still, small voice as it were, encouraging him, and telling him what to do next. And again and yet again, he denounced the idolatry of the King, and then, as he had appeared, so he disappeared, suddenly taken up to heaven according to the old tradition, by a whirlwind in a chariot of fire, with horses of fire.

Amos, the first of the prophets whose writings we have, lived more than a hundred years after Elijah. He was a herdsman, and his early life was a simple one, spent away from cities. The life of a shepherd in Palestine was not an easy one; he had to be very brave and prompt in action, for he often had to face wild beasts, and he had to be ready to protect his flock by day and by night. David gave King Saul an idea of some of the perils a shepherd had to face; "Your servant kept his father's sheep, and there came a lion, and a bear, and took a lamb out of the flock, and I went out after him and smote him and delivered it out of his mouth." Amos must have travelled about a good deal, probably in order to sell his wool, for he seems to have known all about the conditions in different parts of the country. Like Elijah, he appeared suddenly before the people, the first time at a great public festival. He would stay in public for a little, deliver his message, and then vanish.

The vision of Amos was the widest that the Hebrews had yet had placed before them, for he broke away from the old idea that Jehovah was the God of one nation only, and he taught that He was the God of the whole earth. He recited a great deal of their early history to the people, and entreated them to give up their idolatry, and their injustice and oppression of the poor, and he put two new ideas before them: that good acts were better than elaborate ceremonies, and that privileges given to people meant opportunities of service and responsibility for using them. This teaching went a great deal further than the harsh laws Moses had been obliged to make for the ignorant and undisciplined people he had in his care, but the work of the earlier teachers and prophets had been to impress upon Israel that the Lord was their *God*: the work of Amos and of those who came after him was to make known the *character* of the Lord and what He required from those who believed in Him.

FROM THE BOOK OF THE ANCIENT WORLD
By Dorothy Mills

THE STORY OF ASSYRIA

Assyria was the great robber nation of the ancient world. The other nations made war for various reasons: sometimes they were attacked and so had to defend themselves, sometimes they were ruled by an ambitious king who wanted to extend his empire and so made war on his neighbors. But for Assyria war was her chief occupation. She loved wealth, and many of her wars were waged in order to seize the trade of other nations and so add to her riches. The power of Assyria increased with every fresh conquest, and she was feared and hated by everyone, so that when her hour of greatness at length passed and she was destroyed, the whole ancient world rejoiced.

No Assyrian king could be peaceful, and war was looked upon as his rightful occupation. The Assyrian army generally consisted of about fifty or sixty thousand men, and there were war-chariots, horsemen and infantry. The king and the great nobles had tents, but the common soldiers generally slept on the bare ground. A special cooking tent was taken for the king, and his royal chair of state always accompanied him. The soldiers wore bronze helmets and fought with bows and arrows, spears and swords, and they defended themselves with metal or wicker shields. The approach of an Assyrian army spread terror over the land. The Hebrew prophet Isaiah has given us a vivid picture of what it was like:

> They shall come with speed quickly, none shall be weary nor stumble among them; none shall slumber nor sleep; neither shall the girdle of their loins be loosed, nor the latchet of their shoes be broken: whose

arrows are sharp, and all their bows bent, their horses' hoofs shall be counted like flint, and their wheels like a whirlwind; their roaring shall be like a lion, they shall roar like young lions, yea, they shall roar and lay hold of the prey, and shall carry it away safe, and none shall deliver it. And in that day they shall roar against them like the roaring of the sea: and if one look unto the land, behold darkness and sorrow, and the light is darkened in the heavens thereof.

When a city was being besieged, battering rams were used, and every kind of cruelty was practiced on the unfortunate enemy who was taken prisoner.

One king built a great palace. Round each room were a number of alabaster slabs depicting his deeds and wars, and the inscriptions give the history of his reign from year to year. He describes his palace in these words:

A palace for my royal dwelling-place, for the glorious seat of my royalty, I founded forever, and splendidly planned it; I surrounded it with a cornice of copper. Sculptures of the creatures of land and sea carved in alabaster I made, and placed them at the doors. Lofty door posts of cedar I made, and sheathed them with copper, and set them upon the gates. Thrones of costly woods, dishes of ivory containing silver, gold, lead, copper and iron, the spoil of my hand, taken from conquered lands, I deposited therein.

After a victorious war, the Assyrian king would spend a time in feasting and celebrating his triumph. One of his favorite amusements was hunting, more especially lion hunting. In earlier days the king hunted wild lions, and these exploits were always magnificently recorded in sculpture on the walls of his palace. Inscriptions gave all the thrilling details, some of which were doubtless exaggerated in order to impress on the mind of the people the majesty and power of the king. One such inscription runs: "I killed a hundred and twenty lions in my youthful ardor, in the fullness of my manly might on my own feet, and eight hundred lions I killed from my chariot. All kinds of beasts and fowls I added to my hunting spoils." In later times the lions were kept in the royal park and tamed, so when the actual hunt took place, there could have been but little danger and none of the thrill of the earlier hunts.

The most important Assyrian city was Nineveh, but as the Assyrians lived chiefly for war, it never became as great a trading city as Babylon, but caravans went out in all directions, and the Assyrians made good roads over which their merchants as well as their armies could travel. In Nineveh itself there were splendid buildings, temples and palaces, and the latter had gardens and parks attached to them. One king tried to make a kind of botanical garden, in which he planted trees he had found in the foreign lands he had conquered. He gives this account of it:

As for the cedar and the almug, from the countries I have conquered, these trees, which none of the kings my fathers that were before me had planted, I took, and in the gardens of my land I planted, and by the name of garden I called them; whatsoever in my land there was not I took, and I established the gardens of Assyria.

These gardens were generally planted by the river, so that they were kept well watered, and summer houses were often built in the midst of them. This king who cared so much for his garden also brought cultivated grapes into Assyria, and it was evidently so well known that he liked any unusual or curious specimens of natural objects, that once when a King of Egypt wished to honor him with a gift, he sent the Assyrian a crocodile from the Nile.

Nineveh was surrounded by massive double walls, of which the inner one was called the "Wall whose splendor overthrows the Enemy," and the outer, the "Wall that terrifies the Foe." Fifteen gates led into this city, which to the ancient world seemed a symbol of arrogance and pride, for it had been built and made splendid by the tribute taken from conquered people who had been crushed and oppressed by the might of Assyria.

The Assyrians did not make as much use of the rivers as did the other ancient peoples. When an army wanted to cross a stream, bridges of boats were sometimes made, but generally only the chief men were ferried over in boats, and the others had to swim across, though they usually had the help of inflated skins. Their boats were rafts or coracles of skins stretched on a wooden framework.

THE CHOSEN PEOPLE
By Charlotte Yonge

NINEVEH

"Where is the dwelling-place of the lions, and the feeding-place of the young lions?"
—Nahum, 2:11

When the confusion of tongues took place at Babel, and men were dispersed, the sons of Ham's grandson, Cush, remained in Mesopotamia, which took the name of Assyria, from Assur, the officer of Nimrod, the first king. This Assur began building, on the banks of the Tigris, the great city of Nineveh, one of the mightiest in all the world, and the first to be ruined. It was enclosed by a huge wall, so wide that three chariots could drive side by side on the top, and built of bricks made of the clay of the country, dried in the sun and cemented with bitumen, guarded at the base by a plinth fifty feet in height, and with immense ditches round it, about sixty miles in circumference. Within were huge palaces, built of the same bricks, faced with alabaster, and the rooms decked with cedar, gilding, and ivory, and raised upon terraces whence broad flights of steps led down to courts guarded by giant stone figures of bulls and lions, with eagles' wings and human faces, as if some notion of the mysterious

Cherubim around the Throne in Heaven had floated to these Assyrians. The slabs against the walls were carved with representations of battles, hunts, sacrifices, triumphs, and all the scenes in the kings' histories, nay, in the building of the city; and there were explanations in the wedge-shaped letters of the old Assyrian alphabet. The Ninevites had numerous idols, but their honor for the Lord had not quite faded away; and about the time of Amaziah in Judah, and Jeroboam II in Israel, the prophet Jonah was sent to rebuke them for their many iniquities. In trying to avoid the command, by sailing to Tarshish in a Phoenician ship, he underwent that strange punishment which was a prophetic sign of our Lord's Burial and Resurrection; and thus warned, he went to Nineveh and startled the people by the cry, "Yet forty days, and Nineveh shall be destroyed!" At that cry, the whole place repented as one man; and from the king to the beggar all fasted and wept, till God had mercy on their repentance and ready faith, and turned away His wrath, in pity to the 120,000 innocent children who knew not yet to do good or evil.

FROM THE CATECHISM IN EXAMPLES
By Rev. D. Chisholm

THE SECOND EMINENT GOOD WORK: FASTING

Fasting is a virtue which was practiced by the pagans themselves to appease the wrath of Heaven. In the Holy Scriptures we see how the people of Nineveh, when threatened by the prophet of God with entire destruction, endeavored to avert their terrible fate by fasting and works of penance. How much more reason have we, my child, who are the special children of God, obliged to have recourse to the same means to turn away His face from our sins, and blot out all our iniquities!

JONAH AND THE PEOPLE OF NINIVEH

In the book of the prophet Jonah we read: " Now the word of the Lord came to Jonah, saying: Arise, and go to Nineveh the great city, and preach in it: for the wickedness thereof is come up before Me. . . .

"And Jonah arose, and went to Nineveh, according to the word of the Lord: now Nineveh was a great city of three days journey.

"And Jonah began to enter into the city one day's journey: and he cried, and said: Yet forty days, and Nineveh shall be destroyed!

"And the men of Nineveh believed in God: and they proclaimed a fast, and put on sackcloth from the greatest to the least. And the word came to the king of Nineveh: and he rose up from his throne, and cast away his robe from him, and was clothed in sackcloth, and sat in ashes. And he caused it to be proclaimed and published in Nineveh from the mouth of the king and of his princes, saying: Let neither men nor beasts, oxen nor sheep, taste anything:

let them not feed, nor drink water. And let men and beasts be covered with sackcloth, and cry to the Lord with all their strength, and let them turn everyone from his evil way, and from the iniquity that is in their hands. Who can tell if God will turn, and forgive: and will turn away from His fierce anger, and we shall not perish?

"And God saw their works, that they were turned from their evil way: and God had mercy with regard to the evil which He had said that He would do to them, and He did it not.

FROM THE STORY OF THE GREEKS
By H. A. Guerber

EARLY INHABITANTS OF GREECE

Although Greece (or Hellas) is only half as large as the State of New York, it holds a very important place in the history of the world. It is situated in the southern part of Europe, cut off from the rest of the continent by a chain of high mountains which form a great wall on the north. It is surrounded on nearly all sides by the blue waters of the Mediterranean Sea, which stretch so far inland that it is said no part of the country is forty miles from the sea, or ten miles from the hills. Thus shut in by sea and mountains, it forms a little territory by itself, and it was the home of a noted people.

The history of Greece goes back to the time when people did not know how to write, and kept no record of what was happening around them. For a long while the stories told by parents to their children were the only information which could be had about the country and its former inhabitants; and these stories, slightly changed by every new teller, grew more and more extraordinary as time passed. At last, they were so changed that no one could tell where the truth ended and fancy began.

The beginning of Greek history is therefore like a fairy tale; and while much of it cannot, of course, be true, it is the only information we have about the early Greeks. It is these strange fireside stories, which used to amuse Greek children so many years ago, that you are first going to hear.

About two thousand years before the birth of Christ, in the days when Isaac wanted to go down into Egypt, Greece was inhabited by a savage race of men called the Pelasgians. They lived in the forests, or in caves hollowed out of the mountainside, and hunted wild beasts with great clubs and stone-tipped arrows and spears. They were so rude and wild that they ate nothing but raw meat, berries, and the roots, which they dug up with sharp stones or even with their hands.

For clothing, the Pelasgians used the skins of the beasts they had killed; and to protect themselves against other savages, they gathered together in families or tribes, each having a chief who led in war and in the chase.

There were other far more civilized nations in those days. Among these were the Egyptians, who lived in Africa. They had long known the use of fire, had good tools, and were much further advanced than the Pelasgians. They had learned not only to build houses, but to erect the most wonderful monuments in the world, the Pyramids, of which you have no doubt heard.

In Egypt, there were at that time a number of learned men. They were acquainted with many of the arts and sciences, and recorded all they knew in a peculiar writing of their own invention. Their neighbors, the Phœnicians, whose land also bordered on the Mediterranean Sea, were quite civilized too; and as both of these nations had ships, they soon began to sail all around that great inland sea.

As they had no compass, the Egyptian and Phœnician sailors did not venture out of sight of land. They first sailed along the shore, and then to the islands which they could see far out on the blue waters.

When they had come to one island, they could see another still farther on; for, as you will see on any map, the Mediterranean Sea, between Greece and Asia, is dotted with islands, which look like stepping-stones going from one coast to the other.

Advancing thus carefully, the Egyptians and Phœnicians finally came to Greece, where they made settlements, and began to teach the Pelasgians many useful and important things.

FROM OUR OLD WORLD BACKGROUND
By Charles Beard

THE CITY-STATES OF GREECE

In strange contrast to the despotic empires of Egypt and Asia Minor were the governments of Greece. The Greeks were a marvelous shepherd people who in very ancient times moved down in search of pasture into the rugged peninsula that bears their name. They conquered the people who already dwelt there and at the same time learned much from their subjects. Their new homeland was broken into many small regions by the mountains and the sea. It had no great river like the Nile and no vast plains like those of Babylonia.

Though the Greeks lived close together and worshiped the same gods, they could not be permanently united. Many alliances and leagues were formed among them, it is true, but none of these lasted for long. It is true also that the Greeks of Macedonia, under Alexander the Great, built up a huge empire extending from the Danube River to the borders of India; but it did not survive his death in 323 B.C. The peoples of Greece were too independent to bow their necks to a single ruler. They were happiest when divided into tiny states or commonwealths, each managing its own affairs. In desperate battles they beat off Persian kings who tried to subdue them, and not until many centuries had passed did they fall under the sword of the Romans.

In the eighth century before Christ, there were in the Greek peninsula scores of these little countries known as city-states. Among them may be mentioned Corinth, Thebes, Miletus, and Argos. Most famous and important of all were Athens and Sparta.

The Greek state was usually no larger than a county in Ohio or Iowa. It had a sort of capital city with shops, temples, dwellings, and market places. The country around it was laid out into small villages and farms. Each community formed one great family. The members of it believed that they were the descendants of the same god and were thus related. The citizens of each little state were intensely patriotic. They were also enterprising, for they founded colonies all around the shores of the Mediterranean Sea.

Within their city-states the Greeks made many kinds of experiments in governing themselves. There were, however, three forms of government that were most common: the monarchy, or rule of one man; the aristocracy, which meant in practice the rule of the few; and the democracy, or rule of the many. Our very word "democracy" comes from the Greek and means "rule of the people."

A Greek democracy, however, differed very much from our modern notions. In Athens, for example, when the people ruled, the voters did not choose representatives to go to the capital and make laws. On the contrary, the voters all assembled in the open air. They approved or rejected laws proposed to them, and they chose the magistrates or officials of the little state.

In another respect also the Greek city democracy differed from ours. In Athens, for instance, even in the democratic period, there were about as many slaves as there were Athenians. There were five or six slaves for every citizen who had a right to vote in the assembly. At its best, therefore, democracy in Greece was limited to a very small ruling class. The masses did not rule. They were slaves—men and women, usually white, taken captive in war or bought somewhere in a slave market.

From Old World Hero Stories
By Eva March Tappan

HOMER, THE GREAT STORYTELLER

A long, long time ago, perhaps three thousand years or more, there was a man named Homer. No one knows much about him; but there are legends that he was born on the island of Chios and that he was blind. He wandered about the land, homeless, but welcome wherever he chose to go, because he was a poet. He once described how a blind poet was treated at a great banquet, and probably that is the way in which people treated him. He said that when the feast was ready, a page was sent to lead in the honored guest. A silver-studded chair was brought forward for him and set against a pillar. On the pillar, the page hung his harp, so near him that he could touch it if he wished. A little table was placed before him, and on it was put a tray spread with food and wine. When the feasting was at an end, he sang a glorious song of the mighty deeds of men. The Greeks liked to hear stories just as well as the people of today, and they shouted with delight. Then they all went out to the racecourse, the page leading the blind singer carefully along the way. There were races and wrestling matches and boxing and throwing of the discus. After this, the poet took his harp and stepped to the center of the circle. The young men gathered around him eagerly, and he chanted a story of Ares, the war god, and Aphrodite, goddess of beauty and love.

Homer composed two great poems. One is the Iliad, which takes its name from Ilium, or Troy, a town in Asia Minor. For ten long years the Greeks tried to capture Ilium. They had good reason for waging war against the Trojans, for Paris, son of the king of Troy, had stolen away the Grecian Helen, the most beautiful woman in the world. She was the wife of a Greek prince named Menelaus; and the other princes of Greece joined him in attacking Troy. They took some smaller places round about and divided the booty, as the custom was. In the tenth year of the war, Achilles and Agamemnon, two of the greatest of the princes, quarreled about one of these divisions, and here the Iliad begins. Achilles was so angry that he took his followers, the Myrmidons, left the camp, and declared that he would have nothing more to do with the war, he would return to Greece.

Now the Greeks were in trouble, indeed, for Achilles was their most valiant leader, and his men were exceedingly brave soldiers. They sent his friend Patroclus to beg him to come back. Achilles would not yield, even to him; but he finally agreed to allow his followers to return and also to lend his armor and equipments to Patroclus.

When the Trojans saw the chariot and armor of Achilles, they ran for their lives, as Patroclus had expected; but at length Hector, son of King Priam, ventured to face his enemy, and Patroclus fell. Achilles was heartbroken. It was all his own fault, he declared, and he groaned so heavily that his wailing was heard in the depths of the ocean. He vowed that, come what might, he would be revenged. He went back to the camp and made up the quarrel with Agamemnon; and then he rushed forth into battle. The Trojans were so terrified that they all ran back into the city save one, Hector. But when Achilles dashed forward upon him, his heart failed, and he, too, ran for his life. Three times Achilles chased him around the walls of Troy, then thrust him through with his spear. He tied cords to the feet of his fallen enemy and dragged his body back and forth before the eyes of the Trojans; and when the following morning had come, he dragged it twice around the tomb of Patroclus.

The Greeks believed that if a person's body had not received funeral rites, he would be condemned to wander for one hundred years on the banks of the Styx, the gloomy river of the dead; but Achilles declared in his wrath that the body of Hector should be thrown to the dogs. Then King Priam loaded into his litter rolls of handsome cloth, rich garments, and golden dishes, and made his way to the tent of the fierce warrior. "Your father is an old man like me," he pleaded. "Think of him and show pity. I have brought a wealth of ransom. Take it and give me the body of my son." The fiery Achilles yielded and even agreed to a twelve-days' truce so that the funeral might be celebrated with all due honor. The tale ends with the building of an immense pyre and the burning of the body of Hector.

FROM THE CATECHISM IN EXAMPLES
By Rev. D. Chisholm

THE SEVENTH CORPORAL WORK OF MERCY: BURY THE DEAD

The seventh Corporal Work of Mercy is to bury the dead. Our bodies, my child, were made by God to possess the joys of Heaven for all eternity as well as our souls, and therefore a great respect is due to them. They have been consecrated to God by Baptism, and have been the dwelling-place of Jesus when He came into us in Holy Communion. And although, on account of sin, they must fall into corruption for a time, they will one day rise again, never to die. This hope of our resurrection should inspire us with a reverence for the departed, and cause us to place what is human of them with respect in their last earthly home. This work is most pleasing to God and meritorious to ourselves.

FROM STORIES FROM THE CLASSICS
Selected & Arranged by Eva March Tappan

THE WOODEN HORSE AND THE FALL OF TROY
Retold from Homer's Iliad

By Josephine Preston Peabody

Nine years the Greeks laid siege to Troy, and Troy held out against every device. On both sides the lives of many heroes were spent, and they were forced to acknowledge each other enemies of great valor.

Sometimes the chief warriors fought in single combat, while the armies looked on, and the old men of Troy, with the women, came out to watch afar off from the city walls. King Priam and Queen Hecuba would come, and Cassandra, sad with foreknowledge of their doom, and Andromache, the lovely young wife of Hector, with her little son, whom the people called the city's king. Sometimes fair Helen came to look across the plain to the fellow-countrymen whom she had forsaken; and although she was the cause of all this war, the Trojans half forgave her when she passed by, because her beauty was like a spell, and warmed hard hearts as the sunshine mellows apples. So for nine years the Greeks plundered the neighboring towns, but the city Troy stood fast, and the Grecian ships waited with folded wings.

In the tenth year of the war the Greeks, who could not take the city by force, pondered how they might take it by craft. At length, with the aid of Ulysses, they devised a plan.

A portion of the Grecian host broke up camp and set sail as if they were homeward bound; but, once out of sight, they anchored their ships behind a neighboring island. The rest of the army then fell to work upon a great image of a horse. They built it of wood, fitted and carved, and with a door so cunningly concealed that none might notice it. When it was finished, the horse looked like a prodigious idol; but it was hollow, skillfully pierced here and there, and so spacious that a band of men could lie hidden within and take no harm. Into this hiding-place went Ulysses, Menelaus, and the other chiefs, fully armed, and when the door was shut upon them, the rest of the Grecian army broke camp and went away.

Meanwhile, in Troy, the people had seen the departure of the ships, and the news had spread like wildfire. The great enemy had lost heart,—after ten years of war! Part of the army had gone,—the rest were going. Already the last of the ships had set sail, and the camp was deserted. The tents that had whitened the plain were gone like a frost before the sun. The war was over!

The whole city went wild with joy. Like one who has been a prisoner for many years, it flung off all restraint, and the people rose as a single man to test the truth of new liberty. The gates were thrown wide, and the Trojans—men, women, and children—thronged over the plain and into the empty camp of the enemy. There stood the Wooden Horse.

No one knew what it could be. Fearful at first, they gathered around it, as children gather around a live horse; they marveled at its wondrous height and girth, and were for moving it into the city as a trophy of war.

At this, one man interposed, Laocoön, a priest of Neptune. "Take heed, citizens," said he. "Beware of all that comes from the Greeks. Have you fought them for ten years without learning their devices? This is some piece of treachery."

But there was another outcry in the crowd, and at that moment certain of the Trojans dragged forward a wretched man who wore the garments of a Greek. He seemed the sole remnant of the Grecian army, and as such they consented to spare his life, if he would tell them the truth.

Sinon, for this was the spy's name, said that he had been left behind by the malice of Ulysses, and he told them that the Greeks had built the Wooden Horse as an offering to Athene, and that they had made it so huge in order to keep it from being moved out of the camp, since it was destined to bring triumph to its possessors.

At this the joy of the Trojans was redoubled, and they set their wits to find out how they might soonest drag the great horse across the plain and into the city to insure victory. While they stood talking, two immense serpents rose out of the sea and made towards the camp. Some of the people took flight, others were transfixed with terror; but all, near and far, watched this new omen. Rearing their crests, the sea serpents crossed the shore, swift, shining, terrible as a risen water-flood that descends upon a helpless little town. Straight through the crowd they swept, and seized the priest Laocoön where he stood, with his two sons, and wrapped them all round and round in fearful coils. There was no chance of escape. Father and sons perished together; and when the monsters had devoured the three men, into the sea they slipped again, leaving no trace of the horror.

The terrified Trojans saw an omen in this. To their minds punishment had come upon Laocoön for his words against the Wooden Horse. Surely, it was sacred to the Gods; he had spoken blasphemy, and had perished before their eyes. They flung his warning to the winds.

They wreathed the horse with garlands, amid great acclaim; and then, all lending a hand, they dragged it, little by little, out of the camp and into the city of Troy. With the close of that victorious day, they gave up every memory of danger and made merry after ten years of privation.

That very night Sinon the spy opened the hidden door of the Wooden Horse, and in the darkness, Ulysses, Menelaus, and the other chiefs who had lain hidden there crept out and gave the signal to the Grecian army. For, under cover of night, those ships that had been moored behind the island had sailed back again, and the Greeks were come upon Troy.

Not a Trojan was on guard. The whole city was at feast when the enemy rose in its midst, and the warning of Laocoön was fulfilled.

Priam and his warriors fell by the sword, and their kingdom was plundered of all its fair possessions, women and children, and treasure. Last of all, the city itself was burned to its very foundations.

Homeward sailed the Greeks, taking as royal captives poor Cassandra and Andromache and many another Trojan. And home at last went fair Helen, the cause of all this sorrow, eager to be forgiven by her husband, King Menelaus. For she had awakened from the enchantment of Venus, and even before the death of Paris she had secretly longed for her home and kindred. Home to Sparta she came with the king after a long and stormy voyage, and there she lived and died the fairest of women.

But the kingdom of Troy was fallen. Nothing remained of all its glory but the glory of its dead heroes and fair women, and the ruins of its citadel by the river Scamander. There even now, beneath the foundations of later homes that were built and burned, built and burned, in the wars of a thousand years after, the ruins of ancient Troy lie hidden, like moldered leaves deep under the new grass. And there, to this very day, men who love the story are delving after the dead city as you might search for a buried treasure.

From Anecdotes and Examples for the Catechism
By Rev. Francis Spirago

The Wooden Horse of Troy

In the hour of temptation dangerous things appear attractive to us, and hence the greater the need of grace. In ancient history, we read that the Greeks, with an army of 100,000 valiant warriors, laid siege to the city of Troy in Asia Minor. As the city was strongly built and was garrisoned by brave defenders, for ten long years it held out against the Greeks. Finding they were unable to take it by force, the besiegers resolved to have recourse to stratagem. Accordingly they constructed a gigantic wooden horse, dragged it up close to the city walls, and then withdrew to their ships, as if, weary of the protracted hostilities, they were about to return to their own country. A few stragglers were left behind who were instructed to inform the Trojans that the Greeks had constructed the horse to propitiate the gods and obtain favorable winds for their voyage homeward. The Trojans determined to draw the horse into the city as a trophy of their victorious defense of their homes. A few wise men among the inhabitants warned them not to accept this gift from the enemy; one especially, named Laocoön, pronounced these memorable words, "Beware of the Danaos, even when they bring gifts." But their counsel was unheeded; the horse was drawn in triumph into the city. That same night thirty Grecian warriors, who were concealed within the body of the horse, issued forth from their hiding-place, put the sentinels to death, and opened the gates. Then the Greeks, who, meanwhile, had returned to their camp, made their way into the city and slaughtered the inhabitants. Troy was burned to the ground. The enemy of mankind acts in the same way as the Wily Greeks; he invests what will prove dangerous with attraction in our eyes. Unhappy those who fall into his snares.

FROM OLD WORLD HERO STORIES
By Eva March Tappan

THE ODYSSEY

Homer's second poem is the Odyssey. Troy finally fell into the hands of the Greeks, but Ulysses, or Odysseus, one of the leaders, was unfortunate enough to be hated by Poseidon, god of the sea. His home was on the island of Ithaca; but before Poseidon would allow him to return to it, he drove the homesick wanderer back and forth over the Mediterranean Sea for ten long years and made him undergo all sorts of danger. The Odyssey tells the story of his wanderings and his wonderful adventures.

First, he was driven by a storm to the land of the Lotus-eaters. Whoever ate the lotus forgot his home and friends, and cared for nothing but to stay in the lotus country and idle his life away in vain and empty dreams. Some of Odysseus's men tasted this fruit; and he had to drag them on board the ship and even tie them to the benches to keep them from staying behind.

Odysseus's second adventure was in the country of the Cyclopes, monstrous giants, each having one huge eye in the middle of his forehead. One of these giants, Polyphemus, found the Greeks in his cave when he drove home his sheep and goats. He devoured two of the men at once, and others on the following day. But Odysseus was planning revenge. He offered the giant a great bowl of wine, which pleased him mightily. "What is your name?" the Cyclops asked. "No man," replied Odysseus. Then Polyphemus promised him as a great favor that he should be the last of the company to be eaten. But when the giant was sleeping stupidly, Odysseus and his men took a stick of green olive wood as big as the mast of a ship, heated one end in the fire until it was a burning coal, and plunged it into the eye of Polyphemus. He roared with pain, and the other giants ran from all sides to his aid. "What is it? Who is murdering you?" they cried. "No man," howled the giant, "No man is killing me." "If it is no man," they said, "then your illness comes from Zeus, and you must bear it.

We can do nothing," and they went their way.

The Greeks made their escape, but it was not long before they were in trouble again. They landed on the floating island which was the home of Aeolus, god of the winds. He was kind and friendly, and when they departed, he gave Odysseus a leather sack tied up with a silver cord. All the storm winds were safely shut up in this sack; but Odysseus's men supposed it was full of treasure. They were so afraid they would not get their share that while their leader slept, they tore it open. Aeolus had given them a favorable breeze, and they were so close to their own island that they could see men heaping wood on the fires, but now the storm winds rushed out of the bag and the vessel was driven back again over the waters.

They landed on the island of the enchantress Circe, who had an unpleasant habit of changing people into the animals that they most resembled. They passed by the Sirens, beautiful, treacherous maidens who sang so sweetly from a soft green meadow near the shore that no seamen who heard them could help throwing themselves into the water to make their way near to the marvelous music. The wise Odysseus had himself bound to the mast and forbade his sailors to free him, whatever he might say or do. Therefore he was able to hear the magical songs in safety. Neither did he lose his vessel, for he had stopped up the ears of the sailors with wax. They passed between the snaky monster Scylla and the horrible whirlpool Charybdis; and after many long years of wandering and hardship Odysseus arrived on the shore of his beloved Ithaca.

Penelope, wife of Odysseus, had been tormented by a throng of suitors, who for years had been feasting upon her food and wasting her property. Her son Telemachus was only a youth and not yet strong enough to drive them away. Penelope never gave up the hope that Odysseus would return, and to gain time she put the suitors off by every device in her power. When everything else had failed, she began to weave a web in her loom, and promised that when it was done, she would choose among them. She worked at this for three years, and the suitors waited; but in the fourth year her maids found out the secret, that she was pulling out by night what she wove by day. In the very nick of time Odysseus appeared. He and Telemachus slew the wicked suitors and punished all who had been unfaithful in his absence. Then Telemachus and Penelope and the aged father of Odysseus rejoiced, for at last their lord had come to his own again.

These are bits of the stories that Homer tells in the Iliad and the Odyssey; but their greatest charm is in his manner of telling them. He seems to know just how each one of his characters feels. He understands the anger of Achilles, and he sympathizes with the sorrow of Hector's wife when the hero is going forth to battle. He knows how to use words so marvelously well that he can make one line sound like the tramping of horses on a plain and another like the beating of waves against the rocks. He describes every event as if he himself had seen it, and he never forgets to mention the little things which so many people pass over. Best of all, the stories are told so simply and naturally that, even after the many centuries, we can hardly help feeling that Homer is alive and is telling them directly to us.

FROM WONDER STORIES
By Carolyn Sherwin Bailey

HOW THE MYTHS BEGAN

Long ago, when our earth was more than two thousand years younger, there was a wonderful place called Mount Olympus at the top of the world that the ancients could see quite clearly with the eyes of hope and faith. It did not matter that the Greek and Roman people had never set foot on this mountain in the clouds. They knew it in story and reverenced the gods and goddesses who inhabited it.

In the days when the myths were told, Greece was a more beautiful country than any that is the result of civilization to-day, because the national ideal of the Greeks was beauty and they expressed it in whatever they thought, or wrote, or made with their hands. No matter how far away from home the Greeks journeyed they remembered with pride and love their blue bays and seacoast, the fertile valleys and sheep pastures of Arcadia, the sacred grove of Delphi, those great days when their athletes met for games and races at Athens, and the wide plains of Olympia covered and rich with the most perfect temples and statues that the world has ever known. When the Greeks returned the most beloved sight that met their eyes was the flag of their nation flying at Corinth, or the towers of the old citadel that Cadmus had founded at Thebes.

It was the youth time of men, and there were no geographies or histories or books of science to explain to the ancients those things about life that everyone wants to know sooner or later. There was this same longing for truth among the Roman people as well as among the Greeks. The Romans, also, loved their country, and built temples as the Greeks did, every stone of which they carved and fitted as a stepping stone on the way to the abode of the gods.

But who were these gods, and what did a belief in their existence mean to the Greek and Roman people?

There have been certain changes in two thousand years on our earth. We have automobiles instead of chariots, our ships are propelled by steam instead of by a favorable wind, and we have books that attempt to tell us why spring always follows winter and that courage is a better part than cowardice. But we still have hard winters and times when it is most difficult to be brave. We still experience war and famine and crime, and peace and plenty and love in just about the same measure that they were to be found in Greece and Rome. The only difference is that we are a little closer to understanding life than the ancients were. They tried to find a means of knowing life facts and of explaining the miracles of outdoors and of ruling their conduct by their daily intercourse with this higher race of beings, the gods, on Mount Olympus.

There was a gate of clouds on the top of Mount Olympus that the goddesses, who were known as the Seasons, opened to allow the inhabitants of the Mount to descend to the earth and return. Jupiter, the ruler of the gods, sat on the Olympian throne holding thunderbolts and darts of lightning in his mighty hands. The same arts and labors as those of men were practiced by these celestial beings. Minerva and her handmaidens, the Graces, wove garments for the goddesses of more exquisite colors and textures than any that could be made by human hands. Vulcan built the houses of the gods of glittering brass. He shaped golden shoes that made it possible for them to travel with great speed, and he shod their steeds so that their chariots could ride upon the water. Hebe fed the gods with nectar and ambrosia, prepared and served by her own fair hands. Mars loosed the dogs of war, and the music of Apollo's lute was the song of victory and peace when war was ended. Ceres tended and blessed the fields of grain, and Venus, clad in beautiful garments by the Seasons, expressed the desire of the nations, of dumb beasts and of all nature for love.

There were many more than these, making the great immortal family of the gods, like men, but different in their higher understanding of life and its meaning. They lived apart on their Mount, but they descended often to mingle with the people. They stood beside the forge and helped with the harvest, their voices were heard in the rustling leaves in the forest and above the tumult and crash of war. They guarded the flocks and crowned the victors in games and carried brave warriors to Elysian fields after their last battles. They loved adventure and outdoors; they felt joy and knew pain. These gods were the daily companions of the ancients who have given them to us in our priceless inheritance of the classics and art.

When you read the poems of the blind Roman, Homer, and those of Ovid and Virgil; when you see a picture of a columned Greek temple or the statue of the Apollo Belvedere or the Guido Reni painting of Aurora lighting the sky with the torches of day, you, too, are following the age-old stepping stones that led to Mount Olympus. The myths were the inspiration for the greatest writing and architecture and sculpture and painting that the world has ever known. They were more than this.

Among the ruins of the ancient cities there was found one temple with a strange inscription on the altar: "To the unknown God." The temple was placed on Mars Hill as if, out of the horrors of war, this new hope had come to the people.

The word mythology means an account of tales. The myths were just that, tales, but most beautiful and worthwhile stories. So that people who made them and retold them and lived as the gods would have had them live came, finally, to feel that there was need for them to build this other, last altar.

FROM AUNT CHARLOTTE'S STORIES OF GREEK HISTORY
By Charlotte M. Yonge

INTRODUCTION TO GREEK MYTHOLOGY

I am going to tell you the history of the most wonderful people who ever lived. But I have to begin with a good deal that is not true; for the people who lived in the beautiful islands and peninsulas called Greece, were not trained in the knowledge of God like the Israelites, but had to guess for themselves. They made strange stories, partly from the old beliefs they brought from the east, partly from their ways of speaking of the powers of nature—sky, sun, moon, stars, and clouds—as if they were real beings, and so again of good or bad qualities as beings also, and partly from old stories about their forefathers. These stories got mixed up with their belief, and came to be part of their religion and history; and they wrote beautiful poems about them, and made such lovely statues in their honor, that nobody can understand anything about art or learning who has not learnt these stories. I must begin with trying to tell you a few of them.

In the first place, the Greeks thought there were twelve greater gods and goddesses who lived in Olympus. There is really a mountain called Olympus, and those who lived far from it thought it went up into the sky, and that the gods really dwelt on the top of it. Those who lived near, and knew they did not, thought they lived in the sky. But the chief of all, the father of gods and men, was the sky-god—Zeus, as the Greeks called him, or Jupiter, as he was called in Latin. However, as all things are born of Time, so the sky or Jupiter was said to have a father, Time, whose Greek name was Kronos. His other name was Saturn; and as Time devours his offspring, so Saturn was said to have had the bad habit of eating up his children as fast as they were born, till at last his wife Rhea contrived to give him a stone in swaddling clothes, and while he was biting this hard morsel, Jupiter was saved from him, and afterwards two other sons, Neptune (Poseidon) and Pluto (Hades), who became lords of the ocean and of the world of the spirits of the dead; for on the sea and on death Time's tooth has no power. However, Saturn's reign was thought to have been a very peaceful and happy one. For as people always think of the days of Paradise, and believe that the days of old were better than their own times, so the Greeks thought there had been four ages—the Golden age, the Silver age, the Brazen age, and the Iron age—and that people had been getting worse in each of them. Poor old Saturn, after the Silver age, had had to go into retirement, with only his own star, the planet Saturn, left to him; and Jupiter was reigning now, on his throne on Olympus, at the head of the twelve greater gods and goddesses, and it was the Iron age down below. His star, the planet we still call by his name, was much larger and brighter than Saturn. Jupiter was always thought of by the Greeks as a majestic-looking man in his full strength, with thick hair and beard, and with lightnings in his hand and an eagle by his side. These lightnings or thunderbolts were forged by his crooked son Vulcan (Hephæstion), the god of fire, the smith and armorer of Olympus, whose smithies were in the volcanoes (so called from his name), and whose workmen were the Cyclops or Round Eyes—giants, each with one eye in the middle of his forehead. Once, indeed, Jupiter had needed his bolts, for the Titans, a horrible race of monstrous giants, of whom the worst was Briareus, who had a hundred hands, had tried, by piling up mountains one upon the other, to scale heaven and throw him down; but when Jupiter was hardest pressed, a dreadful pain in his head caused him to bid Vulcan to strike it with his hammer. Then out darted Heavenly Wisdom, his beautiful daughter Pallas Athene or Minerva, fully armed, with piercing, shining eyes, and by her counsels he cast down the Titans, and heaped their own mountains,

Etna and Ossa and Pelion, on them to keep them down; and whenever there was an earth-quake, it was thought to be caused by one of these giants struggling to get free, though perhaps there was some remembrance of the tower of Babel in the story. Pallas, this glorious daughter of Jupiter, was wise, brave, and strong, and she was also the goddess of women's works—of all spinning, weaving, and sewing.

Jupiter's wife, the queen of heaven or the air, was Juno—in Greek, Hera—the white-armed, ox-eyed, stately lady, whose bird was the peacock. Do you know how the peacock got the eyes in his tail? They once belonged to Argus, a shepherd with a hundred eyes, whom Juno had set to watch a cow named Io, who was really a lady, much hated by her. Argus watched till Mercury (Hermes) came and lulled him to sleep with soft music, and then drove Io away. Juno was so angry, that she caused all the eyes to be taken from Argus and put into her peacock's tail.

Mercury has a planet called after him too, a very small one, so close to the sun that we only see it just after sunset or before sunrise. I believe Mercury or Hermes really meant the morning breeze. The story went that he was born early in the morning in a cave, and after he had slept a little while in his cradle, he came forth, and, finding the shell of a tortoise with some strings of the inwards stretched across it, he at once began to play on it, and thus formed the first lyre. He was so swift that he was the messenger of Jupiter, and he is always represented with wings on his cap and sandals; but as the wind not only makes music, but blows things away unawares, so Mercury came to be viewed not only as the god of fair speech, but as a terrible thief, and the god of thieves. You see, as long as these Greek stories are parables, they are grand and beautiful; but when the beings are looked on as like men, they are absurd and often horrid. The gods had another messenger, Iris, the rainbow, who always carried messages of mercy, a recollection of the bow in the clouds; but she chiefly belonged to Juno.

All the twelve greater gods had palaces on Olympus, and met every day in Jupiter's hall to feast on ambrosia, a sort of food of life which made them immortal. Their drink was nectar, which was poured into their golden cups at first by Vulcan, but he stumbled and hobbled so with his lame leg that they chose instead the fresh and graceful Hebe, the goddess of youth, till she was careless, and one day fell down, cup and nectar and all. The gods thought they must find another cupbearer, and, looking down, they saw a beautiful youth named Ganymede watching his flocks upon Mount Ida. So they sent Jupiter's eagle down to fly away with him and bring him up to Olympus. They gave him some ambrosia to make him immortal, and established him as their cupbearer. Besides this, the gods were thought to feed on the smoke and smell of the sacrifices people offered up to them on earth, and always to help those who offered them most sacrifices of animals and incense.

The usual names of these twelve were—Jupiter, Neptune, Juno, Latona, Apollo, Diana, Pallas, Venus, Vulcan, Mercury, Vesta, and Ceres; but there were multitudes besides—"gods many and lords many" of all sorts of different dignities. Every river had its god, every mountain and wood was full of nymphs, and there was a great god of all nature called Pan, which in Greek means All. Neptune was only a visitor in Olympus, though he had a right there.

His kingdom was the sea, which he ruled with his trident, and where he had a whole world of lesser gods and nymphs, tritons and sea horses, to attend upon his chariot.

And the quietest and best of all the goddesses was Vesta, the goddess of the household hearth—of home, that is to say. There are no stories to be told about her, but a fire was always kept burning in her honor in each city, and no one might tend it who was not good and pure.

FROM ANECDOTES AND EXAMPLES
ILLUSTRATING THE CATHOLIC CATECHISM
By Rev. Francis Spirago

HERCULES AT THE CROSSROADS

The practice of virtue is frequently irksome to human nature, but it leads to true happiness. The pagan Greeks relate the following fable: A youth named Hercules was standing at a place where two roads met, undecided which to take. Then there came up to him two guides. One was fair to look upon and flattering in her speech, promising him all manner of enjoyments, if he would follow her guidance. The other offered him no present delights, but rather struggle and suffering, but these would be succeeded by supreme happiness. Hercules chose the latter, and followed the second guide. This fable contains a deep truth. The first guide who presented herself to the young man was sin; she gives temporary pleasures to those who follow her, but afterward suffering, both here and hereafter, is their portion. The other guide personates virtue; her service is oftentimes painful and difficult, but it results in happiness, both in time and in eternity.

FROM FIFTY FAMOUS STORIES RETOLD
By James Baldwin

DAMON AND PYTHIAS

A young man whose name was Pythias had done something which the tyrant Dionysius did not like. For this offense, he was dragged to prison, and a day was set when he should be put to death. His home was far away, and he wanted very much to see his father and mother and friends before he died.

"Only give me leave to go home and say good-by to those whom I love," he said, "and then I will come back and give up my life."

The tyrant laughed at him. "How can I know that you will keep your promise?" he said. "You only want to cheat me, and save yourself."

Then a young man whose name was Damon spoke and said,— "O king! put me in prison in place of my friend Pythias, and let him go to his own country to put his affairs in order, and to bid his friends farewell. I know that he will come back as he promised, for he is a man who has never broken his word. But if he is not here on the day which you have set, then I will die in his stead."

The tyrant was surprised that anybody should make such an offer. He at last agreed to let Pythias go, and gave orders that the young man Damon should be shut up in prison.

Time passed, and by and by the day drew near which had been set for Pythias to die; and he had not come back. The tyrant ordered the jailer to keep close watch upon Damon, and not let him escape. But Damon did not try to escape. He still had faith in the truth and honor of his friend. He said, "If Pythias does not come back in time, it will not be his fault. It will be because he is hindered against his will."

At last the day came, and then the very hour. Damon was ready to die. His trust in his friend was as firm as ever; and he said that he did not grieve at having to suffer for one whom he loved so much.

Then the jailer came to lead him to his death; but at the same moment Pythias stood in the door. He had been delayed by storms and shipwreck, and he had feared that he was too late. He greeted Damon kindly, and then gave himself into the hands of the jailer. He was happy because he thought that he had come in time, even though it was at the last moment.

The tyrant was not so bad but that he could see good in others. He felt that men who loved and trusted each other, as did Damon and Pythias, ought not to suffer unjustly. And so he set them both free.

"I would give all my wealth to have one such friend," he said.

From Stories from the Classics
Selected & Arranged by Eva March Tappan

Icarus and Dædalus
By Josephine Preston Peabody

Among all those mortals who grew so wise that they learned the secrets of the gods, none was more cunning than Dædalus.

He once built, for King Minos of Crete, a wonderful Labyrinth of winding ways so cunningly tangled up and twisted around that, once inside, you could never find your way out again without a magic clue. But the king's favor veered with the wind, and one day he had his master architect imprisoned in a tower. Dædalus managed to escape from his cell; but it seemed impossible to leave the island, since every ship that came or went was well guarded by order of the king.

At length, watching the sea-gulls in the air,—the only creatures that were sure of liberty,—he thought of a plan for himself and his young son Icarus, who was captive with him.

Little by little, he gathered a store of feathers great and small. He fastened these together with thread, molded them in with wax, and so fashioned two great wings like those of a bird. When they were done, Dædalus fitted them to his own shoulders, and after one or two efforts, he found that by waving his arms he could winnow the air and cleave it, as a swimmer does the sea. He held himself aloft, wavered this way and that, with the wind, and at last, like a great fledgling, he learned to fly.

Without delay, he fell to work on a pair of wings for the boy Icarus, and taught him carefully how to use them, bidding him beware of rash adventures among the stars. "Remember," said the father, "never to fly very low or very high, for the fogs about the earth would weigh you down, but the blaze of the sun will surely melt your feathers apart if you go too near."

For Icarus, these cautions went in at one ear and out by the other. Who could remember to be careful when he was to fly for the first time? Are birds careful? Not they! And not an idea remained in the boy's head but the one joy of escape.

The day came, and the fair wind that was to set them free. The father bird put on his wings, and, while the light urged them to be gone, he waited to see that all was well with Icarus, for the two could not fly hand in hand. Up they rose, the boy after his father. The hateful ground of Crete sank beneath them; and the country folk, who caught a glimpse of them when they were high above the tree-tops, took it for a vision of the gods,—Apollo, perhaps, with Cupid after him.

At first there was a terror in the joy. The wide vacancy of the air dazed them,—a glance downward made their brains reel. But when a great wind filled their wings, and Icarus felt himself sustained, like a halcyon-bird in the hollow of a wave, like a child uplifted by his mother, he forgot everything in the world but joy. He forgot Crete and the other islands that he had passed over: he saw but vaguely that winged thing in the distance before him that was his father Dædalus. He longed for one draught of flight to quench the thirst of his captivity: he stretched out his arms to the sky and made towards the highest heavens.

Alas for him! Warmer and warmer grew the air. Those arms, that had seemed to uphold him, relaxed. His wings wavered, drooped. He fluttered his young hands vainly,—he was falling,—and in that terror he remembered. The heat of the sun had melted the wax from his wings; the feathers were falling, one by one, like snowflakes; and there was none to help.

He fell like a leaf tossed down the wind, down, down, with one cry that overtook Dædalus far away. When he returned, and sought high and low for the poor boy, he saw nothing but the bird-like feathers afloat on the water, and he knew that Icarus was drowned.

The nearest island he named Icaria, in memory of the child; but he, in heavy grief, went to the temple of Apollo in Sicily, and there hung up his wings as an offering. Never again did he attempt to fly.

FROM THE STORY OF THE GREEKS
By H. A. Guerber

LYCURGUS OF SPARTA

Lycurgus was a thoroughly good and upright man. We are told that the mother of the baby king once offered to put her child to death that Lycurgus might reign. Fearing for the babe's safety, Lycurgus made believe that he agreed to this plan, and asked that the child should be given to him to kill as he saw fit.

Lycurgus, having thus obtained possession of the babe, carried him to the council hall. There the child was named king; and Lycurgus promised that he would watch carefully over him, educate him well, and rule for him until he should be old and wise enough to reign alone.

While he was thus acting as ruler, Lycurgus made use of his power to bring many new customs into Sparta, and to change the laws. As he was one of the wisest men who ever lived, he knew very well that men must be good if they would be happy. He also knew that health is far better than riches; and, hoping to make the Spartans both good and healthy, he won them over little by little to obey a new set of laws, which he had made after visiting many of the neighboring countries, and learning all he could.

The laws which Lycurgus drew up for the Spartans were very strict. For instance, as soon as a babe came into the world, the law ordered that the father should wrap it up in a cloak, and carry it before a council made up of some of the oldest and wisest men.

They looked at the child carefully, and if it seemed strong and healthy, and was neither crippled nor in any way deformed, they said that it might live.

The Spartan children stayed under their father's roof and in their mother's care until they were seven years old. While in the nursery, they were taught all the beautiful old Greek legends, and listened with delight to the stories of the ancient heroes, and especially to the poems of Homer telling about the war of Troy and the adventures of Ulysses.

As soon as the children had reached seven years of age, they were given over to the care of the state, and allowed to visit their parents but seldom. The boys were put in charge of chosen men, who trained them to become strong and brave; while the girls were placed under some good and wise woman, who not only taught them all they needed to know to keep house well, but also trained them to be as strong and fearless as their brothers. All Spartan boys were allowed but one rough woolen garment, which served as their sole covering by night and by day, and was of the same material in summer as in winter.

They were taught very little reading, writing, and arithmetic, but were carefully trained to recite the poems of Homer, the patriotic songs, and to accompany themselves skillfully on the lyre. They were also obliged to sing in the public chorus, and to dance gracefully at all the religious feasts.

As the Spartans were very anxious that their boys should be strong and fearless, they were taught to stand pain and fatigue without a murmur; and, to make sure that they could do so, their teachers made them go through a very severe training.

Led by one of the older boys, the little lads were often sent out for long tramps over rough and stony roads, under the hot sun; and the best boy was the one who kept up longest, in spite of bleeding feet, burning thirst, and great fatigue.

Spartan boys were allowed no beds to sleep in, lest they should become lazy and hard to please. Their only couch was a heap of rushes, which they picked on the banks of the Eurotas, a river near Sparta; and in winter they were allowed to cover these with a layer of cat-tail down to make them softer and warmer.

The Spartan girls, who were brought up by the women, were, like the boys, taught to wrestle, run, and swim, and to take part in gymnastics of all kinds, until they too became very strong and supple, and could stand almost any fatigue.

They were also taught to read, write, count, sing, play, and dance; to spin, weave, and dye; and to do all kinds of woman's work. In short, they were expected to be strong, intelligent, and capable, so that when they married they might help their husbands, and bring up their children sensibly. At some public festivals the girls strove with one another in various games, which were witnessed only by their fathers and mothers and the other married people of the city. The winners in these contests were given beautiful prizes, which were much coveted.

Lycurgus hoped to make the Spartans a strong and good people. To hinder the kings from doing anything wrong, he had the people choose five men, called ephors, to watch over and to advise them.

Then, knowing that great wealth is not desirable, Lycurgus said that the Spartans should use only iron money. All the Spartan coins were therefore bars of iron, so heavy that a yoke of oxen and a strong cart were needed to carry a sum equal to one hundred dollars from one spot to another. Money was so bulky that it could neither be hidden nor stolen; and no one cared to make a fortune, since it required a large space to stow away even a small sum.

When Charilaus, the infant king, had grown up, Lycurgus prepared to go away. Before he left the town, he called all the citizens together, reminded them of all he had done to make them a great people, and ended by asking every man present to swear to obey the laws until he came back.

The Spartans were very grateful for all he had done for them, so they gladly took this oath, and Lycurgus left the place. Sometime after, he came back to Greece; but, hearing that the Spartans were thriving under the rules he had laid down, he made up his mind never to visit Sparta again.

It was thus that the Spartans found themselves bound by solemn oath to obey Lycurgus' laws forever; and as long as they remembered this promise, they were a thriving and happy people.

FROM YOUNG FOLKS' HISTORY OF ROME
By Charlotte Yonge

ITALY

I am going to tell you next about the most famous nation in the world. Going westward from Greece another peninsula stretches down into the Mediterranean. The Apennine Mountains run like a limb stretching out of the Alps to the south eastward, and on them seems formed that land, shaped somewhat like a leg, which is called Italy.

Round the streams that flowed down from these hills, valleys of fertile soil formed themselves, and a great many different tribes and people took up their abode there, before there was any history to explain their coming. Putting together what can be proved about them, it is plain, however, that most of them came of that old stock from which the Greeks descended, and to which we belong ourselves, and they spoke a language, which had the same root as ours and as the Greek. From one of these nations the best-known form of this, as it was polished in later times, was called Latin, from the tribe who spoke it.

THE TIBER

About the middle of the peninsula there runs down, westward from the Apennines, a river called the Tiber, flowing rapidly between seven low hills, which recede as it approaches the sea. One, in especial, called the Palatine Hill, rose separately, with a flat top and steep sides, about four hundred yards from the river, and girdled in by the other six. This was the place where the great Roman power grew up from beginnings, the truth of which cannot now be discovered.

CURIOUS POTTERY

There were several nations living round these hills—the Etruscans, Sabines, and Latins being the chief. The homes of these nations seem to have been in the valleys round the spurs of the Apennines, where they had farms and fed their flocks; but above them was always the hill which they had fortified as strongly as possible, and where they took refuge if their enemies attacked them. The Etruscans built very mighty walls, and also managed the drainage of their cities wonderfully well. Many of their works remain to this day, and, in especial, their monuments have been opened, and the tomb of each chief has been found, adorned with figures of himself, half lying, half sitting; also curious pottery in red and black, from which something of their lives and ways is to be made out. They spoke a different language from what has become Latin, and they had a different religion, believing in one great Soul of the World, and also thinking much of rewards and punishments after death. But we know hardly anything about them, except that their chiefs were called Lucumos, and that they once had a wide power which they had lost before the time of history. The Romans called them Tusci, and Tuscany still keeps its name.

The Latins and the Sabines were more alike, and also more like the Greeks. There were a great many settlements of Greeks in the southern parts of Italy, and they learnt something from them. They had a great many gods. Every house had its own guardian. These were called Lares, or Penates, and were generally represented as little figures of dogs lying by the hearth, or as brass bars with dogs' heads. This is the reason that the bars which close in an open hearth are still called dogs. Whenever there was a meal in the house the master began by pouring out wine to the Lares, and also to his own ancestors, of whom he kept figures;

for these natives thought much of their families, and all one family had the same name, like our surname, such as Tullius or Appius, the daughters only changing it by making it end in *a* instead of *us*, and the men having separate names standing first, such as Marcus or Lucius, though their sisters were only numbered to distinguish them.

The history of these people was not written till long after they had grown to be a mighty and terrible power, and had also picked up many Greek notions. Then they seem to have made their history backwards, and worked up their old stories and songs to explain the names and customs they found among them, and the tales they told were formed into a great history by one Titus Livius [also known as Livy].

OLD WORLD HERO STORIES
Eva March Tappan

HOW ROME WAS FOUNDED

Just as the story of Greece begins with the tales told by the Greek poet Homer, so the story of Rome begins with the stories told by the Latin poet Virgil. Virgil's poem is called the Aeneid, because the hero is Aeneas, one of the brave warriors of Troy. Virgil takes up the tale of the Trojan War very nearly where Homer leaves it. The city was finally captured by a stratagem. The Greeks sailed away until they were out of sight behind an island, and the Trojans thought that they had gone home. They left behind them a monstrous wooden horse just outside the city. While the Trojans were wondering what it could be, a ragged, unkempt Greek was brought in as a captive. He told them that the horse was built as an offering to the goddess Athena, or Minerva, but that if it was only brought within the walls, it would protect the town instead of the makers. The Trojans never guessed that the whole thing was a trick. They made a gap in the wall and pulled in the horse. That night, when all were asleep, the Greeks who were hidden in the horse crept out, and Troy was soon in the hands of its enemies, Aeneas fought until the whole town was in flames and there was no longer any hope in fighting. Then he took his aged father Anchises on his shoulders and with his wife and their little son Ascanius, he fled. In the confusion his wife was lost, and although he ran fearlessly through the burning city, calling her name, she was gone. At length her spirit appeared to him and told him not to mourn, for she had been taken away by the will of the gods, to preserve her both from long years of wandering and from being a slave to the Greeks.

Outside the town, Aeneas met many other Trojans who had also fled from the Greeks. They decided to build boats, and with him for their leader to search for some land where they might make new homes for themselves. They worked away on the vessels, and when spring had come, they bade farewell, with many tears, to the place where Troy had stood, and sailed forth upon the sea, not knowing where the fates would grant them a home.

Thrace was only a little way off, so the wanderers first went there and prepared to sacrifice a bull. Aeneas began to pull up a little bush in order to cover his altar with green leaves, and to his horror, the broken twigs dropped blood. A voice came from the ground, the voice of a murdered kinsman, bidding him flee from the accursed land.

Just as soon as the sea was calm, they hastened away from Thrace. They next landed on the little island of Delos, for here was the oracle of Apollo, and they hoped it would tell them where to go. "Seek your ancient mother," said the oracle; but this was not very helpful, for no one knew what was meant. At last Anchises said he remembered hearing that the Trojans first came from Crete; so to Crete they went. They began to build a city and marked off places for their homes. They ploughed the land and planted their fields. But sickness came upon them, and the fields yielded no crops. What to do next they did not know; but the images of the household gods which Aeneas had brought with him spoke to him one night in a dream and told him that a mistake had been made, that the real founder of the race was Dardanus, and that he had come from Hesperia, or Italy. There was nothing for them to do but to set out for Italy; and now they met troubles upon troubles. At one island where they landed and spread a meal for themselves, a flock of Harpies, horrible birds with the faces of maidens ghastly pale and drawn with hunger, swooped down upon them, and could hardly be driven away by their swords. When they came to Sicily, they had a long night of terror, for they heard the thunders and saw the fires of Mount Aetna. In the morning a wretched man called to them from the shore. He was thin and haggard, his beard was rough and tangled, and his clothes were held together with thorns. He admitted that he was a Greek and that he had fought at Troy; but he pleaded that they would take him away. "Throw me into the deep if you will," he said. "I shall at least have met my death at the hands of men and not monsters." Then he told them that he had been with Odysseus, or Ulysses, as the Romans called him, and had been left behind in this country of the horrible Cyclopes. Just as he finished his story, they saw the Cyclops whom Ulysses had blinded come feeling his way downhill with a pine tree for a staff. He heard their voices and waded out into the sea in pursuit, raising such a bellowing that land and water trembled with the clamor. The dreadful company of giants rushed down to the shore, but the Trojans had escaped.

Aeneas sailed safely between Scylla and Charybdis and was now close to Italy. He would soon have been in his destined home, had not Juno, who hated the Trojans, interfered and commanded Aeolus to send out the storm winds to drive them away. They were thrown upon the shores of Carthage, which was ruled by Queen Dido. She promptly fell in love with Aeneas; and he seemed to be perfectly willing to forget Italy and remain in her city. Jupiter, however, bade him continue his journey; and at last, after his many wanderings, he was at the mouth of the Tiber. Here dwelt Latinus, ruler of the country. His beautiful daughter Lavinia was promised in marriage to Turnus, king of a neighboring people; but a dream had come to Latinus to warn him to give her to a stranger from a foreign land, and he decided that Aeneas must be the stranger. Of course, there was war between Turnus and Aeneas. The Trojans won, and Turnus was slain.

This is the end of the Aeneid, but it is only the beginning of the story of Rome. Aeneas founded a city called Lavinium; but when his son Ascanius became ruler, Lavinium proved to be far too small for the people who wished to live in it. It was an easy matter to settle a town in those days, and Ascanius founded another on a long ridge of a neighboring hill. He named this Alba Longa, or the long white city.

When Alba Longa was three centuries old, Numitor, a descendant of Ascanius, was reigning. His brother Amulius contrived to get possession of the kingdom and drove Numitor from the throne. He killed Numitor's son, and he disposed of the daughter, Rhea Sylvia, by making her one of the maidens who guarded the ever-burning lamp in the temple of the goddess Vesta. He thought that everything was well arranged to give him peace and quiet on the throne; but one day he was told that Rhea Sylvia was the mother of twin sons whose father was the war god Mars. These children were heirs to the throne, and therefore Amulius got them and their mother out of the way as soon as possible. He put the mother to death and ordered one of his men to throw the boys into the river Tiber.

Perhaps the man did not want to destroy the babies. At any rate, he seems not to have thrown them into the river, but to have left them in one of the pools along the bank which were made by the high water. When the river subsided, there were the children, safe and sound, on dry land, but crying with hunger. A she-wolf heard them, bore them to her den, and nursed them as if they had been her own cubs. By and by a shepherd named Faustulus came upon them, took them away from the den, and carried them home to his wife.

The children were called Romulus and Remus. They grew up supposing that they were the sons of Faustulus; but the shepherd had discovered in the meantime who they were, and when they were old enough, he told them that they were the grandsons of Numitor, and that the throne belonged to him, and after him to them. Then the two young men called together their shepherd friends, drove Amulius away from his stolen throne, and put him to death. Numitor was again made ruler of the kingdom.

But the two brothers had no idea of simply waiting for their grandfather to die, and they set to work to build a city near the place where they had been thrown into the water and form a kingdom for themselves. So far, everything had gone on smoothly, but now there was trouble between them. Of course, it was proper that the city should be named for the elder brother, and they were twins! Surely, this was a question for the gods to decide; and they agreed to watch for some sign in the heavens. Romulus climbed the Palatine Hill and Remus the Aventine, and there they watched. All day they sat gazing at the sky; but the gods gave no sign. All night they watched; but they were none the wiser. When the sun rose on the following morning, Remus and his followers gave shouts of delight, for he had seen six vultures fly across his part of the sky. But before they were done shouting, Romulus and his friends cried out joyfully, for Romulus had seen twelve vultures!

The question of naming the city was no nearer a settlement than at first; for it would, indeed, take a very wise man to decide which ought to count more, to see six birds first or twelve birds second. It seems to have been decided in some way in favor of Romulus, and he began to build a wall for the city. Apparently, neither of the brothers felt very good-natured; for when the wall was up a little way, Remus jumped over it and said scornfully, "That is what your enemies will do." "And this is the way they will fare," Romulus retorted, and struck his brother angrily. For this act he grieved all his life long, for Remus fell dead at his feet.

More people were needed for the new town of Rome. It was not hard to get men, for Romulus invited everyone to come, even those who had fled from justice or were outcasts for any other reason. They were all welcomed and all protected. It was a different matter to get women; for the tribes about them looked upon the Romans as a collection of rabble and outlaws and scorned the thought of allowing their daughters to marry such good-for-nothings. They had so much curiosity, however, about the new city that when Romulus sent them cordial invitations to attend some games in honor of Neptune, they came in full numbers, and the Sabines even brought their wives and daughters with them. The strangers were treated with the utmost courtesy, and soon they forgot everything but the games. Suddenly the Romans rushed upon them and seized the young women among their guests and carried them away to become their wives.

The Sabines meant to take some terrible vengeance upon the Romans, but they waited until they were sure they could succeed. Then they advanced upon Rome. Their victory would be certain if they could only capture the citadel, or fortress which protected the city. "What will you take," they asked Tarpeia, the daughter of the Roman commander, "to let us in?" "Give me what you wear on your left arms," she replied eagerly. She meant their heavy golden bracelets; but on their left arms they also carried their shields, and these they threw upon the traitor and so crushed her to death.

The Sabines were now within the city, and a terrible fight began between them and the Romans. But, if the Sabines had been surprised at the games of Neptune, they were thunderstruck now; for right into the midst of the battle ran the stolen women. The Romans had been very kind to them, and they had learned to like their new homes. They begged their husbands not to slay their fathers and brothers, and they begged their fathers and brothers not to slay their husbands. There was no sense in trying to avenge the wrongs of women who did not feel that they had been wronged; and the fighting stopped. The two tribes talked the matter over and became so friendly that they agreed to live together as one nation.

These are the legends that have been handed down for many centuries about the founding of Rome. How much truth there is in them it is hard to tell; but the Roman poets and orators were never tired of referring to the tales; and in the magnificent temple of Jupiter which was afterwards built in Rome there was a large statue of the wolf and the twin brothers.

Unit Eight: The Exile

Theme: Listening for God's Voice

FROM BOOK OF THE ANCIENT WORLD
By Dorothy Mills

HEZEKIAH

In the time of Hezekiah, many more of the Psalms than had been before collected, were written down and applied to the Temple Service. The latter part of the Proverbs of Solomon were first copied out, and the inspired words of the prophets began to be added to the Scriptures. Joel's date is unfixed, but Hosea, Amos, and Jonah, had recently been prophesying, and the glorious evangelical predictions of Isaiah and Micah were poured out throughout this reign, those of Isaiah ranging from the humiliation and Passion of the Redeemer, to the ingathering of the nations to His Kingdom, and Micah marking out the little Bethlehem as the birth-place of "Him whose goings are from everlasting."

Manasseh, the son of the good Hezekiah, in the first years of his reign was savagely wicked, and very idolatrous. It is believed that he caused the great evangelical prophet, Isaiah, to be put to death, and he set up an idol in the Temple itself. He soon brought down his punishment on his head, for the Assyrian captains invaded Judea, and took him captive, dragging him in chains to Babylon. There he repented, and humbled himself with so contrite a heart, that God had mercy on him, and caused his enemies to restore him to his throne; but the free days of Judah were over, and they were thenceforth subjects, paying tribute to the King of Assyria, and Manasseh was only a tributary for the many remaining years of his reign, while he strove in vain to undo the evil he had done by bringing in idolatry.

Meantime the greatness of Nineveh came to an end. The Babylonians and Medes revolted against it, and it was ruined. No one ever lived there again; the river made part a swamp, and the rest was covered with sand brought by the desert winds. It was all ruin and desolation; but of late years many of its mighty remains have been brought to our country, as witnesses of the dealings of God with His people's foes.

From Book of the Ancient World
By Dorothy Mills

The Hebrew Prophets: Isaiah and Jeremiah

The greatest of all the Hebrew prophets was Isaiah, who lived not long after Amos. He was a reformer and a statesman as well as a prophet. Little is known of his life, but his teaching has been kept for us in the great book that bears his name. Isaiah lived in Jerusalem, and it was a very stirring time in the history of Judah. Assyria was at the height of her power and had just captured Damascus and invaded the northern kingdom of Israel. The King of Judah saw the advancing Assyrian army with terror, and Jerusalem gave way to panic. The inhabitants feasted and reveled, "Let us eat, drink and be merry," they said, "for tomorrow we die." Then it was that Isaiah pleaded with them to leave off this mad riot, and he calmed them and restored some confidence and tranquility. It was at this time that the King bought off the Assyrian with the gold from the temple. He came again later, but in the meantime the wise counsel of the prophet-statesman had prevailed, and when he returned, the Assyrian King found a city prepared to resist him.

But Isaiah did not confine his attention to the political affairs of his people, he vigorously attacked the crimes they were committing of oppression and injustice, and he denounced their luxury and their forgetfulness of the Lord in such a way that he gained great influence. Jerusalem was the center of the prophet's life, and in the pages of his book we can read descriptions of the city, how she bore herself in her days of triumph, and how she endured famine and siege, loss and defeat. He tells us of all the rumors that filled her streets on the approach of the enemy. It is a vivid picture of life at a stirring period in the history of a city. He became the trusted friend and adviser of the King, and for forty years Isaiah was in the closest touch with all that concerned the national life and honor. He was a great patriot but there was nothing narrow in his patriotism. He knew that Judah must one day be destroyed by a foreign invader, but he believed that a remnant would be saved, and he desired for his race that this remnant might be guided by the highest ideals to take its part in service to the world.

Isaiah was a man who had vision, he could see in his imagination what lay beyond the present, he knew what standards of uprightness and honor, of goodness and righteousness people might reach if they would only really want to follow those ideals and would believe that it was possible for them to do so, and this made him very discontented with all that was poor and petty and mean. Isaiah showed the Lord to the people as a King of Righteousness, and he has left us pictures in splendid language of what he believed the world would one day become, when, he said, "the earth should be full of the knowledge of the Lord, as the waters cover the sea."

The vision of the prophet-statesman had been a true one, and though it came about long after his death, Jerusalem was besieged and taken by the King of Babylon. Some of the

Hebrews whom he took as captives were sent to Egypt, and with them there went a man who had been preaching to them for a long time. His name was Jeremiah, and he was a lonely man, and had made for himself many enemies. That had made him not only sad, but sometimes very bitter, for he was a man of a very sensitive nature; he had neither the energy of Elijah, nor the calm steadfastness of Isaiah. He was often weary and depressed and sick at heart. Few nations have loved their country with a fiercer or more intense love than the Hebrews, and Jeremiah lived at a time of great humiliation for his country. These experiences, however, taught him yet another conception of the Lord which he gave to his people. Jerusalem and the Temple had been destroyed, but the Lord did not depend for worship on temples made with hands. Out of the suffering and humiliation, which came from the exile of his people, Jeremiah learned that as the Lord was a Spirit, so every soul of man might be His temple, where He could be worshipped in spirit and in truth.

FROM BOOK OF THE ANCIENT WORLD
By Dorothy Mills

ASHURBANIPAL

As the Assyrians grew richer, they grew more luxurious, their palaces became more and more gorgeous, and their feasting more sumptuous. They became skilled in all kinds of craftsmanship, the oldest known transparent glass was found at Nineveh, and they might have contributed great things to the world, but their cruelty and delight in making others suffer made them like tigers, and they failed to use the gifts they had for fine or noble purposes. There was, however, one king, who, though he was a fierce warrior, cared something more than the others for peaceful pursuits. This was Ashurbanipal, to whose care for books we owe so much of our knowledge of ancient Assyria. He had copies made of the history of both his own country and of Babylon, and these books were preserved in the royal library, where they were at the disposal of all who wished to consult them. Ashurbanipal stated several times that the library at Nineveh was "for the use of readers."

Ashurbanipal was one of the last of the great kings of Assyria, and with him ended the splendor of Nineveh. These last kings had been so greedy for conquest that they did not give the nation time to recover from their ceaseless wars, and so they exhausted the nation. Assyria had been famous for her sieges, but at last this "great Besieger was herself besieged," and she fell. The news was carried all over the ancient world, and at first, it could hardly be believed. Nineveh was the greatest city in the world, yet she had fallen! When it was realized that Assyria was destroyed, never to rise again, a wave of exultation passed over the ancient world, and a Hebrew prophet gave voice to the universal feeling:

Woe to the City of Blood,
All of her guile, robbery-full, ceaseless rapine!
Hark the whip,
And the rumbling of the wheel,
And horses galloping,
And the rattling dance of the chariot!
Cavalry at the charge, and flash of sabre,
And lightning of lances,
Mass of slain and weight of corpses,
Endless dead bodies—
They stumble on their dead!
Everyone seeing thee shall shrink from thee and say:
   "Shattered is Nineveh—who will pity her?
   Whence shall I seek for comforters to thee?"
Asleep are they shepherds, O King of Assyria,
Thy nobles do slumber,
Thy people are strewn on the mountains,
Without any to gather,
There is no healing of thy wreck,
Fatal thy wound!
All who hear the bruit of thee shall clap the hand at thee,
For upon whom hath not thy cruelty passed without ceasing?

From Book of the Ancient World
By Dorothy Mills

Life in Ancient Babylon

Like all ancient cities, Babylon was surrounded by high walls. Those of Babylon were so huge that we are told a four-horse chariot could be turned round on the top. Inside the city, there were great buildings of all kinds: temples and palaces, and large and small houses, with streets and shops and gardens The houses were generally built of brick, round a courtyard which often had a well in the center shaded by trees. The smaller houses were of one story only, but the larger had several. The doors were narrow and high, and the few windows were near the ceiling. The rooms generally opened one into the other and the walls were covered with paintings. The royal palace was very large, for all the persons who were attached to the service of the king lived in it. Warehouses, cellars, kitchens, the king's treasury, and all kinds of official apartments required places in the palace itself, and the king alone required about twenty rooms for his private use. Then there were the queen's apartments and her gardens; royal and rich women seldom went about in the city, and the queen was only rarely seen.

There was not a great deal of furniture used in these houses. The floor was covered with rugs or mats, and here and there were chairs, couches and tables. The chairs were so high that footstools were usually needed; cushions were used, and these and the couches and bedsteads were covered with tapestry. The tables were often inlaid with ivory, and tripods of bronze were seen everywhere as stands for vases of water or wine. Vases of all kinds, of every kind of shape, and made of every kind of material were used as ornaments.

In most ancient countries, the women were looked upon as very inferior to the men, but in Babylonia the woman was almost the equal of the man. She was allowed to hold property of her own, and when she married, if she had a large fortune of her own, she was allowed to have the management of it. If, however, she was poor, and the bridegroom provided all the money, the wife was little more than a slave. Children were well looked after, and both boys and girls were educated. For the first three years both boys and girls were entirely looked after by a nurse. The first important ceremony in a child's life was that of choosing a name. Great care had to be taken about this, for the Babylonians believed that certain names would bring good luck, whilst others would be unlucky. Names were very long, and they sometimes included the name of a god; here are some specimens: Merodach-balasu-igbi, Nergal-ina-esi-edher.

A Babylonian school consisted of several rooms. The main door led into a long room where a doorkeeper sat, who probably kept a clay tablet list of those who arrived late. From there the children went into a court which was open to the sky, in one corner of which was a pile of soft clay, which the children might take in order to make new tablets for their writing lessons. School began early, and one of the sayings found in an old Babylonian copy-book is: "He who would excel in the school of the scribes must rise like the dawn." The first thing the pupils were taught was writing, and the cuneiform writing was very difficult, for there were so many different signs to be learnt, but the children were encouraged by being told that "He who shall excel in tablet writing shall shine like the sun." Great stress was evidently laid on good spelling, for in all the letters that have been preserved, there is very seldom a misspelled word. Reading was also taught, and history, foreign languages, law, religion, the study of omens, astrology and map-making. Boys were also taught to shoot with the bow, and to take part in other out-door exercises, so that on the whole the Babylonians were taught a greater variety of things than the Egyptians. Borsippa, a suburb of Babylon, was famous for its schools and college, and from an allusion on a clay tablet, it seems that a medical school was established there.

The dress of both men and women in Babylonia was very much alike: a tunic or shirt, made of linen or wool, and fastened with a girdle; a long robe worn over this, sometimes open in front and ornamented with a fringe (embroidered patterns and fringes were very much used and admired); some kind of felt hat; sandals; and in colder weather a heavy cloak was worn over the rest of the clothing. All Babylonian gentlemen wore a small engraved cylinder or seal attached to the wrist by a chain, so that they could use it for their signature whenever necessary.

How did the Babylonians spend their time? They were great fighters, and war took up a good part of their time, but unlike the Assyrians, war was not their chief occupation, and they put a number of good things into the world We owe to the Babylonians: the idea of the arch in building, the development of arithmetic, the weaving of cloth, the polishing and engraving of precious stones, the study of the stars, the making of bricks, and the idea of a sun-dial for a clock.

The deep blue Eastern sky studded with brilliant stars attracted the gaze of the wise men of Babylon, and they were the first people who made a map of the heavens. They observed twelve groups of stars, through which it seemed to them the sun passed in his journey across the sky, and they called these the Zodiac. Observing seven other great heavenly bodies in the sky, they named them for their gods, each of whom they believed, in different ways, controlled the course of events. This belief in the influence of the stars on the life of men developed into the science of astrology, which was very much studied in Babylon. Modern astronomy still maps out the sky after the old Babylonian plan, though the names of Roman gods have taken the place of those of ancient Babylonia. The Babylonians also made a calendar, in which they divided the year into twelve months of thirty days each, but like the Egyptians they found that a year of three hundred and sixty days did not coincide accurately with what they thought were the movements of the sun, so they adopted the plan of adding a whole month to the calendar in every six years.

In addition to the sundial for a clock, the Babylonians also used the "clepsydra." This word means a "water thief," and in its simplest form it was a vessel of water with a hole in the bottom, through which the water dripped regularly into another vessel placed beneath to receive it. As the level of the water in the upper vessel was lowered, the time it had taken was marked on a scale at the side. The principle of the sun-dial was to show *when* it was a certain hour; that of the clepsydra was to show *how long* a time had elapsed since a given moment. This instrument was much improved and perfected in later centuries by the Greeks, but it was the Babylonians who first put their minds to inventing some method of telling the time.

A stranger wandering through the city of Babylon would have found busy markets where buying and selling were going on, and where merchants from Egypt and all the other ancient nations were exchanging the products of their countries for things made in Babylon. The shops were all in narrow streets, and the goods for sale were set out to view under awnings, instead of in the windows as in our shops. Weavers, dyers and tanners were hard at work, and the shoes of Babylonia were famous in those days, and so were the Babylonian riding saddles. Then there were gold, silver, and coppersmiths, and the goldsmith was required to guarantee that his work was good before he gave it to his customer. One such guarantee reads as follows: "As to the gold ring set with an emerald, we guarantee that for twenty years the emerald will not fall out." If it did, the goldsmith promised to pay a fine. Then, too, there were carpenters, carvers in ivory, porcelain makers, and in fact, just the same kind of craftsmen as we have today. Only there was no machinery, all these workers produced everything entirely by hand, and the articles were generally bought straight from the person who had made them.

As well as craftsmen there were men following many different professions: there were scribes, who were authors; doctors, whose prescriptions were largely mixed up with strange superstitions; bankers and money lenders; and musicians who played a variety of instruments, drums, trumpets, lyres, harps, pipes and cymbals.

Nebuchadnezzar was the King who had made Babylon so prosperous, and he was very proud of it: "Is not this great Babylon," he said, "which I have built for the house of the kingdom, by the might of my power, and the glory of my majesty!"

From Book of the Ancient World
By Dorothy Mills

The Gods of Ancient Babylon

The gods of Babylon were the same as those of Assyria, and both these nations were very superstitious, especially the Babylonian. In the most ancient times of all they had a great many different gods, but after a while, though the others were still worshipped, some became more important than the others. Marduk was the Creator, and Ea was the Spirit of the Water. The gods of the Babylonians were not the kindly gods of the Egyptians, but beings who were supposed to be always wanting to harm men. Ea was an exception. The sea brought intercourse and trade with other lands to Babylon and helped to make her rich, and so Ea was looked upon as the god who delighted in doing good to mankind, and who brought well-being to the world.

But in addition to these chief gods, the Babylonians believed in countless spirits, most of them evil, and on the watch to attack and torment men. One of the chief of these was the Spirit of the South West Wind, a fearful creature who brought disease and death and was a great terror to the popular imagination. It was said of these evil spirits that "door cannot shut them out, nor bolt prevent them from entering; they glide like serpents beneath the door, and creep through the joints of hinges like a puff of wind." To avoid the wicked tricks of these bad spirits, the Babylonians used charms and magic. They dreaded demons in the water they drank, and in the food they ate, so charms had to be learned and recited in order to make them harmless; they thought that sickness, and especially madness was due to evil spirits, so the wise man or magician was called in at such times to drive away the disease. They poured water over the sick, person, and they believed that the number seven had magic powers, so sometimes they bound magic threads seven times round the limbs of the afflicted person. The Babylonians were also so afraid that witches or demons might enter their houses, that they put images to the right and left of the door to scare away any such unwelcome visitors, and these images were so hideous that they would have been enough to frighten away anybody!

All Babylonians believed in the power of the stars, and astrologers, men who gave their lives to the study of the heavens, thought that they could tell the future from the stars, and also the fate and fortune of individuals. The Three Wise Men or Magi, who journeyed from the East to Jerusalem, were probably either Chaldaeans or sages from the still more distant Persia, where the stars were also studied and believed to foretell events. The discovery of a new star, a comet, or an eclipse of the sun, anything strange to them and which they could not understand, was interpreted as having a meaning in connection with some event in the world.

Of course the very superstitious practices were only common amongst the less well-educated Babylonians, the better educated had much nobler ideas about their gods. Hymn to the Moon God, written before the days of Abraham, shows what some of the most ancient people of the land believed.

> Father, long-suffering and full of forgiveness,
> Whose hands uphold the life of all mankind!
> First-born, omnipotent, whose heart is immensity,
> There is none who may fathom it.
> In heaven, who is supreme?
> Thou alone, Thou art supreme.
> On earth, who is supreme?
> Thou alone, Thou art supreme.
> As for Thee, Thy will is made known in heaven,
> And the angels bow their faces.
> As for Thee, Thy will is made known upon earth,
> And the spirits below kiss the ground.

The Babylonians built temples to their gods, but they were of an entirely different form from that of the Egyptian temples. In Babylon, they consisted of towers with a number of stages, each one a little smaller than the one below. Such a temple was called a Ziggurat. The Babylonians had inherited the idea of a Ziggurat from the ancient Sumerians. These people had probably lived in a mountainous region before settling in the plains of the Euphrates, and they thought of "high places" as the dwelling-place of the gods. So when they built their temples, high tower-like structures seemed to them to be the most fitting. The most famous Ziggurat was that in Babylon. It had seven stages, each of which was painted a different color: black, orange, red, gold, pale yellow, deep blue and silver, and each stage was dedicated to a heavenly body: Saturn, Jupiter, Mars, the Sun, Venus, Mercury and the Moon. The shrine of the god was at the top, but it contained no image, this was kept lower down. The statue was of gold, seated on a golden throne and surrounded by altars. The idea in the ancient Hebrew story of the Tower of Babel came from these Babylonian temple towers, for the Hebrews were much influenced by both the Egyptians and the Babylonians. Constant services were held in the temples, and there were many festivals. The seventh day was kept as a day of rest, and there were very strict rules as to what might be done and what was forbidden on that day. No work of any kind might be performed, and there were special rules for the king: he "must not eat flesh cooked at the fire or in the smoke; must not change his clothes; must not put on white garments; must not offer sacrifices; must not drive in his chariot or issue royal decrees." No one might give medicine to the sick on the seventh day.

A great difference between the religion of the Babylonians and that of the Egyptians was that the latter influenced the conduct of men, whereas the former touched it very little. Both religions taught that there was a life after death, but the Egyptians believed that a good man, who had been declared just by Osiris went to heaven, where life was happy, and where the soul wandered blissfully in the Elysian Fields; the Babylonians on the other hand thought that the life they were to lead after death was gloomy and dismal. They called the place to which souls went "The Land of No Return," and there was nothing there but gloom and dreariness. The Goddess of Love once went down into this dismal land in search of one whom she loved, and the old legend which tells the tale gives this description of the land:

> The house of darkness...
> The house men enter, but cannot depart from
> The road men go, but cannot return.
> The house from whose dwellers the light is withdrawn,
> The Place where dust is their food, their nourishment clay.
> The light they behold not, in darkness they dwell.
> They are clothed like birds, all fluttering wings.
> On the door and the gate-posts the dust lieth deep.

Assyria and Babylon were alike in some ways: in their manner of living, their customs and beliefs, their dress, their writing, but the roots of civilization were much stronger and more enduring in Babylon than Assyria, for Assyria originated very little herself, and as we have seen she lived only for war, and destroyed more than she built. But the history of the world is like the working out of a great pattern, in which each nation has its own thread to weave, its own particular color to put in. Sometimes mistakes are made, and it seems as if a part of the pattern must be destroyed in order that a greater advance may be made later. Assyria was this destroying power, but in order to wage her wars, she built roads and made trade routes to and from the countries she conquered, and it was along these routes that later countries carried art and learning and civilization. Assyria herself disappeared quickly and completely, for when about two hundred years later a Greek army passed over the spot that had once been Nineveh, the Greeks never even guessed that beneath their feet was the wreck of one of the proudest cities of the ancient world.

From Book of the Ancient World
By Dorothy Mills

The Babylonian Exile

The carrying away of the Hebrews to Babylon is always spoken of in history as the "Captivity," and it was a sad and sorrowful time for them. They constantly thought of their own land laid waste by the enemy, and in one of the Psalms written at this time, they lament their unhappy state:

> By the rivers of Babylon
> there we sat weeping when we remembered Zion.
> On the poplars in its midst we hung up our harps.
> For there our captors asked us for the words of a song;
> Our tormentors, for joy:
> "Sing for us a song of Zion!"
> But how could we sing a song of the LORD in a foreign land?
>
> *Psalm 137*

But on the whole the Hebrews do not seem to have been badly treated in Babylon. They "built houses and planted gardens," and life was bearable. The land was described by a Hebrew writer of the time as "a land of traffic, a city of merchants, a fruitful soil, and beside many waters." As long as they paid the tax demanded by the King, and kept the law, they were allowed to rule their own community, and were like a little Jewish kingdom in the midst of Babylon. One of the captives, Daniel, even rose to a high position in the kingdom.

The Hebrews learned a great deal from the Babylonians, especially in the way of trading methods, and banking, and they gradually gave up their old agricultural ways. They also learned the importance of keeping better written records. Some of the exiles had been sent to Egypt, and both there and in Babylon they saw how records were kept everywhere, on the temple walls and on obelisks, on clay tablets and on papyrus rolls. From this time onwards they began to be much more systematic in the way in which they kept their own records, and they began to put together what is now part of the Old Testament.

Still, the nation had been destroyed, the Temple was in ruins, and no sacrifices could be offered in a foreign land.

FROM BOOK OF THE ANCIENT WORLD
By Dorothy Mills

NEBUCHADNEZZAR

More than a thousand years after the death of Hammurabi, a very great king was ruling in Babylon. His name was Nebuchadnezzar, and he was the most important king of the later Babylonians who were also known as Chaldeans. Under him, Babylon became a very great empire. He waged great wars, after one of which he conquered the Hebrews and carried them away captive to Babylon. But he also found time to beautify the city. He built temples, and leading from one of these to his palace he made a long avenue which passed through the Ishtar Gate (Ishtar was the goddess of the Evening Star to whom it was dedicated), and the walls on each side of the avenue were covered with sculptured lions. There were probably about a hundred and twenty of them: some of them were white with yellow manes, others were yellow with red manes, and the background was blue. Nebuchadnezzar also built massive walls round the city to protect it, and he laid out beautiful gardens and pleasure places. The most celebrated were those known as the "Hanging Gardens." These were really platforms built up on tiers of arches and covered with earth. Flowers and vines and shrubs grew in these gardens, and they were considered so wonderful, that they were known as one of the Seven Wonders of the World. It is said that Nebuchadnezzar had these gardens built to look like a mountain in order to please his queen. She was a princess who had lived amongst the mountains of Media and missed the hills of her home.

But Nebuchadnezzar was followed by Belshazzar, who was a weak king. He was betrayed by traitors in the city, and Babylon was taken by Cyrus, King of Persia. The night before this happened, Belshazzar gave a great feast to the nobles of the land. At this feast, the gold and silver vessels which Nebuchadnezzar had taken from Jerusalem were brought out, and the Babylonians drank wine from them. In one of the Hebrew writings, the story is told of how a strange writing on the wall appeared as a warning to Belshazzar of what was about to happen to him. This feast was probably the last revel before the attack of the Persians and the defeat of the Babylonians, and in that night Belshazzar the King was slain, and the Persian became lord of the land.

ANCIENT GREECE

FROM ANECDOTES AND EXAMPLES FOR THE CATECHISM
By Rev. Francis Spirago

CROESUS AND SOLON

Solon, one of the sages of antiquity, once paid a visit to King Croesus, the wealthy Asiatic monarch, who exhibited all his treasures to him, and afterwards asked him, "Am I not the richest and most fortunate man in the whole world?" Solon replied, "Call no man happy before he is dead." By this he intended to signify that the king might lose all his immense possessions before his death. And so it came to pass. Soon after the visit of the sage, Croesus entered upon a war with Cyrus, the king of Persia. First of all he sent to the oracle of Delphi, to inquire whether he would conquer. The answer of the oracle was, as usual, ambiguous. "If Croesus crosses the river Halys, he will overthrow a vast kingdom." Croesus interpreted this saying in his own favor, and boldly crossed the river in question. He was defeated by Cyrus and taken prisoner. The conqueror condemned him to be burned upon a funeral pile. When Croesus was bound to the stake, he exclaimed, "Solon, Solon, Solon!" Cyrus heard this, and wondering what the exclamation signified, he caused his captive to be unbound and brought to him. He asked him why he called on the name of Solon, and Croesus related the conversation he had had with the sage. King Cyrus thought in his heart that the same might happen in his own case, and thereupon spared Croesus' life and let him go free. Let no one pride himself on the amount of his wealth and the extent of his possessions, for he may at any moment lose them.

FROM FIFTY FAMOUS PEOPLE
By James Baldwin

The General and the Fox

There was once a famous Greek general whose name was Aristomenes. He was brave and wise; and his countrymen loved him.

Once, however, in a great battle with the Spartans, his army was beaten and he was taken prisoner.

In those days, people had not learned to be kind to their enemies. In war, they were savage and cruel; for war always makes men so.

The Spartans hated Aristomenes. He had given them a great deal of trouble, and they wished to destroy him.

On a mountain near their city, there was a narrow chasm or hole in the rocks. It was very deep, and there was no way to climb out of it.

The Spartans said to one another, "Let us throw this fellow into the rocky chasm. Then we may be sure that he will never trouble us again."

So a party of soldiers led him up into the mountain and placed him on the edge of the yawning hole in the rocks. "See the place to which we send all our enemies," they said. And they threw him in.

No one knows how he escaped being dashed to pieces. Some of the Greeks said that an eagle caught him in her beak and carried him unharmed to the bottom. But that is not likely.

I think that he must have fallen upon some bushes and vines that grew in some parts of the chasm. At any rate he was not hurt much.

He groped around in the dim light, but could not find any way of escape. The rocky walls surrounded him on every side. There was no place where he could set his foot to climb out.

For three days, he lay in his strange prison. He grew weak from hunger and thirst. He expected to die from starvation.

Suddenly he was startled by a noise close by him. Something was moving among the rocks at the bottom of the chasm. He watched quietly, and soon saw a large fox coming towards him.

He lay quite still till the animal was very near. Then he sprang up quickly and seized it by the tail.

The frightened fox scampered away as fast as it could; and Aristomenes followed, clinging to its tail. It ran into a narrow cleft which he had not seen before, and then through a long, dark passage which was barely large enough for a man's body.

Aristomenes held on. At last, he saw a ray of light far ahead of him. It was the sunlight streaming in at the entrance to the passage. But soon the way became too narrow for his body to pass through. What should he do? He let go of the fox, and it ran out. Then with great labor, he began to widen the passageway. Here the rocks were smaller, and he soon loosened them enough to allow him to squeeze through. In a short time he was free and in the open air.

Some days after this the Spartans heard strange news: "Aristomenes is again at the head of the Greek army." They could not believe it.

FROM FIFTY FAMOUS STORIES RETOLD
BY JAMES BALDWIN

THE SWORD OF DAMOCLES

There was once a king whose name was Dionysius. He was so unjust and cruel that he won for himself the name of tyrant. He knew that almost everybody hated him, and so he was always in dread lest someone should take his life.

But he was very rich, and he lived in a fine palace where there were many beautiful and costly things, and he was waited upon by a host of servants who were always ready to do his bidding. One day a friend of his, whose name was Damocles, said to him,—

"How happy you must be! You have here everything that any man could wish."

"Perhaps you would like to change places with me," said the tyrant.

"No, not that, O king!" said Damocles," but I think, that, if I could only have your riches and your pleasures for one day, I should not want any greater happiness."

"Very well," said the tyrant. "You shall have them."

And so, the next day, Damocles was led into the palace, and all the servants were bidden to treat him as their master. He sat down at a table in the banquet hall, and rich foods were placed before him. Nothing was wanting that could give him pleasure. There were costly wines, and beautiful flowers, and rare perfumes, and delightful music. He rested himself among soft cushions, and felt that he was the happiest man in all the world.

Then he chanced to raise his eyes toward the ceiling. What was it that was dangling above him, with its point almost touching his head? It was a sharp sword, and it was hung by only a single horse-hair. What if the hair should break? There was danger every moment that it would do so.

The smile faded from the lips of Damocles. His face became ashy pale. His hands trembled. He wanted no more food; he could drink no more wine; he took no more delight in the music. He longed to be out of the palace, and away, he cared not where.

"What is the matter?" said the tyrant.

"That sword! That sword!" cried Damocles. He was so badly frightened that he dared not move.

"Yes," said Dionysius, "I know there is a sword above your head, and that it may fall at any moment. But why should that trouble you? I have a sword over my head all the time. I am every moment in dread lest something may cause me to lose my life."

"Let me go," said Damocles. "I now see that I was mistaken, and that the rich and powerful are not so happy as they seem. Let me go back to my old home in the poor little cottage among the mountains."

And so long as he lived, he never again wanted to be rich, or to change places, even for a moment, with the king.

OLD WORLD HERO STORIES
Eva March Tappan

SOLON, WHO MADE LAWS FOR THE ATHENIANS

A certain young Athenian named Solon expected to inherit a large fortune; but when his father died, it was found that he had been so generous to all in need as to leave little property to his son. There were wealthy friends who would have willingly supported Solon, but he preferred to support himself, and he became a merchant. In those times, a merchant not only sold goods, but he went from land to land to purchase them. In this business Solon made himself rich and also saw the customs and became familiar with the laws of many countries. People said that he was always eager to learn and that he liked to write poetry. He was a most devoted father. When one of his children died, he wept as if his heart would break. A friend who tried to comfort him pleaded with him not to weep, because it would do no good. "And that is just why I do weep," Solon replied.

At that time, the Athenians were divided into parties, and the members of each party thought far more of having their own way than of acting for the good of the state. Athens became so weak that even the tiny kingdom of Megara ventured to make war against her, and got possession of the island of Salamis, and, what was more, held on to it in spite of the efforts of the Athenians to win it back. At length they gave up all hope of ever regaining it. They even passed a decree that anyone who should suggest making the attempt should be looked upon as an enemy to his country and should be put to death.

Now Salamis was Solon's birthplace, and he could not bear to have it in the hands of enemies. The way he set about regaining it, however, was to shut himself up in his house and send out a report that he had become insane. In reality, he was writing a poem; and when it was done, he sallied forth into the marketplace, always full of people, and mounted the stone from which proclamations were made. There he stood and recited the poem. It was a ringing appeal to his countrymen to recover the island. An insane man could not be put to death for breaking a law; and this poem so aroused the Athenians that they repealed the law, set out for war, put Solon in command, and regained the island.

In another way, Solon was of great help to his countrymen. The Athenian, Cylon, and his friends had raised a revolt and had seized the temple of the goddess Minerva. The magistrates told them that if they would tie a cord to the shrine of the goddess and keep fast hold of it, they would still be under her protection and might come down from the temple and be sure of a fair trial. It chanced that the cord gave way; and at this the magistrates rushed upon them and killed them. Some of the Athenians believed that the many troubles of the state had come upon it because of this broken promise, and they were most grateful to Solon when he induced the magistrates to come to trial. The people of Megara took advantage of the difficulties of the Athenians and seized Salamis again. There is no knowing when the struggle over the island would have come to an end, had not both states finally agreed to leave the decision to five judges appointed by the Spartans. Then each side pleaded its right to Salamis. Solon was the chief speaker for the Athenians. He could reason and argue as well as fight; and he won the victory. Salamis was given to Athens.

Solon now became a maker of laws. No two parties wanted exactly the same thing. Taking the people as a whole, the only change desired by the rich was to be better protected in enjoying their wealth; while the poor thought that all wealth ought to be equally divided among the citizens, whether they had ever done anything to earn it or not. These different classes all had confidence in Solon; and he was chosen archon, or chief magistrate. The men who owned little farms were in the most pressing trouble. If a hard season had made it necessary for a farmer to borrow some money, he had to give so high a rate of interest that there was small hope of his debt ever being paid. In that case, his creditor had a legal right to sell him as a slave. Solon's first laws were made to help these farmers. He allowed them to pay their debts to individuals in coins only three fourths as heavy as the old ones, but counted as of the same value. He forgave all debts of farmers to the state. He decreed that no man should be made a slave because he failed to pay borrowed money; that whoever had seized a man as a slave should set him free, and if he had been sold into a foreign country, should bring him back.

Solon's next reform was in regard to the manner of making the laws. Thus far, they had been made by the nobles, that is, the men of high birth. Solon divided the people into four classes according to their income from land. The wealthiest class alone were to hold the highest offices; but they had to pay the most taxes. The lowest class could hold no office in the state, as they paid no taxes for its support; but every man could rise from one class to another, and every man, rich or poor, had the right to vote in the general assembly.

Solon did not forget to look out for the interests of the children. He forbade people to sell their children as slaves, a thing which had formerly been allowed; and he ordered that every father should teach his son a trade. If he neglected to do this, the law did not oblige the son to care for him in his old age.

The laws to punish crime had been put in shape by Draco about a quarter of a century earlier. They were so severe that they were said to have been written in blood. Even the smallest theft was punished by death. Solon revised them and made them far more reasonable. Then he turned his attention to some of the ways in which money was wasted. He decreed that less should be expended in display at funerals, that not more than three garments should be buried with the body, that there should be no sacrifice of an ox and no hired mourners. A woman going on a journey was permitted to carry only three dresses.

The laws of Solon were written on wooden tablets and set up in places where everyone could read them. There is a tradition that he began to put them into verse, but gave up the attempt. Everyone did read them; and promptly one and all began to find fault. The wealthy nobles had lost a great deal of money by the remitting of debts and the freeing of slaves; and they were indignant that so great a share in the government had also been taken from them. The poor people had supposed that in some mysterious way these changes would make them all rich; and they felt wronged and disappointed. Each little party had its special grievance, and everybody blamed Solon. Besides this, people were constantly appealing to him to know the meaning of one law or another; and at length he concluded that it would be best for him to go away for a while and let the Athenians manage matters for themselves. He made them promise that they would keep his laws for ten years, and then he left the country.

When he returned, he found affairs no better. The people were restless and dissatisfied, and a man named Pisistratus was gaining much influence over them. Pisistratus had a frank, pleasant manner, he was generous, and he had won victories in the Olympian chariot-races. He claimed to be a devoted friend to the poor, and made them feel that if he were only in power, he would do great things for them. One day, with his face smeared with blood, he rode into the market place and declared that his enemies had tried to kill him for being so devoted to the interests of the poor. Pisistratus was a relative of Solon, but the honest old patriot could not endure this, and he cried out, "Pisistratus, you have done this thing to impose upon your countrymen." Nevertheless, the people believed in Pisistratus and allowed him to have a guard of armed men. This guard grew larger and larger, and by and by this "friend of the people" captured the Acropolis, that is, the hill on which stood the finest temples and the strongest fortifications; and Pisistratus was now ruler of Athens. Solon could do nothing to prevent this, and he put his weapons outside his door with these words: "I have done all in my power to defend my country and its laws."

After it was clear that Pisistratus would be able to remain in control, the friends of Solon were afraid of what he might do to the aged man to punish him for his opposition. They begged Solon to flee; but he refused. He stayed in his own house and made verses to the effect that whatever difficulties the Athenians might fall into, it was all their own fault.

Most men of that time, if in the place of Pisistratus, would have at least made Solon's life uncomfortable; but Pisistratus was too wise, and perhaps too good-natured. He always treated Solon with the greatest kindness and respect, asked his advice, and what was more, generally followed it. Solon believed that Pisistratus had no right to rule and that the Athenians would yet be sorry that they had allowed him to seize the government; but since he was in power and could not be put out, Solon thought that the best thing he could do for his state was to help make his rule as excellent as possible. This was the easier for Solon because Pisistratus really ruled extremely well. He gave cattle and seeds and tolls to the poor farmers; he built handsome buildings; and, besides this, he invited all the people who knew the poems of Homer and Hesiod by heart to come together in Athens and compare them as they had been used to reciting them. Then he had copies carefully made of the version that was decided to be the best. That is how it came to pass that we have the poems of these two great poets in almost the same words in which they were composed. Solon always loved Salamis, and when he came to die, he bade his friends carry his ashes across the water and scatter them over his beloved island.

FIFTY FAMOUS PEOPLE
By James Baldwin

A CLEVER SLAVE: A STORY ABOUT AESOP

A long time ago there lived a poor slave whose name was Aesop. He was a small man with a large head and long arms. His face was white, but very homely. His large eyes were bright and snappy.

When Aesop was about twenty years old, his master lost a great deal of money and was obliged to sell his slaves. To do this, he had to take them to a large city where there was a slave market.

The city was far away, and the slaves must walk the whole distance. A number of bundles were made up for them to carry. Some of these bundles contained the things they would need on the road; some contained clothing; and some contained goods which the master would sell in the city.

"Choose your bundles, boys," said the master. "There is one for each of you."

Aesop at once chose the largest one. The other slaves laughed and said he was foolish. But he threw it upon his shoulders and seemed well satisfied. The next day, the laugh was the other way. For the bundle that he had chosen had contained the food for the whole party. After all had eaten three meals from it, it was very much lighter. And before the end of the journey Aesop had nothing to carry, while the other slaves were groaning under their heavy loads.

"Aesop is a wise fellow," said his master. "The man who buys him must pay a high price."

A very rich man, whose name was Xanthus, came to the slave market to buy a servant. As the slaves stood before him he asked each one to tell what kind of work he could do. All were eager to be bought by Xanthus because they knew he would be a kind master. So each one boasted of his skill in doing some sort of labor. One was a fine gardener; another could take care of horses; a third was a good cook; a fourth could manage a household.

"And what can you do, Aesop?" asked Xanthus.

"Nothing," he answered.

"Nothing? How is that?"

"Because, since these other slaves do everything, there is nothing left for me to perform," said Aesop.

This answer pleased the rich man so well that he bought Aesop at once, and took him to his home on the island of Samos.

In Samos the little slave soon became known for his wisdom and courage. He often amused his master and his master's friends by telling droll fables about birds and beasts that could talk. They saw that all these fables taught some great truth, and they wondered how Aesop could have thought of them.

Many other stories are told of this wonderful slave. His master was so much pleased with him that he gave him his freedom. Many great men were glad to call him their friend, and even kings asked his advice and were amused by his fables.

From The Baby's Own Aesop
By Aesop and Walter Crane

The Fox & the Grapes

This Fox has a longing for grapes,
He jumps, but the bunch still escapes.
So he goes away sour;
And, 'tis said, to this hour
Declares that he's no taste for grapes.

THE GRAPES OF DISAPPOINTMENT ARE ALWAYS SOUR

THE COCK & THE PEARL

A rooster, while scratching for grain,
Found a Pearl. He just paused to explain
That a jewel's no good
To a fowl wanting food,
And then kicked it aside with disdain.

IF HE ASK BREAD WILL YE GIVE HIM A STONE?

THE WOLF AND THE LAMB

A wolf, wanting lamb for his dinner,
Growled out—"Lamb you wronged me, you sinner."
Bleated Lamb—"Nay, not true!"
Answered Wolf—"Then 'twas Ewe—
Ewe or lamb, you will serve for my dinner."

FRAUD AND VIOLENCE HAVE NO SCRUPLES

THE FRIGHTENED LION

A Bull Frog, according to rule,
Sat a-croak in his usual pool:
And he laughed in his heart
As a Lion did start
In a fright from the brink like a fool.

IMAGINARY FEARS ARE THE WORST

THE MOUSE & THE LION

A poor thing the Mouse was, and yet,
When the Lion got caught in a net,
All his strength was no use
'Twas the poor little Mouse
Who nibbled him out of the net.

SMALL CAUSES MAY PRODUCE GREAT RESULTS

THE LAZY HOUSEMAIDS

Two Maids killed the Rooster whose warning
Awoke them too soon every morning:
But small were their gains,
For their Mistress took pains
To rouse them herself without warning.

LAZINESS IS ITS OWN PUNISHMENT

THE FOX & THE CROW

Said sly Fox to the Crow with the cheese,
"Let me hear your sweet voice, now do please!"
And this Crow, being weak,
Cawed the bit from her beak—
"Music charms," said the Fox, "and here's cheese!"

BEWARE OF FLATTERERS

THE FOX & THE CRANE

You have heard how Sir Fox treated Crane:
With soup in a plate. When again
They dined, a long bottle
Just suited Crane's throttle;
And Sir Fox licked the outside in vain.

THERE ARE GAMES THAT TWO CAN PLAY AT

THE FOX & THE MOSQUITOES

Being plagued with Mosquitoes one day,
Said old Fox, "pray don't send them away,
For a hungrier swarm
Would work me more harm;
I had rather the full ones should stay."

THERE WERE POLITICIANS IN AESOP'S TIME

THE FOX & THE LION

The first time the Fox had a sight
Of the Lion, he 'most died of fright;
When he next met his eye,
Fox felt just a bit shy;
But the next—quite at ease, & polite.

FAMILIARITY DESTROYS FEAR

The Man That Pleased None

Through the town this good Man & his Son
Strove to ride as to please everyone:
Self, Son, or both tried,
Then the Ass had a ride;
While the world, at their efforts, poked fun.

YOU CANNOT HOPE TO PLEASE ALL—DON'T TRY

The Oak & The Reeds

Giant Oak, in his strength & his scorn
Of the winds, by the roots was uptorn:
But slim Reeds at his side,
The fierce gale did outride,
Since, by bending the burden was borne.

BEND, NOT BREAK

The Fir & the Bramble

The Fir-tree looked down on the Bramble.
"Poor thing, only able to scramble
About on the ground."
Just then an axe' sound
Made the Fir wish himself but a Bramble.

PRIDE OF PLACE HAS ITS DISADVANTAGES

THE BOASTER

In the house, in the market, the streets,
Everywhere he was boasting his feats;
Till one said, with a sneer,
"Let us see it done here!
What's so oft done with ease, one repeats."

DEEDS NOT WORDS

THE PEACOCK'S COMPLAINT

The Peacock considered it wrong
That he had not the nightingale's song;
So to Juno he went,
She replied, "Be content
With thy having, & hold thy fool's tongue!"

DO NOT QUARREL WITH NATURE

BROTHER & SISTER

Twin children: the Girl, she was plain;
The Brother was handsome & vain;
"Let him brag of his looks,"
Father said; "mind your books!
The best beauty is bred in the brain."

HANDSOME IS AS HANDSOME DOES

The Dog & the Shadow

His image the Dog did not know,
Or his bone's, in the pond's painted show:
"T'other dog," so he thought
"Has got more than he ought,"
So he snapped, & his dinner saw go!

GREED IS SOMETIMES CAUGHT BY ITS OWN BAIT

The Crow & the Pitcher

How the cunning old Crow got his drink
When 'twas low in the pitcher, just think!
Don't say that he spilled it!
With pebbles he filled it,
Till the water rose up to the brink.

USE YOUR WITS

The Hen and the Fox

The Hen roosted high on her perch;
Hungry Fox down below, on the search,
Coaxed her hard to descend
She replied, "Most dear friend!
I feel more secure on my perch."

BEWARE OF INTERESTED FRIENDSHIPS

THE HARE AND THE TORTOISE

'Twas a race between Tortoise and Hare,
Puss was sure she'd so much time to spare,
That she lay down to sleep,
And let old Thick-shell creep
To the winning post first!—You may stare.

PERSISTENCE BEATS IMPULSE

THE BEAR & THE BEES

"Their honey I'll have when I please;
Who cares for such small things as Bees?"
Said the Bear; but the stings
Of these very small things
Left him not very much at his ease.

THE WEAKEST UNITED MAY BE STRONG TO AVENGE

THE BUNDLE OF STICKS

To his sons, who fell out, father spake:
"This Bundle of Sticks you can't break;
Take them singly, with ease,
You may break as you please,
So, dissension your strength will unmake."

STRENGTH IS IN UNITY

THE FARMER'S TREASURE

"Dig deeply, my Sons! through this field!
There's a Treasure"—he died: unrevealed
The spot where 'twas laid,
They dug as he bade;
And the Treasure was found in the yield.

PRODUCTIVE LABOUR IS THE ONLY SOURCE OF WEALTH

Unit Nine:
The Return

Theme: Responding to God's Grace

From The Book of the Ancient World
by Dorothy Mills

The Return

When Cyrus, King of Persia, conquered Babylon, he allowed the Hebrews whom he found there to return home to Jerusalem and to begin to rebuild the temple. This took place under the leadership of Ezra and Nehemiah. The rebuilding of the Temple was of great importance to the Hebrews, for though they were not an independent kingdom, yet they had once more a common meeting place in their ancient sanctuary. It had also an importance for the world. The Hebrews never regained political independence, but from this time onward they were all members of the Jewish Church, and they were now called Jews more often than Hebrews. In the centuries following their return to Jerusalem they completed their history, they wrote down their law, and they recorded their great religious experiences. They were always hoping for a political deliverer who would free them from foreign rule; in reality they were unconsciously preparing the way for a spiritual deliverer who would set them free from bondage to the letter of the law.

The rebuilding of the Temple also inspired poets to express their feelings and thoughts in verse and hymns, and to collect the ancient poetry of the nation. In this way the book of Psalms, as we know it, began. It consists of a number of smaller collections written at different times and by different poets, a few of which were from very ancient collections that tradition had always associated with the name of David.

The Story of Cyrus the Great

The Medes first became important in history at the time when the Assyrian empire was destroyed, for it was they who helped the Babylonians to burn Nineveh. The chief city of the King of the Medes was Ecbatana, a name meaning "the meeting place of many roads." It stood in fertile plain, where there were roads in all directions to Babylon, Assyria and Persia. It was a very ancient city and Herodotus tells us that the walls protecting it were arranged in seven circles, with each battlement rising higher than the last and colored differently: white, black, red, blue, orange, silver and gold. Later, when the Medes had been conquered by Persia, the great kings made Ecbatana their summer residence. It was there that the treasure of Croesus was brought by Cyrus, and that the decree allowing the Hebrews to return to Jerusalem was found.

After the fall of Assyria the Medes ruled the northern part of what had once been Assyria, until in their turn they were conquered by the Persians, their own kinsfolk. Herodotus gives the old tradition of how it came about.

A King of the Medes once had a dream, in which he saw a vine springing from his daughter and overshadowing all Asia. Like the Pharaoh and Belshazzar he believed in dreams, and so he sent for his wise men, who told him that his dream meant that his daughter's son would one day rule in his place. This Median princess had married a Persian prince, and so the King of the Medes became very jealous and angry. To prevent his grandson ever usurping his throne, he sent for one of his trusted ministers, and ordered him to take the baby out on the mountains to die. The minister, however, was afraid that one day the King might repent of this cruel deed and would try to hold him responsible. So he gave the baby to a cowherd, telling him to kill the child. Now the baby of the cowherd and his wife had died that very day, and so the mother begged her husband to let her keep the little prince and to leave the body of their baby out on the mountainside in his stead. This was done, and the prince grew up in the cowherd's hut as his son. When he was older, he became very popular with all the boys in the neighborhood and they often played together. A favorite game was to choose one of their number as king of the rest, and to have him rule for a day.

One day, Cyrus, as the prince was called, was chosen king. One of the boys refused to do his bidding, so Cyrus ordered him to be beaten. This boy had a rich and important father, who was so angry that a cowherd should have dared to have his son beaten, that he actually complained to the King about it. Cyrus was sent for, and when asked why he had acted in that way, he said:

> O King, what I did, I did to him justly. The boys in the village and this one among them, chose me as their king in play, because they thought me best suited for the honor. All the other boys performed their tasks, but this one was disobedient and paid no heed to my command, and that is why he was punished. Now if for this crime I deserve chastisement, here I am.

This answer pleased the King, and he began to make enquiries about the boy, and he found out what had happened and that he was his grandson. He asked his wise men if it would be safe to allow the boy to live, and they decided that the dream had already been fulfilled, because Cyrus had reigned as king, even if only in play over the other boys, so Cyrus was allowed to live.

But the King of the Medes, though he was glad that his grandson was alive, was so angry at having been disobeyed by his minister, that he ordered his son to be killed as a punishment. From that time on, the minister was always planning how he might destroy the King, and when Cyrus was a man and had become King of Persia, he planned a pretence of war between the Medes and Persians, but when the time of battle arrived, he gave up his whole army into the hands of Cyrus. In this way Cyrus became King of the Medes as well as of Persia. He treated his grandfather kindly, however, and allowed him to live in his palace until his death, but all his power was taken from him.

Such is the story, as it was believed in ancient times, of how Cyrus became King.

From Fifty Famous People
By James Baldwin

The Young Cupbearer

Long, long ago, there lived in Persia a little prince whose name was Cyrus. He was not petted and spoiled like many other princes. Although his father was a king, Cyrus was brought up like the son of a common man.

He knew how to work with his hands. He ate only the plainest food. He slept on a hard bed. He learned to endure hunger and cold.

When Cyrus was twelve years old he went with his mother to Media to visit his grandfather. His grandfather, whose name was Astyages, was king of Media, and very rich and powerful.

Cyrus was so tall and strong and handsome that his grandfather was very proud of him. He wished the lad to stay with him in Media. He therefore gave him many beautiful gifts and everything that could please a prince. One day King Astyages planned to make a great feast for the lad. The tables were to be laden with all kinds of food. There was to be music and dancing; and Cyrus was to invite as many guests as he chose. The hour for the feast came. Everything was ready. The servants were there, dressed in fine uniforms. The musicians and dancers were in their places. But no guests came.

"How is this, my dear boy?" asked the king. "The feast is ready, but no one has come to partake of it."

"That is because I have not invited any one," said Cyrus. "In Persia we do not have such feasts. If anyone is hungry, he eats some bread and meat, with perhaps a few cresses, and that is the end of it. We never go to all this trouble and expense of making a fine dinner in order that our friends may eat what is not good for them."

King Astyages did not know whether to be pleased or displeased.

"Well," said he, "all these rich foods that were prepared for the feast are yours. What will you do with them?"

"I think I will give them to our friends," said Cyrus.

So he gave one portion to the king's officer who had taught him to ride. Another portion he gave to an old servant who waited upon his grandfather. And the rest he divided among the young women who took care of his mother.

The king's cupbearer, Sarcas, was very much offended because he was not given a share of the feast. The king also wondered why this man, who was his favorite, should be so slighted.

"Why didn't you give something to Sarcas?" he asked.

"Well, truly," said Cyrus, "I do not like him. He is proud and overbearing. He thinks that he makes a fine figure when he waits on you."

"And so he does," said the king. "He is very skillful as a cupbearer."

"That may be so," answered Cyrus, "but if you will let me be your cupbearer tomorrow, I think I can serve you quite as well."

King Astyages smiled. He saw that Cyrus had a will of his own, and this pleased him very much.

"I shall be glad to see what you can do," he said. "Tomorrow, you shall be the king's cupbearer."

You would hardly have known the young prince when the time came for him to appear before his grandfather. He was dressed in the rich uniform of the cupbearer, and he came forward with much dignity and grace.

He carried a white napkin upon his arm, and held the cup of wine very daintily with three of his fingers.

His manners were perfect. Sarcas himself could not have served the king half so well.

"Bravo! bravo!" cried his mother, her eyes sparkling with pride.

"You have done well" said his grandfather. "But you neglected one important thing. It is the rule and custom of the cupbearer to pour out a little of the wine and taste it before handing the cup to me. This you forgot to do."

"Indeed, grandfather, I did not forget it," answered Cyrus.

"Then why didn't you do it?" asked his mother.

"Because I believed there was poison in the wine."

"Poison, my boy!" cried King Astyages, much alarmed. "Poison! poison!"

"Yes, grandfather, poison. For the other day, when you sat at dinner with your officers, I noticed that the wine made you act queerly. After the guests had drunk quite a little of it, they began to talk foolishly and sing loudly; and some of them went to sleep. And you, grandfather, were as bad as the rest. You forgot that you were king. You forgot all your good manners. You tried to dance and fell upon the floor. I am afraid to drink anything that makes men act in that way."

"Didn't you ever see your father behave so?" asked the king.

"No, never," said Cyrus. "He does not drink merely to be drinking. He drinks to quench his thirst, and that is all."

When Cyrus became a man, he succeeded his father as king of Persia; he also succeeded his grandfather Astyages as king of Media. He was a very wise and powerful ruler, and he made his country the greatest of any that was then known. In history, he is commonly called Cyrus the Great.

FROM THE BOOK OF THE ANCIENT WORLD
By Dorothy Mills

THE GREAT KINGS OF PERSIA

The King of Persia was always called the "Great King," and Cyrus was the first who made Persia into a great empire. He made the army strong and powerful, and then set out to conquer more land for Persia.

At this time the chief state in Asia Minor was Lydia, the name of whose King, Croesus, has become famous for all time on account of his enormous wealth. His capital was at Sardis, and it was not only filled with his treasure, but scholars and artists from far and near were invited and welcomed there, and the fame of Croesus spread all over Asia Minor. He developed the trade and commerce of his kingdom, and as far as is known the earliest coins of which we have historical record, came from Lydia.

The Lydians were famous for their horsemanship and were dreaded by their foes, but there was coming from the East a mightier power, before whom even their celebrated horsemen would fall. Cyrus and his great army came and defeated them, and Lydia was added to the Persian land, and according to the Persian custom was compelled to offer the Great King earth and water as a token of submission. Then the Greek cities on the coast fell, until at last all Asia Minor called Cyrus King. But he was not yet content, and in 540 B.C. Babylon fell before his conquering army, and Persia was an Empire.

Cyrus was both a good general and a wise statesman. He did not try to force those whom he had conquered to obey him by crushing and oppressing them, he endeavored to secure their loyalty by acts of kindness. He rebuilt the walls of Babylon and restored the temples, and he treated all his subjects in the same way. In one of his inscriptions he says: "The gods whose sanctuaries from of old had lain in ruins I brought back again to their dwelling places and caused them to reside there forever. All the citizens of these lands I assembled and I restored them to their homes." Wherever it was possible, Cyrus allowed native princes to rule over the different parts of his empire, and in all that he did he showed the mind of a great statesman.

Cyrus was one of the great hero figures of the ancient world. His good looks, his courage and his fine statesmanship made him looked up to as the ideal king, and in the next century a Greek writer wrote of him in a way that was perhaps exaggerated, but which gives us some idea of the great extent of his influence. The men of the ancient world were always more ready to be influenced by a great leader than by an idea, and Cyrus was just such a leader, and in his ideals he stands far above most of the other rulers of his time.

His tomb can still be seen, though it was plundered in ancient times and now stands empty. His body was placed in a gilt coffin which rested on a couch with golden feet and was covered with rich purple tapestries, and the walls of the tomb were hung with tapestry from Babylon. In the chamber there were rich suits of clothes and weapons and jewels, and the King's own shield and sword and bow. A very simple inscription told who was buried there. It ran: "O man, I am Cyrus, who founded the greatness of Persia and ruled Asia. Grudge me not this monument."

From The Chosen People
By Charlotte Yonge

The Return to Jerusalem

When Cyrus was about forty years old one of the kings in Asia Minor made war on him, and he not only overthrew this monarch, but won that whole country, which was kept by the Persians for many years. Afterwards, he marched against Assyria, which had insulted him. He beat Belshazzar in battle, and then besieged him in his city; but the Babylonians had no fears; they trusted to their walls and brazen gates, and knew that he could not starve them out, as they had so much corn growing within the walls. For two years, they remained in security, and laughed at the Persian army outside; but at last, Cyrus devised a new plan, and set his men to dig trenches to draw off the water of the Euphrates, and leave the bed of the river dry. Still there were the great gates upon the river, which he expected to have to break down; but on the very day his trenches were ready, Belshazzar was giving a great feast in his palace, and drinking wine out of the golden vessels that Nebuchadnezzar had brought from the Temple.

In the midst of his revelry a strange sight appeared. Near the seven-branched Candlestick that once had burnt in Jerusalem's Holy Place, came forth a bodiless hand, and the fingers wrote upon the wall in characters such as no man knew. The hearts of the revelers failed them for fear, and the king's knees knocked together! Then Nitocris, his mother, a brave and wise woman, remembered all that Daniel had done in the days of Nebuchadnezzar, and at her advice he was called for. He knew the words; they were in the Hebrew tongue, the language of his own Scriptures, the same in which the Finger of God revealed the Commandments. He read them, and they said, "God has numbered your kingdom, and finished it. You are weighed in the balances, and found wanting. Your kingdom is divided, and given to the Medes and Persians!"

At that moment, Cyrus and his Persians were entering by the river gates, which had been left open in that time of careless festivity. One end of the city did not know that the other was taken; and before the night was past Belshazzar lay dead in his palace, and the Assyrian empire was over forever.

It was 170 years since, by the mouth of Isaiah, God had called Cyrus by name. God had said He would give the nations as dust to his sword, and stubble to his bow; had said of him that he was His anointed and His shepherd, and that he would build up the Holy City and Temple, and let the captives go free without money or price. Moreover, it was seventy years since Daniel himself had been carried away from the pleasant land, and well had he counted the weary days prophesied of by Jeremiah; till now he hoped the time was come, and most earnestly he prayed, looking towards Jerusalem, as Solomon had entreated, when his people should turn to God in the land of their captivity, pleading God's goodness and mercy, though admitting that Judah had behaved wickedly. Even while he was yet speaking came the answer by the mouth of the Angel Gabriel; and not only was it the present deliverance that it announced, but that from the building of the street and wall in troubled times, seventy weeks of years were appointed to bring the Anointed, so long promised, the real Deliverer.

Daniel's prayers had won, and the joyful decree was given that Judah should return, build up the city and Temple, and receive back their sacred vessels and treasure from the king, to aid them in their work. Daniel being nearly ninety years old, did not go with them, but remained to protect them at the court of Babylon.

FROM CATECHISM IN EXAMPLES
By Rev. D. Chisholm

EZRA READS THE LAW OF GOD TO THE PEOPLE

In the Old Testament, it is related that when the children of Israel returned from the captivity of Babylon to Jerusalem, Ezra the Scribe assembled the people together, that they might hear the law of God read to them. And when all the people were assembled, Ezra stood upon a high place that he might be seen and heard by the multitude. As soon as he had opened the book, and had begun to read, all the people became silent, and stood up through reverence for the Word of God. And although the reading of the law continued till midday from the early morning, the people listened with attention, and wept with joy, as they heard the Word of God explained to them.

In like manner, my children, whenever you read a holy book, or hear it read to you, imitate the example of these people, and give God thanks for granting you the grace of reading it or of listening to it.

FROM THE BOOK OF THE ANCIENT WORLD
By Dorothy Mills

KING DARIUS

Cyrus was succeeded by his son, who conquered Egypt, and he, in his turn, was followed by another great King, Darius, who added part of India to the Persian Empire, so that the Great King now ruled over an empire which stretched from the river Indus in the East to the Nile in the West. The Persians boasted that "the kingdom extended so far to the South that man cannot live there because of the heat, and Northward to where they cannot exist because of the cold." The world had never seen such an empire before.

The Persians had changed very much from the early days when they were simple shepherd tribes in the mountains. Darius ruled over a well-organized empire. The capital was at Susa, and this great city must have been a wonderful sight as the traveler over the vast plain first caught a glimpse of it with its citadel and palaces, and flourishing marketplace. A great road, called the Royal Road, was built from Susa to Sardis. It was counted as a three months' journey for a man on foot, but the swift mounted eastern messengers could cover the ground in fifteen days. A postal system was organized within the empire and other good roads were made. Darius also made trading easier by a greater use of coins as money, and the gold Daric, accepted everywhere, because of the purity of the metal, became the standard coin of the ancient trading world. This empire was so large that Darius divided it into twenty provinces called Satrapies, and the governor of each was called a Satrap. But this great empire was held together by the will of one man, and not by the loyal allegiance of many parts to one whole, and Darius was always afraid that some of his satraps might be disloyal and raise up a rebellion. To prevent this, royal officials were sent by the King to live at each court, and it was their duty to report anything that seemed suspicious. They were called the "King's Eyes," and the "King's Ears." Darius also built up a navy and Persia became a sea as well as a land power. But the Persian people themselves were not naturally sailors, and the fleet was chiefly made up of the ships of the seafaring nations that had been subdued.

The Persians were not original in their buildings; they had great halls filled with columns such as the Egyptians had built before them; they copied the winged bulls of Assyria, as well as walls of enameled brick. Magnificent palaces were built by Darius and his son Xerxes at Persepolis, parts of which can still be seen. They took other ideas, too, from the Assyrians, they learned from them to be luxurious and so they lost their old simple habits.

Darius ruled over nearly all the world, but he was not content, and when from over the blue Aegean Sea, dotted with islands, there came a band of men who helped a rebellious tribe to burn one of his cities, Darius determined, first, to punish the invaders, and then, hearing how fair was their land, nothing would satisfy him but that he must add it to his empire. But the story of how the Persian met the Greek belongs to the history of Greece rather than to that of Persia, and so that story must be told in another place. Never before in the history of the world had there been so great an empire which required government on so large a scale. The Persians were the first great organizers, but the many nations that made up the empire had no voice in the government. One man alone controlled that mighty empire, and from the North to the South, and from the Nile to India, the word of the Great King was law, the "law of the Medes and Persians that changeth not."

Cyrus and Darius were Great Kings in every sense of the word, and the ancient world had never seen anything like them before. Some of the Pharaohs had been equally magnificent and as great generals, but they had never ruled over so vast an empire made up of so many different nations, and none of them had been governed by ideals such as those which governed Cyrus. But the power of the Great Kings did not last. The Persian empire received its death blow when the Greeks defeated Xerxes, who had succeeded Darius. For though few in numbers, the Greeks were fighting for the cause of freedom, and they prevailed. From that time onwards the Persian power grew less, until at last the Great Kings fell before another conqueror, and Alexander the Great ruled over their land.

FROM THE BOOK OF THE ANCIENT WORLD
By Dorothy Mills

THE STORY OF THE BEHISTUN ROCK

Near the site of the ancient city of Ecbatana, the old capital of the Median kings, on a rocky hillside, are three inscriptions and a great slab of sculpture engraved on the stone. They have been there for centuries, exposed to wind and weather and seemingly out of the reach of man. The modern Persian natives who could not have read them, even if they had clambered up the face of the rock to see them, called them by a word which means "Treasure Story," and there was a legend attached to the strange carvings. It was said that they told the secret of where a great treasure could be found, and that whoever was able to read them should have the treasure. Little did the natives imagine what the treasure was, not one of gold or silver or precious stones, but a key that would open the door to a priceless store of historical records. This treasure was found by an Englishman, Henry Rawlinson, a soldier and a scholar, who scaled the rock and read the inscriptions. It was a perilous undertaking, for they are more than a hundred feet from the ground on the steep side of a rock that is seventeen hundred feet high, and even when the rock was scaled it was a difficult task to make drawings and copy the inscriptions. But it must have been an even more perilous undertaking for the ancient sculptors to have climbed up and to secure a foothold while they carved. This rock is known as the Behistun Rock, and like the Rosetta Stone in Egypt, it gave the key to the deciphering of the old cuneiform writing.

Above the inscriptions is a slab of sculpture on which stands Darius the King, with a bow in his left hand and his right hand raised as he pronounces sentence on nine prisoners who stand before him. Their hands are tied behind them and a rope is round their necks. One prisoner lies prostrate beneath the feet of the King, entreating for mercy, but the King tramples on him ruthlessly. Behind the King stand his quiver-bearer and other attendants, and above him floats the god, Ahuramazda, giving him his blessing and a ring as a token of his kingship.

The inscriptions are written in three scripts, in Persian, in Babylonian cuneiform, and in the form of Babylonian used in Susa. The second and third inscriptions are translations of the first, and as the Persian script had already been deciphered it gave a key to the decipherment of the cuneiform. These inscriptions were put there by Darius on this great rock that can be clearly seen from the caravan route that passes there, so that all travelers might see this record of his triumph over his foes. First the King gives honor to the great god of the Persians, and then he goes on to say that the Great King of Persia is the King of Kings, King of the countries which have many peoples, King of the great earth even to afar. Then he briefly recounts his chief exploits and ends with laying the curse of Ahuramazda on whomsoever should destroy the inscriptions, but promising to those who leave them undisturbed that they shall live long and that the god will be their friend forever.

As time went by the Great Kings lost their power and their empire was broken up, but the tale of the greatness of one of them still stands on the lonely rock where it has stood for more than two thousand years.

From Old World Hero Stories
By Eva March Tappan

Darius of Persia Is Repulsed at Marathon

In the year 522, King Darius was on the Persian throne. He already held all that had belonged to Babylon; he had pushed to the east and conquered northwestern India; he had forced many towns in Thrace and Macedonia to yield to him; and now he was ready to attack Greece. He had a good excuse for making the attack. Some time before this, the Ionians, an ancient name for the people of Athens, had made settlements on the coast of Lydia. These had fallen into the hands of the Persians. In course of time they had revolted against Persia, and the Athenians had helped them. When Darius heard what the Athenians had done, he vowed that he would be revenged upon them, and he gave to a slave the command, "Whenever I seat myself to eat, do you cry aloud thrice, 'O king, remember the Athenians!'"

Darius remembered them. Just as soon as he could make ready, he sent a fleet and an army against them, not very safe in a calm and extremely dangerous in bad weather. Just as the vessels were off Mount Athos, the end of the promontory, a furious storm arose and dashed them upon the rocks. So many ships were destroyed and so many men were drowned that there was nothing for the Persians to do but to call back the army that had been sent by land and return to Persia.

Darius was not the kind of man to give up, and before long he was ready to try again. First, however, he sent envoys to the different states of Greece to demand that they send him earth and water. This was a token of submission. Some of the states yielded, but the Athenians were so indignant that they hurled the envoys into a chasm. The Spartans were quite as regardless of the rights of messengers and threw the envoys sent to them into a well, crying out, "There's your earth and water. Take your fill."

A very angry man was King Darius of Persia. He did not wait for a calm day to sail around Mount Athos, but went straight across the sea to Attica. His troops knew just where to land, for on board of one of the vessels was a Greek named Hippias who knew the country well. He was the son of Pisistratus; and after his father's death, he had become ruler of Athens; but he was so tyrannical that he was driven out of the kingdom. He fled to Persia; and now he thought that if Darius could only conquer Athens, he himself might again become its ruler. Hippias told the Persians to land at the plain of Marathon. It was so wide and level, he said, that it would give plenty of room for using the cavalry.

The Athenian army was commanded by ten generals who took turns in ruling for one day. Five of them wished to engage in battle; the other five did not think this was wise. There was one other person who had a vote, the minister of war. Miltiades, a general who wished to fight, went to him secretly and persuaded him to favor a battle. So it was that the famous battle of Marathon was fought. Miltiades was in command. He drew up his lines in front of the hills at the edge of the plain. The Persians, ten times the number of the Greeks, were on the plain between them and the sea. Off the shore were the ships and the chains in which they planned to carry away the Greeks into captivity. The first charge was a vast surprise to the Persians, for the Greeks dashed upon them with no bowmen and no cavalry for protection. Then the two lines met in deadly conflict. Near the end of the engagement, the Greek wings routed the Persian wings; but the Persian center broke through the Greek center. Then the Greek wings faced about and burst upon the enemy so furiously that the Persians, who had felt so sure of their victory, ran for their lives across the plain and down the slope of the shore. They splashed through the shallow water and clambered into their vessels as if fiends instead of Greeks were after them; but before they could get away, the Greeks had captured seven of their vessels.

The Persians did not give up, but hurried away as fast as their oars could drive them. Not a moment's rest was there for the weary Greeks, for the vessels were pointed toward Athens. The soldiers marched off at full speed; and when the Persians arrived and saw them encamped on a little river close to the city, they went back to their own country.

Sometimes a small battle is far more important than many a large one. The number of men who fought at Marathon was not great; but it was a momentous engagement, because it saved the liberty-loving Greeks from becoming the slaves of the Persians.

All honor was shown to Miltiades and to the minister of war, who had been slain in the battle. Their statues were even placed among those of the gods. It was the custom to bring home for burial the bodies of men who had fallen; but as a mark of special honor the Greeks agreed to bury the heroes of Marathon on the field. Over them were raised two mighty mounds of earth. Stately marble pillars were reared, whereon was written the name of every man, be they commander or slave, who had died in that place to save the freedom of Greece. The pillars have long since disappeared, but the great mounds of earth still remain and are pointed out to everyone who visits the battlefield.

FROM OLD WORLD HERO STORIES
By Eva March Tappan

XERXES OF PERSIA TRIES TO CONQUER GREECE

Xerxes, who followed Darius as king of Persia, would much rather have stayed at home and enjoyed himself; but his counselors insisted that it would never do not to punish those insolent Greeks who had beaten his father's forces at Marathon. When once he had yielded, he set to work with energy to make ready for an invasion. He cut a canal across the promontory of Mount Athos, and he built two bridges of boats across the Hellespont. He put up great storehouses along his proposed line of march and filled them with food. Then he fell into a fury, for a storm had swept away his bridges. Not even the Hellespont had any right to oppose the king of Persia, he thought, and as a punishment for this impertinence he bade his men give the waters three hundred lashes.

The mighty Persian army marched to the Hellespont. A marble throne was built for Xerxes on a hilltop, and there he sat gazing at the hundreds of thousands of men encamped below him. Suddenly he began to weep, because the thought had struck him that a hundred years from then not one of those men would be alive. This was undoubtedly true, but no able commander would have had time to think of it on the eve of an invasion.

On the following day came the crossing of the bridges, and the most superb procession that the world has ever seen. There was Xerxes himself in a magnificent war-chariot, and there was the even more magnificent chariot of the sun-god with its eight white horses. There were the Ten Thousand Immortals, the special guard of the king, who marched gravely and steadily with crowns on their heads. There were troops from the many nations subject to Xerxes. Some of them wore coats of mail, some wore linen corselets, and some wore long cloaks. They carried all sorts of weapons; spears, daggers, bows, and arrows, and even heavy clubs knotted with iron, according to the customs of their countries. There were long lines of camels and servants with provisions. There were also more than four thousand ships gathered together in the waters. Fortunately, for all folk who like to hear a good story, there was a little four-year-old boy then living in Asia Minor named Herodotus. When he grew up, he traveled to many places where interesting things had happened, learned all that he could about them, and wrote what he had learned. It is he who tells us about the expeditions of the Persians and this crossing of the bridges of boats by the greatest army that was ever brought together. The Greeks were in so great anxiety that some of them were ready to send earth and water at once. Others were determined to resist even the mighty Persian sovereign. But they were so jealous of one another that even in their trouble they quarreled about the leadership. At length Athens, Sparta, and a few other states agreed to stand together, and the command was given to Leonidas, the Spartan king.

The Persians were marching nearer and nearer, keeping close to the shore. Xerxes heard that a few of the Greeks were at the Pass of Thermopylae but with his hundreds of thousands of men that was a small matter, and he marched on. He had just lost four hundred ships in a storm, and the Greeks were guarding the Euripus, the strait between the island of Euboea and the mainland, or else he might have carried his men to Attica by water if he had thought it was worthwhile.

At Thermopylae the mountains jut out into the sea and leave only a narrow passage between them and the water. Here Leonidas with three hundred Spartans and about six thousand men from other tribes took their stand against the enormous numbers of the Persians. There were two days of terrible fighting. Then a traitor, who hoped for a great reward, told Xerxes that there was a footpath by which his men could go over the mountains and around the Pass. When Leonidas found that the path had been discovered, he knew that he could not hold Thermopylae. Nevertheless, he would not withdraw. "The laws of our country forbid that we should leave the place that we have been sent to guard," he said. The others made their way to their homes; but the Spartans and also the Thespians refused to retreat. The Persians came upon them from above and from below. They fought with their weapons, then with their teeth, with their fists, with stones, with anything that would make a wound or strike a blow, until every man of them was slain. The Persians had won the Pass of Thermopylae, and they set out for Athens.

There was now no reason for guarding the Euripus, and the Greek warships sailed through it toward the south. The commander of the Athenian vessels was Themistocles, a man who had fought at Marathon. He was a far-seeing man, and at the time when the Greeks were rejoicing because they had driven away Darius, he was serious and grave. The Persians will come again," he declared, "and we must learn to defend ourselves on the water as well as on the land." His constant cry was, "Build ships, build ships." The Athenians were slow to yield, but finally a fleet was built. This was the fleet which Themistocles was bringing down the Euripus.

This commander never overlooked any chances. He knew that there must be Ionians, who were of Greek descent, in the army of Xerxes, and he cut messages for them on the rocks along the way. "Men of Ionia," these inscriptions said, "come over to our side if possible; if you cannot do this, we pray you stand aloof from the contest, or at least fight backwardly."

The Persians were aiming first at Athens; and the other kingdoms had abandoned her to her fate. The states lying to the south of the Isthmus of Corinth, the Peloponnesus, as that part of the country was called, were working night and day to build a high wall across the Isthmus to protect themselves and their own cities; and the Persians swept down upon Athens. They plundered and burned and destroyed till there was hardly one stone left standing upon another. The people of the city were saved; for just before the coming of the Persians they had been crowded into boats and carried to safe places.

Long before this, the Athenians had sent to the oracle at Delphi for advice. One line of it was, "Holy Salamis, thou shalt destroy the offspring of women." But who could say whether the "offspring of women" meant Greeks or Persians? Themistocles believed that it meant the Persians, and that a naval victory at Salamis was the only hope of the Greeks.

The men of the Peloponnesus who were building the wall objected. "We will fight at the Isthmus," they said, "and then if we are defeated, we can retreat to our homes; but we will not go out to fight on the water." Themistocles believed that the oracle had promised a victory at Salamis and nowhere else, and he resolved to make the objectors fight, whether they would or not. He sent a faithful slave to Xerxes to say that the Greeks were divided, that some were for him and some were against him. "Now is your chance to win a glorious victory," the message ended. The Persians were made to think that this message was sent by some Greek commander who favored their side.

The envoys of the states met again and talked far into the night. While they debated, a message was brought to Themistocles: "There is one without who would speak to you." It was an Athenian named Aristides. He, too, had been at Marathon. He was so upright and honorable that he was known as "the Just." He had believed that Themistocles was entirely in the wrong in urging the building of ships. He had opposed the course of his rival so strongly that at length the matter was brought to the test of ostracism. This was a peculiar custom of the Athenians. If it was thought that any one man was gaining too much power, the citizens were called together, and each was requested to write on a shell (ostrakon) the name of any one who he thought might endanger the liberty of the state. If any one person received six thousand votes, he was banished for ten years. It was in this way that Aristides had been banished. The Greeks had permitted all those to return who had been sent away, lest they should join the Persians; and here was Aristides in the darkness of the night, bringing a message to his old opponent Themistocles.

Aristides was so earnest a patriot that he was perfectly willing to help even Themistocles to win glory if by so doing he could save his country, and he whispered, "The Persian ships are at the entrance of the strait." Then Themistocles was delighted. He saw that his trick had deceived the enemy and that now the Greeks would have to fight on the water.

So it was that the battle of Salamis came about. The Greek ships formed in a line extending from Attica to Salamis. The Persian vessels lay to the south of them. Then the conflict began. All day long the battle raged. Both sides fought with the utmost courage. Indeed, the Persians would have done better if their commanders had not been quite so fearless. Every one of them was eager to do some brave deed under the eye of the king, have his name set down by the royal secretaries as one of the king's "benefactors," and win the reward and honors that would await him. The result of this was that when the foremost Persian ships were put to flight, the vessels coming up behind them pressed on so zealously that they knocked against them and against one another. Rudders were destroyed, oars were snapped off, and the ships of the invaders drifted about helplessly, were rammed by the Greeks, and sank by the score. The Greeks were here, there, and everywhere; and wherever a Grecian vessel went, it ran its sharp prow into the sides of the Persian ships. The Greeks even sailed around the Persian fleet and attacked it from the rear. When night came, they had won the victory. Xerxes started for home, sailing as fast as a ship would carry him, for he was terribly alarmed lest the Greeks should destroy the bridges over the Hellespont before his troops could march across them. Herodotus says that if all the men and women in the world had advised him to stay, he would not have done it. One of his generals was eager to try again, and he remained with three hundred thousand men. By this time, the states had learned that they must unite. There was a savage battle at Plataea. The Greeks were victorious, and this ended the attempt of the great king of Persia to overpower the little country of Greece.

From Fifty Famous Stories Retold
By James Baldwin

The Brave Three Hundred

All Greece was in danger. A mighty army, led by the great King of Persia, had come from the east. It was marching along the seashore, and in a few days would be in Greece. The great king had sent messengers into every city and state, bidding them give him water and earth in token that the land and the sea were his. But they said,— "No: we will be free."

And so there was a great stir through-out all the land. The men armed themselves, and made haste to go out and drive back their foe; and the women stayed at home, weeping and waiting, and trembling with fear.

There was only one way by which the Persian army could go into Greece on that side, and that was by a narrow pass between the mountains and the sea. This pass was guarded by Leonidas, the King of the Spartans, with three hundred Spartan soldiers.

Soon the Persian soldiers were seen coming. There were so many of them that no man could count them. How could a handful of men hope to stand against so great a host?

And yet Leonidas and his Spartans held their ground. They had made up their minds to die at their post. Someone brought them word that there were so many Persians that their arrows darkened the sun.

So much the better," said the Spartans; "we shall fight in the shade."

Bravely they stood in the narrow pass. Bravely they faced their foes. To Spartans there was no such thing as fear. The Persians came forward, only to meet death at the points of their spears.

But one by one the Spartans fell. At last, their spears were broken; yet still they stood side by side, fighting to the last. Some fought with swords, some with daggers, and some with only their fists and teeth.

All day long, the army of the Persians was kept at bay. But when the sun went down, there was not one Spartan left alive. Where they had stood there was only a heap of the slain, all bristled over with spears and arrows.

Twenty thousand Persian soldiers had fallen before that handful of men. And Greece was saved.

Thousands of years have passed since then; but men still like to tell the story of Leonidas and the brave three hundred who died for their country's sake.

From Old World Hero Stories
By Eva March Tappan

Pericles and His Age

After the Persians had been driven away from Greece, the Athenians returned to their city. It was in ruins; but they were so jubilant over their victories that they hardly thought of their losses. They rebuilt their homes, and then they began to rebuild the city walls. The Spartans were not pleased. They were willing that Athens should be almost as strong as Sparta, but not quite. They sent messengers to suggest that it was not well to wall in the city; for if the Persians should ever succeed in capturing it, the walls would make a strong shelter for them. But the Athenians only worked the faster; and before long the walls had risen so high that they could be as independent as they pleased.

The Athenians were then divided into two parties. One thought it best to keep on good terms with Sparta; the other believed that, no matter how hard they tried, Sparta would never be really friendly; and this party declared that the wisest course was to make Athens as strong as possible, and then Sparta might be friendly or unfriendly as she liked. The leader of this second party was Pericles. He was calm and sensible, and when he spoke to the people, he was so reasonable and so eloquent that the Athenians were easily persuaded to follow his advice. Athens was an inland city, four miles from her seaport, Piraeus. Pericles reminded the citizens that, although Athens was strong and Piraeus was strong, yet an enemy might come in between and shut the city from her port. He advised them to build two parallel walls from Athens to Piraeus. This was done. These walls were sixty feet high, and so wide that two chariots could drive abreast on them.

Next, Pericles induced the Spartans to make a treaty of peace that was to last for thirty years. He had made Athens strong, and now he was free to carry out his plan of making her the most beautiful city in the world. The Athenians loved everything beautiful, and they were ready to fall in with his wishes. It was nothing new to them to have handsome buildings and noble statues; but Pericles planned to build on the Acropolis a group of temples that should be more magnificent than anything the world had ever seen. The noblest of them all was the Parthenon, or temple of Athena. This was of pure white marble, with long rows of columns around it. Three styles of columns were used by the Greeks. One was the Corinthian. The capital, or heading, of this looks as if the top of the column were surrounded with a cluster of marble leaves. The second style was the Ionic, whose capital is carved into two coils a little like snail shells. The third style was the Doric, which has a plain, solid capital. The Corinthian and Ionic are beautiful, but the Doric looks strong and dignified; and therefore the Doric was chosen for the Parthenon. A frieze, or band of sculpture, ran around the whole building. This showed the famous procession which took place every four years to present to the statue of Athena a new peplum, or robe. This robe was exquisitely embroidered by maidens from the noblest families in Athens. The statue was thirty-nine feet high. It was wrought of ivory and gold, and the pupils of the eyes were probably made of jewels. Another of the buildings on the Acropolis was the Erechtheum, which was sacred to Athena and Poseidon. Out under the open sky stood a second statue of Athena; and this was made of bronze captured from the Persians at Marathon.

Pericles entrusted this work to the artist Phidias, and he could not have made a better choice, for from that day to this, people have never ceased to discover new beauties in the Parthenon. Phidias was so anxious to make everything as perfect as possible that when people came to see his work, he used to stand just out of sight and listen to what was said. If anyone discovered a fault, he did not rest until he had corrected it.

Pericles also improved the theatre of Dionysus. A Greek theatre was not a covered building, but consisted of many rows of stone seats rising up the side of a hill. At the base of the hill was a level space where the actors stood. Some of the plays were tragedies. These were serious and grave. They were most frequently about the gods or the noble deeds of the early Greeks. Others were merry comedies which made fun of the whims and fancies of the day. The tragedies taught the listeners to be religious and patriotic, and the comedies made them think about what was going on around them. Both were so valuable to the people that Pericles thought no one ought to be kept away by poverty. Therefore he brought it about that the state should pay the admittance fee. Twice a year twelve plays were acted, and a prize was given to the author whose work was counted best. Thirteen times it was presented to the poet Aeschylus. He was soldier as well as poet, and had fought bravely at Marathon and Salamis. Another poet was Sophocles. The Athenians liked his plays because they were not quite so formal and his characters seemed more like real people. The third of the great tragic poets was Euripides. His plays were lighter than those of Sophocles, and were more like scenes in everyday life.

The greatest writer of comedy was Aristophanes. He amused himself by making fun of his fellow citizens in a witty, good-humored fashion which was vastly entertaining to them. The Athenians thought that to go to court and listen to lawsuits was the finest amusement in the world; and in Aristophanes' play "The Birds," he takes for chief characters two Athenians who are so tired of lawsuits that they have fled from men to the birds. Herodotus, who gave so vivid a description of the crossing of the Hellespont by the forces of Xerxes, lived in the time of Pericles. So did another famous historian named Thucydides. Herodotus was a born storyteller; but Thucydides writes so simply and clearly that he is always interesting.

Pericles made some important changes in the laws. He believed that all citizens ought to have the same right to hold office. But as a poor man could not afford to leave his work in order to serve as a magistrate, he persuaded the Athenians to pass laws to give salaries to officeholders. More than this, if the men went to the meetings of the general assembly, they were paid; and if they served as jurymen, they were paid. Sometimes hundreds of jurymen sat on a single case. Soldiers had never received any wages before this time; they had defended their country as they would have defended their own houses; but now soldiers, too, were paid for their services. Indeed, in one way or another, a very large number of the citizens were paid by the state for doing what the Greeks had before this thought was only their duty. The years between 480 B.C. and 404 B.C. are known as the Age of Pericles. Athens was then the strongest of the states of Greece and the most beautiful. She had a protecting wall seven miles in length; she had the most powerful navy of the time, and the city was the richest in the world in superb temples and marvelous statues.

The Age of Pericles was a happy time for the citizens. With so much building going on, there was enough to do for workmen of all kinds; and if a man could work in gold, brass, stone, or wood, he was sure of good wages. There were ships enough for commerce, and there was commerce enough for the ships. The Athenians knew how to make all sorts of earthenware; they did wonderfully fine work in metal; and other countries were eager to trade with them.

The homes of the Athenians were comfortable, but very simple. The house was usually built around an open court, and into this, all the rooms opened. The Greeks lived so much in the open air that they looked upon a house as being chiefly a shelter from stormy weather and a place for their property. Their furnishings were not expensive, but the chairs and couches and bowls and jars were sure to be of graceful form and color; for the Athenians were such lovers of beauty that anything ugly really made them uncomfortable.

The children had tops and kites and carts and swings just like the children of today. The little girls learned at home to read and write and care for a house; but the boys were sent to school. Greek parents would not allow a boy to go to school alone, but always sent with him a slave called a pedagogue to see that he behaved properly on the street. The boy was taught to read clearly and well. He learned to write with a stylus, or pointed piece of metal or bone, on a tablet covered with wax. When his tablet was covered, the wax could be smoothed, and then it was ready for the next day's work. Boys wrote a great deal from dictation, and often this dictation was taken from the Iliad or the Odyssey. They learned to reckon, to sing, to play on the lyre, and perhaps to draw. They must learn to throw the discus, to wrestle, to leap, and to run. No one expected that all the boys would become champion athletes, but it was looked upon as a disgrace for a boy not to be taught to carry himself well and use his muscles properly.

The peace which Pericles had arranged with Sparta lasted for only fifteen years. Then war broke out. Pericles was managing the defense of Athens with the greatest wisdom; but the plague came down upon the city, and soon the great Athenian lay dying. The friends about his bedside were talking of his victories, when he suddenly opened his eyes and said, "Many other generals have performed the like; but you take no notice of the most honorable part of my character, that no Athenian through my means ever put on mourning.

— ❦ —

The Athenian Oath

This oath was taken by the young men of ancient Athens when they reached the age of seventeen.

We will never bring disgrace on this our City by an act of dishonesty or cowardice.
We will fight for the ideals and Sacred Things of the City both alone and with many.
We will revere and obey the City's laws, and will do our best to incite a like reverence and respect in those above us who are prone to annul them or set them at naught.
We will strive increasingly to quicken the public's sense of civic duty.

Thus in all these ways we will transmit this City, not only not less, but greater and more beautiful than it was transmitted to us.

— ❦ —

FROM THE JUNIOR CLASSICS, VOLUME SEVEN: STORIES OF COURAGE AND HEROISM
Selected and Arranged by William Patten

HOW PHIDIAS HELPED THE IMAGE-MAKER
By Beatrice Harraden

During the time when Pericles was at the head of the state at Athens, he spared no pains and no money to make the city beautiful. He himself was a lover and patron of the arts, and he was determined that Athens should become the very center of art and refinement, and that she should have splendid public buildings and splendid sculptures and paintings. So he gathered round him all the great sculptors and painters, and set them to work to carry out his ambitious plans; and some of you know that the "Age of Pericles" is still spoken of as an age in which art advanced towards and attained to a marvelous perfection.

On the Acropolis, or Citadel of Athens, rose the magnificent Temple of Athena, called the Parthenon, built under the direction of Phidias, the most celebrated sculptor of that time, who adorned it with many of his works, and especially with the huge statue of Athena in ivory, forty-seven feet in height. The Acropolis was also enriched with another figure of Athena in bronze—also the work of Phidias.

The statue was called the "Athena Promachus"; that is "The Defender." If you turn to your Grecian History, you will find a full description of the Parthenon and the other temples of the gods and heroes and guardian deities of the city. But I want to tell you something about Phidias himself, and little Iris, an image-maker's daughter.

It was in the year 450 B.C., in the early summer, and Phidias, who had been working all the day, strolled quietly along the streets of Athens.

As he passed by the Agora (or market place), he chanced to look up, and he saw a young girl of about thirteen years sitting near him. Her face was of the purest beauty; her head was gracefully poised on her shoulders; her expression was sadness itself. She looked poor and in distress. She came forward and begged for help; and there was something in her manner, as well as in her face, which made Phidias pause and listen to her.

"My father lies ill," she said plaintively, "and he cannot do his work, and so we can get no food: nothing to make him well and strong again. If I could only do his work for him I should not mind; and then I should not beg. He does not know I came out to beg—he would never forgive me; but I could not bear to see him lying there without food."

"And who is your father?" asked Phidias kindly.

"His name is Aristæus," she said, "and he is a maker of images—little clay figures of gods and goddesses and heroes. Indeed, he is clever; and I am sure you would praise the 'Hercules' he finished before he was taken ill."

"Take me to your home," Phidias said to the girl; as they passed on together he asked her many questions about the image-maker. She was proud of her father; and Phidias smiled to himself when he heard her speak of this father as though he were the greatest sculptor in Athens. He liked to hear her speak so enthusiastically.

"Is it not wonderful," she said, "to take the clay and work in into forms? Not everyone could do that—could you do it?"

Phidias laughed.

"Perhaps not so well as your father," he answered kindly. "Still, I can do it."

A sudden thought struck Iris.

"Perhaps you would help father?" she said eagerly. "Ah! but I ought not to have said that."

"Perhaps I can help him," replied Phidias good-naturedly. "Anyway, take me to him."

She led him through some side streets into the poorest parts of the city, and stopped before a little window, where a few roughly wrought images and vases were exposed to view. She beckoned to him to follow her, and opening the door, crept gently into a room which served as their workshop and dwelling-place. Phidias saw a man stretched out on a couch at the farther end of the room, near a bench where many images and pots of all sorts lay unfinished.

"This is our home," whispered Iris proudly, "and that is my father yonder."

The image-maker looked up and called for Iris.

"I am so faint, child," he murmured. "If I could only become strong again I could get back to my work. It is so hard to lie here and die."

Phidias bent over him.

"You shall not die," he said, "if money can do you any good. I met your little daughter, and she told me that you were an image-maker; and that interested me, because I, too, can make images, though perhaps not as well as you. Still, I thought I should like to come and see you and help you; and if you will let me, I will try and make a few images for you, so that your daughter may go out and sell them, and bring you home money. And meanwhile, she shall fetch you some food to nourish you."

Then he turned to Iris, and putting some coins into her hands bade her go out and bring what she thought fit. She did not know how to thank him, but hurried away on her glad errand, and Phidias talked kindly to his fellow-worker, and then, throwing aside his cloak, sat down at the bench and busied himself with modeling the clay.

It was so different from his ordinary work that he could not help smiling.

"This is rather easier," he thought to himself, "than carving from the marble a statue of Athena. What a strange occupation!" Nevertheless, he was so interested in modeling the quaint little images that he did not perceive that Iris had returned, until he looked up, and saw her standing near him, watching him with wonder, which she could not conceal.

"Oh, how clever!" she cried. "Father, if you could only see what he is doing!"

"Nay, child," said the sculptor, laughing; "get your father his food, and leave me to my work. I am going to model a little image of the goddess Athena, for I think the folk will like to buy that, since that rogue Phidias has set up his statue of her in the Parthenon."

"Phidias, the prince of sculptors!" said the image-maker. "May the gods preserve his life; for he is the greatest glory of all Athens!"

"Ay," said Iris, as she prepared her father's food, "that is what we all call him—the greatest glory of all Athens."

"We think of him," said Aristæus, feebly, "and that helps us in our work. Yes, it helps even us poor image-makers. When I saw the beautiful Athena I came home cheered and encouraged. May Phidias be watched over and blessed all his life!"

The tears came into the eyes of Phidias as he bent over his work; it was a pleasure to him to think that his fame gained for him a resting-place of love and gratitude in the hearts of the poorest citizens of Athens. He valued this tribute of the image-maker far more than the praises of the rich and great. Before he left, he saw that both father and daughter were much refreshed by the food which his bounty had given to them, and he bade Aristæus be of good cheer, because he would surely regain his health and strength.

"And because you love your art," he said, "I shall be a friend to you and help you. And I shall come again tomorrow and do some work for you—that is to say, if you approve of what I have already done, and then Iris will be able to go out and sell the figures."

He hastened away before they were able to thank him, and he left them wondering who this new friend could be. They talked of him for a long time, of his kindness and his skill; and Aristæus dreamt that night about the stranger who had come to work for him.

The next day Phidias came again, and took his place at the image-maker's bench, just as if he were always accustomed to sit there. Aristæus, who was better, watched him curiously, but asked no questions.

But Iris said to him: "My father and I talk of you, and wonder who you are."

Phidias laughed.

"Perhaps I shall tell you some day," he answered. "There, child, what do you think of that little vase? When it is baked it will be a pretty thing."

As the days went on, the image-maker recovered his strength; and meanwhile Phidias had filled the little shop with dainty-wrought images and graceful vases, such as had never been seen there before.

One evening, when Aristæus was leaning against Iris, and admiring the stranger's work, the door opened and Phidias came in.

"What, friend," he said cheerily, "you are better tonight I see!"

"Last night," said Aristæus, "I dreamt that the friend who held out a brother's hand to me and helped me in my trouble was the great Phidias himself. It did not seem wonderful to me, for only the great do such things as you have done for me. You must be great."

"I do not know about that," said the sculptor, smiling, "and after all, I have not done so much for you. I have only helped a brother-workman: for I am an image-maker too—and my name is Phidias."

Then Aristæus bent down and reverently kissed the great sculptor's hands.

"I cannot find words with which to thank you," he murmured, "but I shall pray to the gods night and day that they will forever bless Phidias, and keep his fame pure, and his hands strong to fashion forms of beauty. And this I know well: that he will always have a resting-place of love and gratitude in the poor image-maker's heart."

And Phidias went on his way, tenfold richer and happier for the image-maker's words. For there is something lovelier than fame and wealth, my children; it is the opportunity of giving the best of one's self and the best of one's powers to aid those of our fellow-workers who need our active help.

FROM OLD WORLD HERO STORIES
By Eva March Tappan

Two Philosophers, Socrates and Plato

About a century before the Age of Pericles, someone asked a very wise man, "What is a philosopher?" He replied: "At the games, some try to win glory, some buy and sell for money, and some watch what the others do. So it is in life; and philosophers are those who watch, who study nature, and search for wisdom." Now during the time of Pericles a young man lived in Athens who was to become famous as a philosopher, though perhaps no one thought so at the time. His father was a sculptor. The son followed the same occupation, and probably worked with hammer and chisel upon some of the statues that were making Athens beautiful.

This young man, whose name was Socrates, studied with some of the teachers of the time; but he was not satisfied with their teaching, and he made up his mind that the best way for him to find out what was true was to think for himself. One of his conclusions was that, as the gods needed nothing, so the man who needed least was in that respect most like them. Therefore he trained himself to live on coarse and scanty food; he learned to bear heat and cold; and even when he served in the army and had to march over ice and snow, he did not give up his habit of going barefooted.

Socrates was not handsome. He had a flat nose, thick lips, and prominent eyes. He became bald early in life. He walked awkwardly, and used to astonish people by sometimes standing still for hours when he wanted to think out something. On the other hand, he had a beautiful voice, he was bright and witty and brave and kindhearted. As he grew older, he used to spend the whole day wherever people were to be found. He went to the market place, to the workshops, and to the porticoes where the Athenians were accustomed to walk up and down and talk together. He was ready to talk with anyone, rich or poor, old or young, and to teach them what he believed to be right and true. His way of doing this was by asking questions and so making them think for themselves. For instance, his pupil Plato represents him as having a talk with a boy named Lysis. "Of course your father and mother love you and wish you to be happy?" he asked. "Certainly," replied the boy. "Is a slave happy, who is not allowed to do what he likes?"

"No!" "Then your parents, wishing you to be happy, let you do as you choose? Would your father let you drive his chariot in a race?" "Surely not," said Lysis. "But he lets a hired servant drive it and even pays him for so doing," Socrates continued. "Does he care more for this man than for you?" "No, he does not." "As your mother wishes you to be happy, of course she lets you do as you like when you are with her," said the philosopher. "She never hinders you from touching her loom or shuttle when she is weaving, does she?" Lysis laughed and replied, "She not only hinders me, but I should be beaten if I touched them." "When you take the lyre, do your parents hinder you from tightening and loosening any string that you please? How is this? "I think it is because I know the one, but not the other," the boy replied thoughtfully. "So it is," said Socrates, "and all persons will trust us in those things wherein they have found us wise."

This was the philosopher's manner of teaching an honest boy; but if a man was not sincere, Socrates would tangle him up with his questions until the man had said that sickness and health, right and wrong, and black and white were the same things. He prayed and offered sacrifices to the gods as the laws required; but he believed that there was one God overall, and that to be honest and good was better than sacrifices. He taught his followers to say this prayer: "Father Jupiter, give us all good, whether we ask it or not; and avert from us all evil, though we do not pray thee so to do. Bless all our good actions, and reward them with success and happiness."

Socrates had made many enemies. The rulers hated him because he declared, among other remarks of the sort, that to govern a state was far more difficult than to steer a vessel; but that, although no one would attempt to steer a vessel without training, everyone thought himself fit to govern a state. He was accused of preaching new gods and of giving false teaching to the young and was condemned to die. He was perfectly calm and serene. He told his judges that it was a gain to him to die; but that it was unjust for them to put him to death, and therefore they would suffer for it. He would not allow his family to come before them to plead for his life, and he would not escape when his friends offered to open the way.

It was thirty days from the time that he was sentenced until his death. He spent much of this time in talking with his pupils. One of those whom he loved best was Plato; and Plato afterwards wrote an account of the last days of his master. Socrates said that his death was only going "to some happy state of the blessed." He was asked in what manner he wished to be buried; and he replied with a smile, "Just as you please, if only you can catch me." He was to die by poison. When the cup was brought, he drank it as calmly as if it had been wine, and he comforted his disciples, who were weeping around him. At the last, he called to one of the young men, "Crito, we owe a cock to Aesculapius; pay it, therefore, and do not neglect it." Aesculapius was the god to whom a man who was grateful for his recovery from illness made a sacrifice; and Socrates was so sure of a happier life to come that he felt as if death was passing from sickness to health. It is no wonder that his pupil Plato said, "This man was the best of all of his time that we have known, and, moreover, the most wise and just."

After the death of Socrates, Plato traveled from one country to another. He studied the people, the laws, and the customs. If there were philosophers in the land, he learned all that he could from them. "Plato, how long do you intend to remain a student?" one of his friends asked. He replied, "As long as I am not ashamed to grow wiser and better." In the course of his travels, he went to Syracuse, on the island of Sicily. The ruler of Syracuse was Dionysius. He was called a tyrant, which meant that he had seized the throne unlawfully. Dionysius himself wrote poems, and he was always glad to welcome philosophers and scholars to his court. Unluckily, he and Plato fell into an argument. Plato not only got the better of it, but dared to make some bold remarks about tyrants. Dionysius was so angry that he came near putting his honored guest to death. He did bribe someone to sell the philosopher as a slave on his homeward journey. This was done, but Plato's friends bought his freedom.

At length Plato returned to Athens. A little way outside of the city was a large public garden or park, along the Cephissus River. Here grew plane trees and olive trees. Here were temples and statues. This was called the Academy, in honor of one Academus, who had left it to the city for gymnastics. Plato's father seems to have owned a piece of land near this park; and here Plato opened a school for all who chose to become learners. It took its name from the park and was known as the Academy. The most brilliant young men of the time were eager to come to the Academy to study with Plato. He discussed difficult questions with his students and he wrote on the deepest subjects, but with so much humor and sweetness that many people fancied him to be descended from Apollo, the god of eloquence. Long afterwards, Cicero, the greatest Roman orator, declared that if Jupiter were to speak Greek, he would use the language of Plato.

One of Plato's sayings was, "To conquer one's self is the highest wisdom." He not only taught self-control, but he practiced it. A friend came upon him one day unexpectedly and asked why he was holding his arm up as if to strike. "I am punishing a passionate man," Plato replied. It seemed that he had raised his arm to strike a disobedient slave; but had stopped because he found himself in a passion. It was a rare event for him to lose his self-control. Even when he was told that his enemies were spreading false stories about him, he did not fly into a fit of anger; he only said quietly, "I will live so that none will believe them." He was simple and friendly in his manner. There is a tradition that some strangers who met him at the Olympian games were so pleased with him that they accepted gladly his invitation to visit him in Athens. When their visit was near its end, they said, "But will you not introduce us to your famous namesake, the philosopher Plato?" They were greatly surprised when their host replied quietly, "I am the person whom you wish to see."

When Plato died, he was buried in his garden. His followers raised altars and statues in his memory, and for many years the day of his birth was celebrated among them with rejoicing.

FROM FIFTY FAMOUS PEOPLE
By James Baldwin

A STORY OF OLD ROME

There was a great famine in Rome. The summer had been very dry and the corn crop had failed. There was no bread in the city. The people were starving.

One day, to the great joy of all, some ships arrived from another country. These ships were loaded with corn. Here was food enough for all.

The rulers of the city met to decide what should be done with the corn.

"Divide it among the poor people who need it so badly," said some.

"Let it be a free gift to them from the city."

But one of the rulers was not willing to do this. His name was Coriolanus, and he was very rich.

"These people are poor because they have been too lazy to work," he said. "They do not deserve any gifts from the city. Let those who wish any corn bring money and buy it."

When the people heard about this speech of the rich man, Coriolanus, they were very angry.

"He is no true Roman," said some.

"He is selfish and unjust," said others.

"He is an enemy to the poor. Kill him! kill him!" cried the mob. They did not kill him, but they drove him out of the city and bade him never return.

Coriolanus made his way to the city of Antium, which was not far from Rome. The people of Antium were enemies of the Romans and had often been at war with them. So they welcomed Coriolanus very kindly and made him the general of their army.

Coriolanus began at once to make ready for war against Rome. He persuaded other towns near Antium to send their soldiers to help him.

Soon, at the head of a very great army, he marched toward the city which had once been his home. The rude soldiers of Antium overran all the country around Rome. They burned the villages and farmhouses. They filled the land with terror.

Coriolanus pitched his camp quite near to the city. His army was the greatest that the Romans had ever seen. They knew that they were helpless before so strong an enemy.

"Surrender your city to me," said Coriolanus. "Agree to obey the laws that I shall make for you. Do this, or I will burn Rome and destroy all its people."

The Romans answered, "We must have time to think of this matter. Give us a few days to learn what sort of laws you will make for us, and then we will say whether we can submit to them or not."

"I will give you thirty days to consider the matter," said Coriolanus.

Then he told them what laws he would require them to obey. These laws were so severe that all said, "It will be better to die at once."

At the end of the thirty days, four of the city's rulers went out to beg him to show mercy to the people of Rome. These rulers were old men, with wise faces and long white beards. They went out bareheaded and very humble.

Coriolanus would not listen to them. He drove them back with threats, and told them that they should expect no mercy from him; but he agreed to give them three more days to consider the matter.

The next day, all the priests and learned men went out to beg for mercy. These were dressed in their long flowing robes, and all knelt humbly before him. But he drove them back with scornful words.

On the last day, the great army which Coriolanus had led from Antium was drawn up in battle array. It was ready to march upon the city and destroy it.

All Rome was in terror. There seemed to be no way to escape the anger of this furious man.

Then the rulers, in their despair, said, "Let us go up to the house where Coriolanus used to live when he was one of us. His mother and his wife are still there. They are noble women, and they love Rome. Let us ask them to go out and beg our enemy to have mercy upon us. His heart will be hard indeed if he can refuse his mother and his wife."

The two noble women were willing to do all that they could to save their city. So, leading his little children by the hand, they went out to meet Coriolanus. Behind them followed a long procession of the women of Rome. Coriolanus was in his tent. When he saw his mother and his wife and his children, he was filled with joy. But when they made known their errand, his face darkened, and he shook his head.

For a long time his mother pleaded with him. For a long time his wife begged him to be merciful. His little children clung to his knees and spoke loving words to him.

At last, he could hold out no longer. "O mother," he said, "you have saved your country, but have lost your son!" Then he commanded his army to march back to the city of Antium.

Rome was saved; but Coriolanus could never return to his home, his mother, his wife and children. He was lost to them.

A Story from Ancient Rome
From Fifty Famous Stories Retold
BY James Baldwin

Horatius at the Bridge

Once there was a war between the Roman people and the Etruscans who lived in the towns on the other side of the Tiber River. Porsena, the King of the Etruscans, raised a great army, and marched toward Rome. The city had never been in so great danger.

The Romans did not have very many fighting men at that time, and they knew that they were not strong enough to meet the Etruscans in open battle. So they kept themselves inside of their walls, and set guards to watch the roads.

One morning the army of Porsena was seen coming over the hills from the north. There were thousands of horsemen and footmen, and they were marching straight toward the wooden bridge which spanned the river at Rome.

"What shall we do?" said the white-haired Fathers who made the laws for the Roman people. "If they once gain the bridge, we cannot hinder them from crossing; and then what hope will there be for the town?"

Now, among the guards at the bridge, there was a brave man named Horatius. He was on the farther side of the river, and when he saw that the Etruscans were so near, he called out to the Romans who were behind him.

"Hew down the bridge with all the speed that you can!" he cried. "I, with the two men who stand by me, will keep the foe at bay."

Then, with their shields before them, and their long spears in their hands, the three brave men stood in the road, and kept back the horsemen whom Porsena had sent to take the bridge.

On the bridge the Romans hewed away at the beams and posts. Their axes rang, the chips flew fast; and soon it trembled, and was ready to fall.

"Come back! come back, and save your lives!" they cried to Horatius and the two who were with him.

But just then Porsena's horsemen dashed toward them again.

"Run for your lives!" said Horatius to his friends. "I will keep the road."

They turned, and ran back across the bridge. They had hardly reached the other side when there was a crashing of beams and timbers. The bridge toppled over to one side, and then fell with a great splash into the water.

When Horatius heard the sound, he knew that the city was safe. With his face still toward Porsena's men, he moved slowly backward till he stood on the river's bank.

A dart thrown by one of Porsena's soldiers put out his left eye; but he did not falter. He cast his spear at the foremost horseman, and then he turned quickly around. He saw the white porch of his own home among the trees on the other side of the stream;

> "And he spake to the noble river
>   That rolls by the walls of Rome:
> 'O Tiber! father Tiber!
>   To whom the Romans pray,
>
> A Roman's life, a Roman's arms,
>   Take thou in charge today.'"

He leaped into the deep, swift stream. He still had his heavy armor on; and when he sank out of sight, no one thought that he would ever be seen again. But he was a strong man, and the best swimmer in Rome. The next minute he rose. He was half-way across the river, and safe from the spears and darts which Porsena's soldiers hurled after him.

Soon he reached the farther side, where his friends stood ready to help him. Shout after shout greeted him as he climbed upon the bank. Then Porsena's men shouted also, for they had never seen a man so brave and strong as Horatius. He had kept them out of Rome, but he had done a deed which they could not help but praise.

As for the Romans, they were very grateful to Horatius for having saved their city. They called him Horatius Cocles, which meant the "one-eyed Horatius," because he had lost an eye in defending the bridge; they caused a fine statue of brass to be made in his honor; and they gave him as much land as he could plow around in a day.

And for hundreds of years afterwards—

> "With weeping and with laughter,
>   Still was the story told,
> How well Horatius kept the bridge
>   In the brave days of old."

FROM FIFTY FAMOUS STORIES RETOLD
By James Baldwin

THE STORY OF CINCINNATUS

There was a man named Cincinnatus who lived on a little farm not far from the city of Rome. He had once been rich, and had held the highest office in the land; but in one way or another he had lost all his wealth. He was now so poor that he had to do all the work on his farm with his own hands. But in those days it was thought to be a noble thing to till the soil.

Cincinnatus was so wise and just that everybody trusted him, and asked his advice; and when any one was in trouble, and did not know what to do, his neighbors would say,—

"Go and tell Cincinnatus. He will help you."

Now there lived among the mountains, not far away, a tribe of fierce, half-wild men, who were at war with the Roman people. They persuaded another tribe of bold warriors to help them, and then marched toward the city, plundering and robbing as they came. They boasted that they would tear down the walls of Rome, and burn the houses, and kill all the men, and make slaves of the women and children.

At first the Romans, who were very proud and brave, did not think there was much danger. Every man in Rome was a soldier, and the army which went out to fight the robbers was the finest in the world. No one stayed at home with the women and children and boys but the white-haired "Fathers," as they were called, who made the laws for the city, and a small company of men who guarded the walls. Everybody thought that it would be an easy thing to drive the men of the mountains back to the place where they belonged.

But one morning five horsemen came riding down the road from the mountains. They rode with great speed; and both men and horses were covered with dust and blood. The watchman at the gate knew them, and shouted to them as they galloped in. Why did they ride thus? and what had happened to the Roman army?

They did not answer him, but rode into the city and along the quiet streets; and every-body ran after them, eager to find out what was the matter. Rome was not a large city at that time; and soon they reached the market place where the white-haired Fathers were sitting. Then they leaped from their horses, and told their story.

"Only yesterday," they said, "our army was marching through a narrow valley between two steep mountains. All at once a thousand savage men sprang out from among the rocks before us and above us. They had blocked up the way; and the pass was so narrow that we could not fight. We tried to come back; but they had blocked up the way on this side of us too. The fierce men of the mountains were before us and behind us, and they were throwing rocks down upon us from above.

We had been caught in a trap. Then ten of us set spurs to our horses; and five of us forced our way through, but the other five fell before the spears of the mountain men. And now, O Roman Fathers! send help to our army at once, or every man will be slain, and our city will be taken."

"What shall we do?" said the white-haired Fathers. "Whom can we send but the guards and the boys? and who is wise enough to lead them, and thus save Rome?"

All shook their heads and were very grave; for it seemed as if there was no hope. Then one said, "Send for Cincinnatus. He will help us."

Cincinnatus was in the field plowing when the men who had been sent to him came in great haste. He stopped and greeted them kindly, and waited for them to speak.

"Put on your cloak, Cincinnatus," they said, "and hear the words of the Roman people."

Then Cincinnatus wondered what they could mean. "Is all well with Rome?" he asked; and he called to his wife to bring him his cloak.

She brought the cloak; and Cincinnatus wiped the dust from his hands and arms, and threw it over his shoulders. Then the men told their errand.

They told him how the army with all the noblest men of Rome had been entrapped in the mountain pass. They told him about the great danger the city was in. Then they said, "The people of Rome make you their ruler and the ruler of their city, to do with everything as you choose; and the Fathers bid you come at once and go out against our enemies, the fierce men of the mountains."

So Cincinnatus left his plow standing where it was, and hurried to the city. When he passed through the streets, and gave orders as to what should be done, some of the people were afraid, for they knew that he had all power in Rome to do what he pleased. But he armed the guards and the boys, and went out at their head to fight the fierce mountain men, and free the Roman army from the trap into which it had fallen.

A few days afterward there was great joy in Rome. There was good news from Cincinna-tus. The men of the mountains had been beaten with great loss. They had been driven back into their own place.

And now the Roman army, with the boys and the guards, was coming home with ban-ners flying, and shouts of victory; and at their head rode Cincinnatus. He had saved Rome.

Cincinnatus might then have made himself king; for his word was law, and no man dared lift a finger against him. But, before the people could thank him enough for what he had done, he gave back the power to the white-haired Roman Fathers, and went again to his little farm and his plow.

He had been the ruler of Rome for sixteen days.

From Old World Hero Stories
By Eva March Tappan

Socrates and His House

There once lived in Greece a very wise man whose name was Socrates. Young men from all parts of the land went to him to learn wisdom from him; and he said so many pleasant things, and said them in so delightful a way, that no one ever grew tired of listening to him.

One summer he built himself a house, but it was so small that his neighbors wondered how he could be content with it.

"What is the reason," said they, "that you, who are so great a man, should build such a little box as this for your dwelling house?"

"Indeed, there may be little reason," said he"; but, small as the place is, I shall think myself happy if I can fill even it with true friends."

From Anecdotes and Examples for the Catechism
By Rev. Francis Spirago

Is the Persian King Happy?

Virtue, and not earthly possessions, renders man truly happy. Socrates, the sage, was once asked whether he considered the king of Persia a happy man. The answer he gave was this, "I cannot tell, for I do not know whether he is proficient in knowledge and virtue; they alone make men happy."

From Anecdotes and Examples for the Catechism
By Rev. Francis Spirago

The Disciple of Zeno

Christ taught by word and example, and thus showed us the necessity of reducing to practice what we learn. In the order of virtue, an ounce of practice is worth tons of pure theory. A youth, who had been sent to the famous Greek philosopher Zeno to finish his studies, was asked by his father on his return home, "Well, what have you learned?" "You shall see presently," the young man answered, and added not another word. His father, thinking his silence to be an evidence of stupidity or neglect of study, abused him roundly, saying, "This, forsooth, is the result of all the expense I have been to." Then noticing the youth's patience and submission to it all, he inquired, "What means this silence, sir?" "That," replied the youth, "is what Zeno taught me."

FROM ANECDOTES AND EXAMPLES FOR THE CATECHISM
By Rev. Francis Spirago

DEMOSTHENES RELATES A FABLE

There are many who take no interest in higher things, and care only for the enjoyments of time and sense. Demosthenes, Greece's most renowned orator, was once addressing a large assembly on matters pertaining to the welfare of their common country. Although he spoke with enthusiasm and eloquence, his audience paid little attention to his discourse; some yawned, others talked to one another, or even went to sleep. Observing this, the orator left off speaking on serious subjects and related a fable about the ass and its shadow. Instantly silence prevailed, his hearers pricked up their ears as if some matter were being propounded on which all their happiness depended. Too often Christian people act in a similar manner; they display complete indifference regarding weighty matters relating to their eternal salvation. Sermons and spiritual books have no attraction for them, yet they take a lively interest in the amusements and diversions of the day and even in such slight and trifling things as society gossip, stories in newspapers, etc. They neglect what is of primary importance and give the first place to secondary matters. What supreme folly!

FROM ANECDOTES AND EXAMPLES FOR THE CATECHISM
By Rev. Francis Spirago

DIOGENES AND THE THREE SESTERTII

Man must not forget his highest and final end. Once upon a time Diogenes, the Grecian sage, set up a tent in the market-place at Athens, and wrote up outside it: "Wisdom is sold here." A gentleman, seeing this notice, laughed heartily at it, and calling one of his servants, he gave him three sestertii (twelve cents) and said to him: "Go and ask that braggart how much wisdom he will let you have for three sestertii." The servant went as he was desired, handed the money to Diogenes, and delivered his master's message. Diogenes pocketed the three sestertii, and said: "Tell this to your master: 'In all your actions look to the end.'" The gentleman approved so highly of this axiom, when it was repeated to him, that he caused it to be inscribed in letters of gold over the entrance to his house, that both he himself and everyone who entered might be reminded of the end of life. Now, no one ever reminded us mortals of the highest end and aim of our existence more frequently and more forcibly than Jesus Christ did. Would that every Christian kept his eyes constantly fixed upon his final end! Everlasting happiness—our last end—should be the guiding star of our existence, the lodestone of all our affections.

From Fifty Famous Stories Retold
By James Baldwin

Diogenes the Wise Man

At Corinth, in Greece, there lived a very wise man whose name was Diogenes. Men came from all parts of the land to see him and hear him talk.

But wise as he was, he had some very queer ways. He did not believe that any man ought to have more things than he really needed; and he said that no man needed much. And so he did not live in a house, but slept in a tub or barrel, which he rolled about from place to place. He spent his days sitting in the sun, and saying wise things to those who were around him.

At noon one day, Diogenes was seen walking through the streets with a lighted lantern, and looking all around as if in search of something.

"Why do you carry a lantern when the sun is shining?" someone said.

"I am looking for an honest man," answered Diogenes.

When Alexander the Great went to Corinth, all the foremost men in the city came out to see him and to praise him. But Diogenes did not come; and he was the only man for whose opinions Alexander cared.

And so, since the wise man would not come to see the king, the king went to see the wise man. He found Diogenes in an out-of-the-way place, lying on the ground by his tub. He was enjoying the heat and the light of the sun.

When he saw the king and a great many people coming, he sat up and looked at Alexander. Alexander greeted him and said,—

"Diogenes, I have heard a great deal about your wisdom. Is there anything that I can do for you?"

"Yes," said Diogenes. "You can stand a little on one side, so as not to keep the sunshine from me."

This answer was so different from what he expected, that the king was much surprised. But it did not make him angry; it only made him admire the strange man all the more. When he turned to ride back, he said to his officers,—

"Say what you will; if I were not Alexander, I would like to be Diogenes."

FROM FIFTY FAMOUS STORIES RETOLD
By James Baldwin

A LACONIC ANSWER

Many miles beyond Rome, there was a famous country which we call Greece. The people of Greece were not united like the Romans; but instead there were several states, each of which had its own rulers.

Some of the people in the southern part of the country were called Spartans, and they were noted for their simple habits and their bravery. The name of their land was Laconia, and so they were sometimes called Lacons.

One of the strange rules which the Spartans had, was that they should speak briefly, and never use more words than were needed. And so a short answer is often spoken of as being laconic; that is, as being such an answer as a Lacon would be likely to give.

There was in the northern part of Greece a land called Macedon; and this land was at one time ruled over by a war-like king named Philip.

Philip of Macedon wanted to become the master of all Greece. So he raised a great army, and made war upon the other states, until nearly all of them were forced to call him their king. Then he sent a letter to the Spartans in Laconia, and said, "If I go down into your country, I will level your great city to the ground."

In a few days, an answer was brought back to him. When he opened the letter, he found only one word written there.

That word was "IF."

It was as much as to say, "We are not afraid of you so long as the little word 'if' stands in your way."

FROM FIFTY FAMOUS STORIES RETOLD
By James Baldwin

THE UNGRATEFUL GUEST

Among the soldiers of King Philip of Macedon, there was a poor man who had done some brave deeds. He had pleased the king in more ways than one, and so the king put a good deal of trust in him.

One day this soldier was on board of a ship at sea when a great storm came up. The winds drove the ship upon the rocks, and it was wrecked. The soldier was cast half-drowned upon the shore; and he would have died there, had it not been for the kind care of a farmer who lived close by.

When the soldier was well enough to go home, he thanked the farmer for what he had done, and promised that he would repay him for his kindness.

But he did not mean to keep his promise. He did not tell King Philip about the man who had saved his life. He only said that there was a fine farm by the seashore, and that he would like very much to have it for his own. Would the king give it to him?

"Who owns the farm now?" asked Philip.

"Only a churlish farmer, who has never done anything for his country," said the soldier.

"Very well, then," said Philip. "You have served me for a long time, and you shall have your wish. Go and take the farm for yourself."

And so the soldier made haste to drive the farmer from his house and home. He took the farm for his own.

The poor farmer was stung to the heart by such treatment. He went boldly to the king, and told the whole story from beginning to end. King Philip was very angry when he learned that the man whom he had trusted had done so base a deed. He sent for the soldier in great haste; and when he had come, he caused these words to be burned in his forehead:—

"THE UNGRATEFUL GUEST.

Thus, all the world was made to know of the mean act by which the soldier had tried to enrich himself; and from that day until he died all men shunned and hated him.

FROM FIFTY FAMOUS STORIES RETOLD
By James Baldwin

ALEXANDER AND BUCEPHALUS

One day King Philip bought a fine horse called Bucephalus. He was a noble animal, and the king paid a very high price for him. But he was wild and savage, and no man could mount him, or do anything at all with him.

They tried to whip him, but that only made him worse. At last the king bade his servants take him away.

"It is a pity to ruin so fine a horse as that," said Alexander, the king's young son. "Those men do not know how to treat him."

"Perhaps you can do better than they," said his father scornfully.

"I know," said Alexander, "that, if you would only give me leave to try, I could manage this horse better than anyone else."

"And if you fail to do so, what then?" asked Philip.

"I will pay you the price of the horse," said the lad.

While everybody was laughing, Alexander ran up to Bucephalus, and turned his head toward the sun. He had noticed that the horse was afraid of his own shadow.

He then spoke gently to the horse, and patted him with his hand. When he had quieted him a little, he made a quick spring, and leaped upon the horse's back.

Everybody expected to see the boy killed outright. But he kept his place, and let the horse run as fast as he would. By and by, when Bucephalus had become tired, Alexander reined him in, and rode back to the place where his father was standing.

All the men who were there shouted when they saw that the boy had proved himself to be the master of the horse.

He leaped to the ground, and his father ran and kissed him.

"My son," said the king, "Macedon is too small a place for you. You must seek a larger kingdom that will be worthy of you."

After that, Alexander and Bucephalus were the best of friends. They were said to be always together, for when one of them was seen, the other was sure to be not far away. But the horse would never allow any one to mount him but his master.

Alexander became the most famous king and warrior that was ever known; and for that reason he is always called Alexander the Great. Bucephalus carried him through many countries and in many fierce battles, and more than once did he save his master's life.

FROM THE CHOSEN PEOPLE
By Charlotte Yonge

ALEXANDER THE GREAT

"When they have conquered Asshur and conquered Eber,
They too shall perish forever."
—Numbers 24:24

Mountain lands, small islets, and peninsulas broken into by deep bays and gulfs, rise to the northward of the east end of the Mediterranean, and were known to the Jews as the Isles of the Gentiles. The people who lived in them have been named Greeks; they were the race whom God endowed, above all others, with gifts of the body and mind, though without bestowing on them the light of His truth. They had many idols, of whom Zeus, the Thunderer, was the chief; but they did not worship them with cruel rites like the Phoenicians, and some of their beautiful stories about them were full of traces of better things. Their best and wisest men were always straining their minds to feel after more satisfying knowledge of Him, Who, they felt sure, must rule and govern all things; and sometimes these philosophers, as they were called, came very near the truth. Every work of the Greeks was well done, whether poems, history, speeches, buildings, statues, or painting; and the remains have served for patterns ever since. At first, there were many separate little states, but all held together as one nation, and used to meet for great feasts, especially for games. There were the Olympian games, by which they reckoned the years, and the Isthmean, which were held at the Isthmus of Corinth. Everyone came to see the wrestling, boxing, racing, and throwing heavy weights, and to hear the poems sung or recited; and the men who excelled all the rest were carried high in air with shouts of joy, and crowned with wreaths of laurel, bay, oak, or parsley, one of the greatest honors a

Greek could obtain. Of all the cities, Athens had the ablest men, and Sparta the most hardy; and these two had been the foremost in beating and turning back the great Persian armies of Darius and Xerxes; but since that time there had been quarrels between these two powers, and they grew weak, so that Philip, King of Macedon, who had a kingdom to the north of them, and was but half a real Greek, contrived to conquer them all, and make them his subjects.

The symbol of Macedon was a he-goat, the rough goat that Daniel had seen in his vision; and the time was come for the fall of the Ram of Persia. Philip's son, Alexander, set his heart on conquering the old enemy of Greece; and as soon as he came to the crown, in the year 336, although he was only twenty years old, he led his army across the Hellespont into Asia Minor. His army was very brave, and excellently trained by his father, and he himself was one of the most highly gifted men who ever lived, brave and prudent, seldom cruel, and trying to do good to all who fell under his power. The poor weak luxurious Persian King, Darius, could do little against such a man, and indeed did not come out to battle in the way to conquer; for he carried with him all the luxuries of his palace, his mother, and all his wives and slaves. Before his army marched a number of men carrying silver altars, on which burnt the sacred fire; then came three hundred and sixty-five youths in scarlet robes, to represent the days of the year; then the Magi, and the gilded chariot and white horses of the Sun; and next, the king's favorite soldiers, called the Immortal Band, whose robes were white, their breastplates set with jewels, and the handles of their spears golden. They had small chance with the bold active Greeks; and at the Battle of the Issus they were routed, and Darius fled away, leaving all his women to the mercy of the conqueror. The poor old Persian Queen, his mother, had never met with such gentle respect and courtesy as Alexander showed to her old age; he always called her mother, never sat down before her but at her request, and never grieved her but once, and that was by showing her a robe that his mother and sisters had spun, woven, and embroidered for him, and offering to have her grandchildren taught the like works. She fancied this meant that he was treating them like slaves, and he could hardly make her understand that the Greeks deemed such works an honor to the highest ladies, and indeed thought their goddess of wisdom presided over them.

While Darius fled away, Alexander came south to Palestine, and laid siege to Tyre upon the little isle, to which he began to build a causeway across the water. The Tyrians had an image of the Greek god Apollo, which they had stolen from a temple in Greece, and they chained this up to the statue of Moloch, their own god, to hinder Apollo from going over to help the Greeks; but neither this precaution nor their bravery could prevent them from being overcome, as the prophet Zechariah had foretold, "The Lord will cast her out, and will smite her power in the sea, and she shall be devoured with fire."

"Gaza also shall see it, and shall be very sorrowful." Alexander took this brave Philistine city after a siege of two months, and behaved more cruelly there than was his custom. It was the turn of Jerusalem next; but the Lord had promised to "encamp about His House, because of him that passes by;" and in answer to the prayers and sacrifices offered up by the Jews, God appeared to the High Priest, Jaddua, in a dream, and told him to adorn the city, and go out to meet the conqueror in his beautiful garments, with all his priests in their ephods. They obeyed, and as Alexander came up the hill Sapha, in front of the city, be beheld the long ranks of priests and Levites in their white array, headed by the High Priest with his robes bordered with bells and pomegranates, and the fair miter on his head, inscribed with the words "Holiness unto the Lord." One moment and Alexander was down from his horse, adoring upon his knees. His friends were amazed, but he told them he adored not the man, but Him who had given him the priesthood, and that just before he had left home, the same figure had stood by his bed, and told him that he should cross the sea, and win all the chief lands of Asia. He then took Jaddua by the hand, and was led by him into the Temple, where he attended a sacrifice, and was shown Daniel's prophecies about him as the brazen thighs, the he-goat and the leopard; he was much pleased, and promised all Jaddua asked, that the Jews might follow their own laws, and pay no tribute on the Sabbath years, when the land lay fallow.

Alexander next passed on to Egypt, where he built, at the mouth of the Nile, the famous city that still is called by his name, Alexandria; indeed he founded cities everywhere, and made more lasting changes than ever did conqueror in the short space of twelve years. He then hunted Darius into the mountain parts of the north of Persia, and after two more victories, the Greeks found the poor Persian king dying on the ground, from wounds given by his own subjects. So the soft silver of Persia yielded to the brazen might of Greece. After this, Alexander called himself King of Persia, and wore the tiara like an eastern king. He took his men on to the borders of India, but they thought they were getting beyond the end of the world, and grew so frightened that he had to turn back. All that the Medes and Persians had possessed now belonged to him, and he wanted to make Babylon his capital. He made his court there, and received messengers who paid him honor from all quarters; but he was hurt by so much success; he grew proud and passionate; he feasted and drank too much, and did violent and hasty things, but worst of all, he fancied himself a god, and insisted that at home, in Greece, sacrifices should be offered to him. He tried to restore Babylon to what it had been, and set multitudes to work to clear away the rubbish, and build up the Temple of Bel. But when he ordered the Jews to share in the work, they answered that it was contrary to their Law to labor at an idol temple, and he listened to them, releasing them from the command. He wished to turn the waters of the Euphrates back into their stream, and drain the swamps into which they had spread; but Babylon was under the curse of God, and was never to recover. Alexander caught a fever while going about surveying the unwholesome swamps, and after trying to hold out against it for nine days, his strength gave way. He said there would be a mighty strife at his funeral, perhaps recollecting how the prophecy had said that his kingdom should not continue; and instead of trying to choose an heir, he put his ring on the finger of his friend, and very soon died. He was only thirty-two, and had not reigned quite twelve years; but perhaps no one ever did greater things in so short a time. He died in the year 323; and so the great horn of the goat was broken when it was at the strongest. No one hated him; for though sometimes violent, he had generally been kind; he was frank, open, and freehanded, warm-hearted to his friends, and seldom harsh to his enemies, and he had done his best to educate and improve all the people whom he conquered. It was owing to him that Greek manners and habits prevailed, and the Greek language was spoken everywhere around the eastern end of the Mediterranean, though Persia itself soon fell back into the old eastern ways. Babylon became almost deserted after his death; the swamps grew worse, till no one could live there, and at last, the only use of the great walls was to serve as an enclosure for a hunting ground, where the wild beasts had their home, and kept court for ever.

FROM FIFTY FAMOUS STORIES RETOLD
By James Baldwin

A LESSON IN JUSTICE

Alexander, the king of Macedon, wished to become the master of the whole world. He led his armies through many countries. He plundered cities, he burned towns, he destroyed thousands of lives.

At last, far in the East, he came to a land of which he had never heard. The people there knew nothing about war and conquest. Although they were rich, they lived simply and were at peace with all the world.

The shah, or ruler of these people, went out to meet Alexander and welcome him to their country. He led the great king to his palace and begged that he would dine with him.

When they were seated at the table the servants of the shah stood by to serve the meal. They brought in what seemed to be fruits, nuts, cakes, and other delicacies; but when Alexander would eat he found that everything was made of gold.

"What!" said he, "do you eat gold in this country?"

"We ourselves eat only common food," answered the shah. "But we have heard that it was the desire for gold which caused you to leave your own country; and so, we wish to satisfy your appetite."

"It was not for gold that I came here," said Alexander. "I came to learn the customs of your people."

"Very well, then," said the shah, "stay with me a little while and observe what you can."

While the shah and the king were talking, two countrymen came in. "My lord," said one, "we have had a disagreement, and wish you to settle the matter."

"Tell me about it," said the shah.

"Well, it is this way," answered the man: "I bought a piece of ground from this neighbor of mine, and paid him a fair price for it. Yesterday, when I was digging in it, I found a box full of gold and jewels. This treasure does not belong to me, for I bought only the ground; but when I offered it to my neighbor he refused it."

The second man then spoke up and said, "It is true that I sold him the ground, but I did not reserve anything he might find in it. The treasure is not mine, and therefore I am unwilling to take it."

The shah sat silent for a while, as if in thought. Then he said to the first man, "Have you a son?"

"Yes, a young man of promise," was the answer.

The shah turned to the second man: "Have you a daughter?"

"I have," answered the man, "—a beautiful girl."

"Well, then, this is my judgment. Let the son marry the daughter, if both agree, and give them the treasure as a wedding portion."

Alexander listened with great interest. "You have judged wisely and rightly," said he to the shah, "but in my own country we should have done differently."

"What would you have done?"

"Well, we should have thrown both men into prison, and the treasure would have been given to the king."

"And is that what you call justice?" asked the shah.

"We call it policy," said Alexander.

"Then let me ask you a question," said the shah. "Does the sun shine in your country?"

"Surely."

"Does the rain fall there?"

"Oh, yes!"

"Is it possible! But are there any gentle, harmless animals in your fields?"

"A great many."

"Then," said the shah, "it must be that the sun shines and the rain falls for the sake of these poor beasts; for men so unjust do not deserve such blessings."

FROM FIFTY FAMOUS STORIES RETOLD
By James Baldwin

THE STORY OF REGULUS

On the other side of the sea from Rome there was once a great city named Carthage. The Roman people were never very friendly to the people of Carthage, and at last a war began between them. For a long time it was hard to tell which would prove the stronger. First the Romans would gain a battle, and then the men of Carthage would gain a battle; and so the war went on for many years.

Among the Romans there was a brave general named Regulus,—a man of whom it was said that he never broke his word. It so happened after a while, that Regulus was taken prisoner and carried to Carthage. Ill and very lonely, he dreamed of his wife and little children so far away beyond the sea; and he had but little hope of ever seeing them again. He loved his home dearly, but he believed that his first duty was to his country; and so he had left all, to fight in this cruel war.

He had lost a battle, it is true, and had been taken prisoner. Yet he knew that the Romans were gaining ground, and the people of Carthage were afraid of being beaten in the end. They had sent into other countries to hire soldiers to help them; but even with these they would not be able to fight much longer against Rome.

One day some of the rulers of Carthage came to the prison to talk with Regulus.

"We should like to make peace with the Roman people," they said, "and we are sure, that, if your rulers at home knew how the war is going, they would be glad to make peace with us. We will set you free and let you go home, if you will agree to do as we say."

"What is that?" asked Regulus.

"In the first place," they said, "you must tell the Romans about the battles which you have lost, and you must make it plain to them that they have not gained anything by the war. In the second place, you must promise us, that, if they will not make peace, you will come back to your prison."

"Very well," said Regulus, "I promise you, that, if they will not make peace, I will come back to prison."

And so they let him go; for they knew that a great Roman would keep his word.

When he came to Rome, all the people greeted him gladly. His wife and children were very happy, for they thought that now they would not be parted again. The white-haired Fathers who made the laws for the city came to see him. They asked him about the war.

"I was sent from Carthage to ask you to make peace," he said. "But it will not be wise to make peace. True, we have been beaten in a few battles, but our army is gaining ground every day. The people of Carthage are afraid, and well they may be. Keep on with the war a little while longer, and Carthage shall be yours. As for me, I have come to bid my wife and children and Rome farewell. Tomorrow I will start back to Carthage and to prison; for I have promised."

Then the Fathers tried to persuade him to stay.

"Let us send another man in your place," they said.

"Shall a Roman not keep his word?" answered Regulus. "I am ill, and at the best have not long to live. I will go back, as I promised."

His wife and little children wept, and his sons begged him not to leave them again.

"I have given my word," said Regulus. "The rest will be taken care of."

Then he bade them good-by, and went bravely back to the prison and the cruel death which he expected.

This was the kind of courage that made Rome the greatest city in the world.

FROM FIFTY FAMOUS STORIES RETOLD
By James Baldwin

CORNELIA'S JEWELS

Cornelia Scipionis Africana was the second daughter of Publius Cornelius Scipio Africanus, the hero of the Second Punic War, and Aemilia Paulla. She is remembered as the perfect example of a virtuous Roman woman.

It was a bright morning in the old city of Rome many hundred years ago. In a vine-covered summer-house in a beautiful garden, two boys were standing. They were looking at their mother and her friend, who were walking among the flowers and trees.

"Did you ever see so handsome a lady as our mother's friend?" asked the younger boy, holding his tall brother's hand. "She looks like a queen."

"Yet she is not so beautiful as our mother," said the elder boy. "She has a fine dress, it is true; but her face is not noble and kind. It is our mother who is like a queen."

"That is true," said the other. "There is no woman in Rome so much like a queen as our own dear mother."

Soon Cornelia, their mother, came down the walk to speak with them. She was simply dressed in a plain white robe. Her arms and feet were bare, as was the custom in those days; and no rings nor chains glittered about her hands and neck. For her only crown, long braids of soft brown hair were coiled about her head; and a tender smile lit up her noble face as she looked into her sons' proud eyes.

"Boys," she said, "I have something to tell you."

They bowed before her, as Roman lads were taught to do, and said, "What is it, mother?"

"You are to dine with us today, here in the garden; and then our friend is going to show us that wonderful casket of jewels of which you have heard so much."

The brothers looked shyly at their mother's friend. Was it possible that she had still other rings besides those on her fingers? Could she have other gems besides those which sparkled in the chains about her neck?

When the simple outdoor meal was over, a servant brought the casket from the house. The lady opened it. Ah, how those jewels dazzled the eyes of the wondering boys! There were ropes of pearls, white as milk, and smooth as satin; heaps of shining rubies, red as the glowing coals; sapphires as blue as the sky that summer day; and diamonds that flashed and sparkled like the sunlight.

The brothers looked long at the gems.

"Ah!" whispered the younger; "if our mother could only have such beautiful things!"

At last, however, the casket was closed and carried carefully away.

"Is it true, Cornelia, that you have no jewels?" asked her friend. "Is it true, as I have heard it whispered, that you are poor?"

"No, I am not poor," answered Cornelia, and as she spoke she drew her two boys to her side; "for here are my jewels. They are worth more than all your gems."

I am sure that the boys never forgot their mother's pride and love and care; and in after years, when they had become great men in Rome, they often thought of this scene in the garden. And the world still likes to hear the story of Cornelia's jewels.

Unit Ten: Maccabean Revolt

Theme: Remaining Faithful

From The Catechism in Examples
By Rev. D. Chisholm

FAITH

The ninth fruit of the Holy Ghost is Faith. By this is meant that life of faith by which we look on all things, good or evil, as coming from God, and are constantly looking forward, as St. Paul did, to the reward promised to those who while on earth live and labor for God alone and for Heaven.

St. Seranus the Gardener

Whosoever lives a life of faith will find means of instructing himself and of sanctifying himself at every step he takes. St. Seranus was only a simple gardener, but as he looked on the plants and flowers amongst which he labored daily growing up until they arrived at maturity, he would say to himself : This is how I ought to live to reach the end for which I was made ; it is my duty to labor without ceasing to advance from virtue to virtue, and to perform all my actions, direct all my thoughts, and regulate all my desires, so as to attain that perfection that God requires of me."

From Book of the Ancient World
By Dorothy Mills

After the Return to Jerusalem

The Jews remained under Persian rule, until Persia was in its turn conquered by Alexander the Great. At his death, his vast empire was divided up and Palestine was a much coveted piece of land owing to its favorable position. Egypt and Syria in turn possessed the land, and the latter persecuted the Jews in the hope of making them renounce their religion and customs. The Jews made a vigorous resistance to this persecution under a heroic leader Judas Maccabaeus. He was a brilliant general and he inspired his army with courage. He had only

CONNECTING WITH HISTORY VOL. 1 COMPANION READER

a small and poorly equipped following, but the men who composed it were patriots and inspired by an intense enthusiasm for their religion. They had against them well-trained soldiers, armed with the best weapons of the time, and amongst them were Jews who had deserted their own side, who knew every inch of the country and who could spy out all their movements. But in spite of these odds, Judas Maccabaeus succeeded in gaining victories, until he was able to enter Jerusalem and restore the Temple and its services. But peace did not last very long, and when another Syrian army invaded the land, Judas Maccabaeus was killed in battle and the Jewish cause was lost.

This defeat was a deathblow to the Jewish hopes for independence, but still there was no peace. Ceaseless strife prevailed, until at last Rome interfered and the troubled land of Palestine passed under her control. She was not popular with the people, but her strong hand kept peace and she sent governors to maintain her authority. These rulers grew in power until in 37 B.C. Herod, the ruler of the time, was given the title of King.

Herod was a tyrant, and he only kept the peace at the point of the sword, but when he had made himself quite secure as King, he devoted much time to erecting great buildings, and he rebuilt the Temple with great splendor and magnificence.

But the time was coming when the Jews were to live in Palestine no longer. The rulers under the Romans were tyrannical and the people grew more and more angry at the indignities heaped upon them, until at last open rebellion broke out, and there was war. It reached its height in 70 A.D. when Titus, son of the Roman Emperor came against Jerusalem and besieged it. The city was crowded for the Feast of the Passover, and famine and pestilence soon appeared in the city. Titus broke through the outer walls and at last the Jews took refuge in the Temple, which was almost like a fortress. Then a Roman soldier threw a flaming torch into the Temple, and a blazing fire broke out. After that the end soon came; the Temple was burnt and the whole city razed to the ground, except three towers and a part of the wall, which were left in order that the world might know how strong was the city taken by Rome. Those of the Jews who had survived, and a few of the vessels from the Temple which had escaped destruction, were taken to be shown as triumphal spoils when Titus returned to Rome.

Was this the end of the Jewish hopes, of the new and better world that Isaiah had predicted, of the Deliverer whom they expected? At this time the laws of the Jews had become definite, their religious beliefs very rigid; long years of oppression had given a tinge of melancholy to their thought and had taken the joyousness out of life. The very fact that they were a small and politically unimportant nation made them cling to all their old traditions and customs, and this made them narrow and intolerant.

But, whatever their faults, they had developed an enthusiastic zeal for the things of God's kingdom, and they never wavered in their belief that underneath all history there was a plan. The experiences of their history had taught them that there was only one God, and that belief brings with it the recognition that everything in human life is part of one ordered plan. They had learned what was the character of God, and so they believed that there would come a day when Righteousness would reign throughout the world. They needed an interpreter whose character and teaching would show them, and through them the world, the way to the fulfillment of all that was best and noblest in their hopes.

In the fullness of time, the Teacher came. At Bethlehem, in the days of Herod the King, seventy years before the destruction of Jerusalem, Christ was born, Who by His life and teaching made possible the fulfillment of the ancient visions.

The Chosen People
By Charlotte Yonge

The Maccabees

Never was there a time when God left Himself without a witness; and in these darkest times of the Jewish history, He raised up a defender of His Name. There was a small town, named Modin, near the seashore, where a Greek officer called Apelles was sent to force the people into idolatry. He set up an altar to one of his gods, and having ordered all the inhabitants to assemble, insisted on their doing sacrifice. Among them came a family of priests, who, from their ancestor, Hasmon, were known as the Hasmoneans. The father, Mattathias, declared with a loud voice that he would permit no such dishonor to his God, and the first Jew who approached to offer incense, was struck down and slain by him. Then with his five brave sons, and others emboldened by his example, he fell upon Apelles, drove him away, and pulled down the idolatrous altar. He then fled away to the hills, where so many people joined him, that he had a force sufficient to defend themselves from their enemies; and he went round Judea, circumcising the children, and rescuing the copies of the Law which the Greeks had seized from the synagogues. Some of these holy books, which had been defiled by paintings of the heathen idols, were destroyed, by order of Mattathias, after the writing had been carefully copied. It was at this time that the Jews began to read Lessons from the Prophets in the synagogue, because Antiochus had only forbidden reading the Law, without specifying the prophetic books. Mattathias, who was already an old man, soon fell sick; and gathering his sons about him, reminded them of the deeds that God had done by the holy men of old, and exhorting them to do boldly in defense of His Covenant. He appointed as their leader his third son, Judah, who for his warlike might was called Maccabæus, or the Hammerer; and the second, Simon, surnamed Thassi, (one who increases,) was to be his chief adviser.

In the year 166, Judah Maccabæus set up his standard, with the motto, "Who is like unto Thee, O Lord, among the gods?" the first letters of which words in Hebrew made his surname, Maccabee. He went through the land, enforcing the Law, and putting the cities in a state of defense. Antiochus, meantime, was holding a mad and hateful festival; but on hearing of the revolt of the Jews, he went into a great rage, and sent a huge army to punish them. Maccabæus defeated this force, drove it back to Antioch, and then marched to Jerusalem, and forced the Greek garrison to take refuge in a fortress called Akra, on Mount Zion. The courts of the Temple were overgrown with shrubs which stood like a forest, the priests' chambers had been pulled down, and the Sanctuary lay desolate. These brave men tore their clothes and wept at the sight; and then set at once to repair the holy place, their priest-leader choosing out the most spotless among them for the work. They pulled down the Altar that had been defiled, and setting aside its stones, built a new one, and out of the spoil that was in their hands, renewed the Candlestick, the table of the Bread of the Presence, and the Altar of incense; and then they newly dedicated the Temple, after three years of desolation. The anniversary was ever after kept with gladness, and was called the winter feast of dedication. Still Judah was not strong enough to take the castle on Mount Zion; but he built strong walls round the Temple, so that it too became a fortress, and he then went to Bethshan to defend the south border of Judea against the Edomites.

These tidings terribly enraged Antiochus, who was gone on an expedition to Persia, and he planned to form a league with his neighbors for the utter destruction of the Jews; but "he came to his end, and none could help him," after overturning his chariot. He became so ill that he could not bear people to come near him. Horrible fears tormented him, and in his remorse he repented of all the evil he had done to the Jews, and sent them a letter assuring them of his favor; but it was now too late, and he died in great misery.

His son, Antiochus Eupator, was only nine years old, and his affairs were managed by a governor named Lysias, who continued the persecution, and led an army to relieve the garrison in Mount Zion. Judah marched out to meet him, but was repulsed with the loss of six hundred men. His younger brother, Eleazar, who saw an elephant of huge size, with a tower of unusual height on its back, thought the king himself must be there. He ran beneath it, stabbed it and was crushed by its fall. Lysias then advanced upon Jerusalem, and laid siege to it, placing the Jews in extreme peril.

Another regent rose up against Lysias, and he made a hasty peace with Maccabæus, and was admitted into the city; but when he saw its strength, he broke his promises, and overthrew the wall.

Judah then gained a victory, and wrote to ask for an alliance and protection from the Romans; but by the time that the answer to his letter arrived he had been killed in a battle with the Syrians. His brothers, Jonathan and Simon, took up his body, and buried it at Modin, in the tomb of their fathers; and they continued to lead the faithful Jews.

It was the plan of the Romans to take the part of a weak nation against a strong one, because it afforded them an excuse for conquering the mightier of the two, so they gave notice that the quarrels of the Jews were their own; and after much fighting, Jonathan obtained two years of peace, and became high-priest. He was later killed by the Syrians.

Simon Thassi was the only survivor of the brave Maccabaean brothers, but he finished their work, and obtained from Rome, Egypt, and Syria, an acknowledgment that the Jews were a free people, and that he was their prince and priest. He took the castle on Mount Zion from the Syrians, and so fortified the Temple, that it became like another citadel, and he was honored by all his neighbors. He built a noble tomb for all his family at Modin, consisting of seven pyramids, in honor of his father and mother, and their five sons; all covered in by a portico, supported on seven pillars, the whole of white marble, and the pediment so high that it served for a mark for sailors at sea.

FROM OLD WORLD HERO STORIES
By Eva March Tappan

HANNIBAL, WHO FOUGHT AGAINST ROME

"Lay your hand upon the sacrifice" said Hamilcar to his nine-year-old son Hannibal, "and swear that you will never be a friend to the Roman people." The little boy laid his hand upon the sacrifice and solemnly repeated the words, "I swear that I will never be a friend to the Roman people." Then he and his father and the soldiers left Carthage and sailed away to Spain.

This Carthage was where the old legends said that Aeneas had landed on his way to make a new home for the Trojans in Italy. It had become a wealthy city, and so powerful that Rome feared it as a rival. There had already been one war between the two states, and in this war Hamilcar had distinguished himself as a general. It was now a time of peace; but everyone knew that another war would follow, and he was on his way to Spain to get money from the Spanish silver mines. After some years, Hamilcar was slain in battle in Spain, and as soon as his son was old enough, the Carthaginians put him in his father's place as commander.

Hannibal was only twenty-six, but he had some definite ideas about overcoming the Romans. He believed that the proper way to attack them was not to fall upon the towns here and there along the coast, but to come down into Italy from the north and so push into the very heart of the country. This was a most excellent plan; the only difficulty was how to carry it out, for rivers and mountains and long stretches of wild and savage country lay between Spain and Italy. Nevertheless, he set out with good courage. He marched through Spain, crossed the Pyrenees, and made his way to the banks of the Rhone. Most of the tribes in that part of the country were at swords' points with the Romans, and had not the least objection to allowing him to pass through their lands. When he came to the Rhone, however, he found that the tribes on the farther bank were ready to fight, though those about him were friendly. He hired all the boats that belonged to these friendly folk and cut down trees to make others. The night before he meant to cross, he sent part of his troops twenty-two miles up the stream. They cut down trees and built some rude rafts, and by means of these made their way to the opposite shore. Hannibal and his men got into the boats all ready to start. The hostile Gauls were waiting for them, brandishing their weapons and shouting their war cries. But away beyond them Hannibal saw a thin line of smoke slowly rising. This was the signal. He pushed across the river, and the horses swam after him, some of the soldiers holding their bridles. The forces that had gone upstream now appeared. The Gauls were shut in between the two bodies of troops; and they ran for their lives.

The elephants were still on the other side, and elephants are not fond of crossing rivers in small boats. Hannibal tried his best to make them think that they were on dry land by covering great rafts with earth. The elephants were too wise to be cheated in this fashion, and when the rafts began to move, some of them jumped overboard. Fortunately, they made their way to the farther shore, and before long the army was again on the march.

The next difficulty was to cross the Alps. The mountaineers came to meet Hannibal with wreaths on their heads and branches of trees in their hands and gave him a most friendly greeting. They would sell him cattle, they said, if he wished, and they would show him the best paths over the maintains. He felt a little suspicious of them, but they seemed so sincere that at length he accepted some of them as guides. But they led him and his men into a narrow defile; then from the heights above they rolled down great stones and masses of rock. Hannibal with some of his infantry climbed the cliff and drove the crafty mountaineers back, while the cavalry and the baggage-carriers made their way out of the defile.

Up, up, the weary soldiers struggled until they were on the summit of the Alps. They were cold and exhausted and many had died; but Hannibal pointed to a valley below them and cried, "Italy! There is Italy, and yonder lies the way to Rome." After a little rest, they began the descent. It was wet and slippery. The track was often covered with snow. In one place an avalanche had swept it away entirely for three hundred yards, and they had to stop and build a road; and a road wide enough and strong enough to satisfy the elephants was not to be made in a day. At last the Alps had been crossed, but half of the men were dead. The others were worn out with cold and hunger and toil. And this was the army that had come to conquer the most powerful nation in the world!

The Romans sent out their forces to meet Hannibal, but he overcame them in three great contests. For many years they had been accustomed to victories, and they were almost thunderstruck at these defeats. Of course they appointed a dictator, Quintus Fabius Maximus. He did not dare to engage in an open battle, for if he had lost, this conquering army would have marched straight upon Rome; but he kept as near Hannibal as possible; and if any Carthaginian troops were separated from the main army, they seldom returned, for Fabius was always ready to cut them off. He harassed Hannibal in every way that he could. "Fabius is a traitor," the Romans cried angrily. They clamored for a battle, and they called him scornfully the "Cunctator," the delayer. Later, they saw how wise he had been, and "Cunctator" became a title of honor.

The following year Hannibal overcame the Romans at Cannae and sent home to Carthage a peck of gold rings from the fingers of the conquered soldiers. The Romans were in terror lest he should enter their city. For some reason he did not attempt it, but spent the winter in Capua. The soldiers rested and feasted and drank and enjoyed themselves. This was no way to strengthen an army; and in the spring, he was no longer a victorious commander, but a commander in difficulties. It was true that the Romans were not strong enough to drive him out of the country; but neither was he strong enough to conquer Rome. Carthage was not generous in sending money; troops coming to aid him were captured by his enemies; and a young Roman general named Scipio succeeded in driving the Carthaginians out of Spain and inducing the Spaniards to stand by Rome.

This young Scipio was a shrewd man. He made up his mind that the best way to get Hannibal out of Italy was to attack the Carthaginians in their own country. He felt sure that then they would order all their troops home to defend Carthage. The senate did not agree with him, and the wary Cunctator did not agree; but Scipio had become consul, and no one could well hinder him from carrying out his plans, especially as the common people believed in him and promptly volunteered to fill up his lines. It resulted just as he had hoped. He overcame the Carthaginian army in Africa, and Hannibal was called home. There was a terrible battle between the two armies at Zama, and the forces of Hannibal were destroyed. Then the Romans saw how wise Scipio had been, and they gave him the title of Africanus in honor of his victories in Africa. When he came home, he had a more magnificent triumph than had ever been seen in Rome before. Carthage was crushed. She had to give up her elephants and warships, to pay Rome an immense tribute, and agree to wage no wars without the consent of her conqueror.

This was the end of the second war between Carthage and Rome, but it was not the end of Hannibal's career. He became chief magistrate of his city. He found that some of its officials were taking possession of the state revenues. He put a stop to this and managed so wisely that even the enormous annual tribute could be paid to Rome without taxing the citizens severely. He showed himself as great a statesman as soldier, and in spite of all her troubles, Carthage became prosperous again. Rome in her jealousy demanded that Hannibal should be given up; but he fled to Syria. It is said that he and Scipio Africanus met in Asia Minor and had many friendly talks together. The story is told that Scipio once asked Hannibal whom he regarded as the greatest general. Hannibal replied, "Alexander." "Whom next?" asked Scipio. "Pyrrhus," was the reply. "And whom next?" "Myself." "Where, then, would you have ranked yourself if you had conquered me?" "Above Alexander, above Pyrrhus, and above all other generals," said the Carthaginian.

Hannibal fled from one king to another; but wherever he went, the Romans pursued. He had long realized that he could not hope to escape from them, and in a ring which he wore he always carried about with him a fatal poison. The time soon came when he must choose between falling into the hands of the Romans and taking his own life. He chose the latter. Thus ended the days of one of the greatest generals of ancient times.

The rest of the story of Carthage is soon told. She had been forbidden to wage war, but enemies attacked her. As was to have been expected, the Romans would do nothing, and she defended herself. This was just the excuse that the Romans wanted, and they commanded the Carthaginians to destroy their own city and make a new settlement ten miles from the sea. The Carthaginians fought to the death. For three long years they resisted all the power of Rome; then the end came. The town was burned, its site was ploughed up, and all of its people who had not died in its defense were sold as slaves.

A few years later, there was a revolt in Spain. This was overcome, and in 133 b.c. Rome ruled the ring of countries about the Mediterranean Sea. These made up "the world." Therefore the tiny village of Romulus and Remus had become the ruler of the world.

FROM OLD WORLD HERO STORIES
By Eva March Tappan

JULIUS CAESAR, THE FIRST EMPEROR OF ROME

When Julius Caesar was a young man, he was taken by pirates. He sent his servants to collect money for his ransom, and then he set to work to make merry with his captors. When he was tired, he told them to keep quiet and let him sleep. When he wanted to be amused, he told them to dance and entertain him and the strange part of it is that they obeyed. He composed verses and orations and ordered the pirates to listen to them. They did not know what to make of either him or his verses, and he berated them for their stupidity. "You don't know poetry when you hear it," he said. "You think you can scoff at my verses and orations because I am your prisoner. I'll take you prisoners some day, and then you shall have your pay." "What will it be?" they demanded with shouts of laughter. "I'll crucify every one of you," he replied quietly. Not so very long after this, he kept his word.

A few years later, Caesar was made governor of Spain. As a general thing, when a man became governor of a province, his chief aim was to get as much money from the provincials as possible; but Caesar behaved as if he were really interested in his people and wanted to help them. He completed the conquest of Spain, and he straightened out the financial affairs of the province. Then he returned to Rome. The people's party made him consul; but the nobles succeeded in electing one of their own party to be the second consul. Caesar was so much stronger than he that the jokers of the time used to date their papers, "In the consulship of Julius and Caesar."

There were now in Rome three men of power: Crassus, who was enormously rich; Pompey, who had long been a successful general; and Caesar, who had not yet accomplished so very much, but who had the power to make people believe that he could do whatever he chose to undertake. These three men, the First Triumvirate, as they are called, bargained together to help one another and divide the Roman world among them.

Caesar's share in this division was Gaul, the present France, and he set off to conquer the country. Before long, wonderful stories came back to Rome of great victories and the capture of thousands of prisoners. Trees were cut down in the forest, and in a few days they had been made into complicated bridges. Great chiefs yielded and cities surrendered. There were tales of forced marches, of sudden surprises, of vast amounts of booty, also of a mysterious land across the water to the northwest. It was called Britain, and tin was brought from there, but no one knew much about it, not even whether it was an island or not. By and by, Caesar visited this Britain. He wrote a book about the country and his conquests there and about his campaigns in Gaul. It is called his "Commentaries," and is so clear and simple and concise that it is a model of military description.

The Triumvirate had agreed that Pompey should give up his command in Spain and Caesar his command in Gaul at the same time; but Pompey remained near Rome, and he induced the senate to allow him to continue as governor of Spain for five years longer. Then Caesar was aroused. At the end of the five years, he would be only a private citizen, while Pompey would be commander of a great army. Crassus was dead. "Either decree that Pompey and I shall give up our provinces at the same time, or allow me to stand for the consulship before I enter Rome," Caesar urged. The senate refused and, moreover, threatened two magistrates, called tribunes of the people, who stood by Caesar. They fled to his camp on the farther side of the little river Rubicon.

It was a law in Rome that any Roman general who brought his army across the Rubicon should be regarded as an enemy to his country. Caesar could declare now, however, that he was coming, not as an enemy, but to defend the people and their tribunes against Pompey and the nobles. It is said that he hesitated, then exclaimed, "The die is cast," and plunged into the river, followed by his army.

Pompey fled. Caesar made himself master of Italy and then pursued. At Pharsalus in Thessaly a great battle was fought, and Caesar won. Pompey fled to Egypt for protection; but the Egyptian councilors were afraid of Caesar and killed the fugitive. Caesar returned to Rome the ruler of the world. He had a magnificent triumph, and he gave the people feasts and money and combats of wild beasts, their favorite amusement. The senators were thoroughly humbled. They made him dictator for life; they changed the name of his birth-month from Quintilus (fifth) to Julius (July); they stamped their money with his image; they even dedicated temples and altars to him as to a god.

Caesar's head was not turned by this flattery; but the heads of those who had opposed him were almost turned with astonishment and relief. Some years before this, one general named Marius and then another one named Sulla had held sole rule in Rome, and each of them had put to death some thousands of the people who had been against him. The Romans supposed that Caesar would behave in the same way; but he made no attempt to revenge himself. Indeed, his only thought seemed to be to do what was best for Rome. He made just laws for rich and poor, and was especially thoughtful of the good of the provincials. He planned to collect a great library, to put up magnificent temples and other public buildings, to rebuild Carthage, to make a road along the Apennines, and to drain the Pontine Marshes, which were near the city.

Caesar ruled nobly, but a plot was formed against him. The chief conspirators were Cassius and Brutus. Cassius was envious of his great power; Brutus believed that if Caesar were slain, the old forms of government would be restored and Rome would be again a republic. These men pressed about Caesar in the senate house as if they wished to present him a petition. At a signal, they drew their swords. Caesar defended himself for a moment; then he saw among them the face of Brutus, the one to whom he had shown every favor and to whom he had given a sincere affection. He cried, "You, too, Brutus!" drew his robe over his face, and fell dead.

It was the custom for an oration to be delivered at a funeral, and the conspirators very unwisely permitted Caesar's friend Antony to speak at his funeral. He also read Caesar's will, in which he had left a gift of money to every citizen and had been especially generous to some of the very men who had become his murderers. The people were aroused to such a pitch of fury that the assassins were glad to flee from the city. The senate appointed Antony to see that the will was carried out, and they agreed to accept as ruler a grandnephew of Caesar whom he had named as his successor. This grandnephew was a young man named Octavianus, who afterwards became the emperor Augustus.

From Fifty Famous Stories Retold
By James Baldwin

Julius Caesar

Nearly two thousand years ago there lived in Rome a man whose name was Julius Caesar. He was the greatest of all the Romans.

Why was he so great?

He was a brave warrior, and had conquered many countries for Rome. He was wise in planning and in doing. He knew how to make men both love and fear him.

At last, he made himself the ruler of Rome. Some said that he wished to become its king. But the Romans at that time did not believe in kings.

Once when Caesar was passing through a little country village, all the men, women, and children of the place came out to see him. There were not more than fifty of them, all together, and they were led by their mayor, who told each one what to do.

These simple people stood by the roadside and watched Caesar pass. The mayor looked very proud and happy; for was he not the ruler of this village? He felt that he was almost as great a man as Caesar himself.

Some of the fine officers who were with Caesar laughed. They said, "See how that fellow struts at the head of his little flock!"

"Laugh as you will," said Caesar, "he has reason to be proud. I would rather be the head man of a village than the second man in Rome!"

At another time, Caesar was crossing a narrow sea in a boat. Before he was halfway to the farther shore, a storm overtook him. The wind blew hard; the waves dashed high; the lightning flashed; the thunder rolled.

It seemed every minute as though the boat would sink. The captain was in great fright. He had crossed the sea many times, but never in such a storm as this. He trembled with fear; he could not guide the boat; he fell down upon his knees; he moaned, "All is lost! all is lost!"

But Caesar was not afraid. He bade the man get up and take his oars again.

"Why should you be afraid?" he said. "The boat will not be lost; for you have Caesar on board."

Sources

THE CATECHISM IN EXAMPLES
by Rev. D. Chisholm

FIFTY FAMOUS STORIES RETOLD
by James Baldwin

FIFTY FAMOUS PEOPLE: A BOOK OF SHORT STORIES
by James Baldwin

ANECDOTES AND EXAMPLES ILLUSTRATING THE CATECHISM
Selected and Arranged by Rev. Francis Spirago
Edited by Rev. James J. Baxter, DD

THE CHOSEN PEOPLE, A COMPENDIUM OF SACRED AND CHURCH HISTORY
FOR SCHOOL-CHILDREN
by Charlotte M. Yonge

THE BOOK OF THE ANCIENT WORLD FOR YOUNGER READERS:
AN ACCOUNT OF OUR COMMON HERITAGE FROM THE DAWN OF CIVILIZATION
TO THE COMING OF THE GREEKS
by Dorothy Mills, M.A.

OUR OLD WORLD BACKGROUND
by Charles A. Beard

JOSEPH THE DREAMER
by Amy Steedman

THE BABE IN THE BULRUSHES
by Amy Steedman

A BOOK OF DISCOVERY: THE HISTORY OF THE WORLD'S EXPLORATION,
FROM THE EARLIEST TIMES TO THE FINDING OF THE SOUTH POLE
by Margaret Bertha Synge

CONNECTING WITH HISTORY VOL. 1 COMPANION READER

RUTH, THE GLEANER
by Amy Steedman

SAMUEL, THE LITTLE SERVER
by Amy Steedman

DAVID THE SHEPHERD BOY
by Amy Steedman

THE STORY OF THE GREEKS
by H. A. Guerber

OLD WORLD HERO STORIES
by Eva March Tappan

STORIES FROM THE CLASSICS
Selected & Arranged by Eva March Tappan

WONDER STORIES
by Carolyn Sherwin Bailey

AUNT CHARLOTTE'S STORIES OF GREEK HISTORY
by Charlotte M. Yonge

YOUNG FOLKS' HISTORY OF ROME
by Charlotte M. Yonge

THE BABY'S OWN AESOP
by Aesop and Walter Crane

THE JUNIOR CLASSICS, VOLUME SEVEN: STORIES OF COURAGE AND HEROISM
Selected and Arranged by William Patten

CPSIA information can be obtained
at www.ICGtesting.com
Printed in the USA
BVHW091308250821
614913BV00002B/6

9 780692 239148